Maya Cultural Activism
in Guatemala

Maya Cultural Activism in Guatemala

Edited by
Edward F. Fischer
and
R. McKenna Brown

University of Texas Press, Austin
Institute of Latin American Studies

First Edition, 1996

Requests for permission to reproduce material from this work should be sent to Permissions, University of Texas Press, P.O. Box 7819, Austin, Texas 78713-7819

♾ The paper used in this publication meets the minimum requirements of American National Standard for Information Sciences—Permanence of Paper for Printed Library Materials, ANSI Z39.48–1984.

Library of Congress Cataloging-in-Publication Data

Maya cultural activism in Guatemala / edited by Edward F. Fischer and R. McKenna Brown.
    p.   cm. — (Critical reflections on Latin America series)
    Includes bibliographical references and index.
    ISBN 0-292-70850-5 (cloth : alk. paper) — ISBN 0-292-70851-3 (pbk. : alk. paper)
    1. Mayas—Ethnic identity. 2. Mayas—Social life and customs. 3. Mayas—Politics and government. 4. Ethnicity—Guatemala. 5. Guatemala—Politics and government. 6. Guatemala—Social life and customs. I. Fischer, Edward F. , 1966– .   II. Brown R. McKenna, 1954– .
III. Series.
F1435.3E72M39 1996
972.81' 004974—dc20   96-28480
                                                                        CIP

Contents

Acronyms

As the reader familiar with Guatemala knows, the landscape of social institutions in that country is marked by a plethora of acronyms, the juggling of which can be problematic even to the most astute scholar. For that reason we have compiled the following handy reference list of the most common acronyms.

AEMG	Asociación de Escritores Mayances de Guatemala (Association of Mayan Writers of Guatemala)
ALMG	Academia de las Lenguas Mayas de Guatemala (Academy of Mayan Languages of Guatemala)
CEDIM	Centro de Documentación e Investigación Maya (Center of Mayan Documentation and Research)
CIRMA	Centro de Investigaciones Regionales de Mesoamérica (Center for Regional Research of Mesoamerica)
COCADI	Coordinadora Cakchiquel [sic] de Desarrollo Integral (Kaqchikel Coordinator for Integral Development)
COMG	Consejo de Organizaciones Mayas de Guatemala (Council of Mayan Organizations of Guatemala)
CONALFA	Comisión Nacional de Alfabetización (National Commission on Alphabetization)
IGER	Instituto Guatemalteco de Educación Radiofónica (Guatemalan Institute for Radio Education)
IIN	Instituto Indigenista Nacional (National Indigenist Institute)
ILV	Instituto Lingüístico de Verano (Summer Institute of Linguistics [SIL], which is an arm of the Wycliffe Bible Translators)
OKMA	Oxlajuuj Keej Maya' Ajtz'iib' (13 Deer Mayan Writers, a group of Maya linguists named after the date in the Maya calendar on which it was formed)

PLFM   Proyecto Lingüístico Francisco Marroquín (Francisco
              Marroquín Linguistic Project)
PRODIPMA   Proyecto de Desarrollo Integral del Pueblo Maya
              (Integral Development Project of the Mayan People, a
              USAID-funded project administered by the
              Universidad Rafael Landívar)
PRONEBI   Programa Nacional de Educación Bilingüe (National
              Program of Bilingual Education)
SIL   *See* ILV
USAID   United States Agency for International Development
UNESCO   United Nations Educational, Scientific, and Cultural
              Organization

Maya Cultural Activism
in Guatemala

1.
Introduction:
Maya Cultural Activism in Guatemala

Edward F. Fischer (Vanderbilt University)
R. McKenna Brown (Virginia Commonwealth University)

> We will always be liable to be seen (correctly) as old colonizers in a new guise as long as we understand critical, emancipatory anthropology as doing our critique to help them—be they the Third World, the working classes, the disinherited, women. . . . Who are we to "help" them! We need critique (exposure of imperialist lies, of the workings of capitalism, of the misguided ideas of scientism, and all the rest) to help ourselves. The catch is, of course, that "ourselves" ought to be them as well as us.
>
> —Fabian (1991)

This book takes a new approach to a recent phenomenon and in so doing marks a new era in Guatemalan studies. The essays that follow all deal with an emergent movement among the Maya of Guatemala, variously called Maya nationalism (Smith 1991), the pan-Maya movement (Fischer 1993, 1996), the Maya revitalization movement (Wilson 1993; Sturm, this volume), or, simply, the Maya movement (*el movimiento maya* being the preferred term among Maya activists themselves). This diversity in nomenclature reflects both the many facets of the movement and the varied views on the nature and impact of its efforts.

The idea for this volume grew in part out of a desire to present the work of a recent generation of Guatemalan Maya scholars, the first generation of Maya Mayanists, pioneers in what Kay Warren calls the field of Maya studies (1992: 192). Over the last several years, the work of these Maya scholars has become generally highly regarded among North American academics, and though analytical disagreements between Maya and North Americans exist, scholars writing on contemporary Maya culture in Guatemala widely cite Maya authors in their English works (e.g., England 1992a; Smith 1991; Tedlock 1992; Warren n.d.; Watanabe 1995; Wilson 1995). This volume presents English translations of original works by four of Guatemala's top Maya scholars, making their scholarship directly available for the first time to the English-reading scholarly community. Complementing the four chapters written by Maya are ten others written by a total of ten North Americans and one German, including anthropologists, linguists, and an art historian. In bringing together scholars from different cultural, disciplinary, and theoretical backgrounds, we hope to give the reader a look at the complexity, richness, and multifaceted nature of contemporary Maya activism.

Taken as a whole, the volume is an elaborately constructed dialogue between Maya and Western scholars over the future of Guatemalan studies and of the Maya people. John M. Watanabe has called for just such a dialogue as an answer to the postmodern dilemma of multivocality; he argues that dialogues should be created "through texts, not just within them," and that the development of an indigenous tradition in Maya anthropology needs to be encouraged, because

> in a world rife with multiple voices, contested meanings, and
> situated, emergent cultural realities, anthropology must still hold
> the courage of its convictions enough to address its others directly
> and to admit their replies. . . . Maya anthropologists would bring to
> anthropology a personal, pragmatic, and passionate engagement
> that goes beyond scientific objectivity or literary self-reflection.
> The courage of their convictions would remind all anthropologists
> that anthropology sometimes does matter in the real world.
> (Watanabe 1995: 41)

What Watanabe foresaw has already come to pass. A growing number of Maya students and professionals are turning to the social sciences to support their political advocacy for the Maya people, and their approach does indeed go "beyond scientific objectivity or literary self-reflection." These Maya scholars (like human beings everywhere) have varied, sometimes competing allegiances. They are at once erudite scholars, upwardly mobile members of a social minority group, and advocates for the well-being of their ethnic group as a whole, though they themselves probably would not compartmentalize their social roles in a like fashion. Indeed, there is a general reluctance on the part of these Maya scholars/ activists/individuals to erect clear boundaries between the discrete (from a Western scientific point of view) social domains in which they live and work, and this blurring of public and private, personal and corporate, political and scholarly frequently confounds the Western observer who strives to separate the objective from the subjective and the political from the scholarly.[1]

The Maya have long been denied a voice in academic representations of their culture and history, and Maya scholars are resentful of the manner in which their culture and history have been appropriated by the non-Maya academy, noting that much "objective" and seemingly apolitical scholarship has had dire political consequences for the Maya people (There can be no doubt that control over the representation of culture and history has practical implications in Guatemala; Ladino elites, for example, often cite the violence of precontact Maya society and the uncivilized nature of modern Indian culture as justifications of the brutality of contemporary counterinsurgency campaigns directed against the Maya people.) The politico-scholarly agenda of Maya cultural activists is based foremost on regaining at least partial control over scholarly and popular representations of the Maya people, for many of its critiques of the present Guatemalan state are based on historico-cultural comparisons. In establishing the historical and cultural basis for their political agenda, Maya scholars have tended toward the sort of essentialist analyses widely employed by U.S. and European academics well through the first half of this century (Watanabe 1990, 1992) and still popular among non-Indian writers in Guatemala. Hobsbawm (1983), Anderson (1983), and others have pointed out the importance of "invented" (and reinvented) traditions in establishing ethnonational unity, and such traditions typically seek definitiveness, leaving little room for contentious representations.

As Maya scholars have turned to essentialism, North American and European academics have begun to reject this traditional analytic style, striving instead for more fluid paradigms that focus attention on the ambiguity and the many layers of contested meanings that underlie cultural data and its collection. This analytical and stylistic divergence notwithstanding, many North American Guatemalanists are sympathetic to—if not actively supportive of—Maya causes, continuing, albeit in novel form, the tradition of advocacy in Guatemalan anthropology that started with Sol Tax in the 1930s. Indeed, the much-discussed "crisis of representation" in Western social sciences is closely associated with an increased emphasis on the ethical implications of fieldwork and scholarly representation. Over the last few decades a growing number of anthropologists have adopted a stance of advocacy, seeing their role as presenting and interpreting indigenous political agendas for a wider audience, involving those studied more fully into the research process (gathering information from "collaborators" rather than the "informants" of yesteryear) and simply trying to empower marginalized peoples by writing sympathetic ethnographies that better represent (in the foreign anthropologist's eyes) the native's view of things (see England 1992a; Osborne 1993; Watanabe 1995; Wilson 1995).

Westerners' attempts at empowerment of indigenous peoples, however, are inherently delicate situations, because, while well-intentioned, they often appear to the intended beneficiaries as simply the old colonialism in a new guise (Fabian 1991: 264): Western scholars, simply because they are from the United States or Europe, are part of the academic tradition that has suppressed indigenous representations in the past, and so their attempts to empower native peoples have paternal-istic implications to which Maya scholars are understandably very sensitive. Ironically, as they seek to proffer the elixir of empowerment, postmodernists are actually eroding the epistemological basis for the authoritative voice central to Maya scholarly activism through their rhetoric of multivocality and relational values, which denies authority to individual representations.

Native peoples around the world (be they peasants, ethnic groups, or, more simply, Others) are no longer unaware of the larger political, economic, and social systems of which they are (willingly or not) a part. Nor are they unaware of the power cultural analyses have in influencing these larger systems. From the Kayapó of the remote Brazilian Amazon to impoverished native Americans living on reservations in the United States to the Maya of Guatemala, native peoples are using culture as a powerful political tool to resist unwelcome meddling by neocolonial entities. The development of current Maya cultural politics owes much to the efforts of foreign (mostly U.S.) scholars to empower the Maya people by training them in the social sciences. Due to the structural position they occupy in Guatemalan society, the Maya have needed, accepted, and benefited from the assistance of non-Maya social scien-tists. Yet, as is common in such relationships of tutelage, a break in the connection between Maya and foreign scholars seems imminent as Maya scholars begin to contest more vigorously the validity and ethical implications of non-Maya scholarship on the Maya. Ideally, the outcome of such a break would be the initiation of a dialogue in which Maya scholars enjoy more equal footing with their foreign colleagues. The present volume seeks to foster just such a dialogue, while offering a partial solution to the problems of voice and multivocality that trouble contemporary ethnographic writers, by dividing its pages between Maya and Westerners, letting the Maya speak for themselves alongside foreign social scientists.

The differences between Maya and North American scholarship are many, as will be apparent to the reader in the following chapters. The most conspicuous difference is simply in the style of presentation. The articles by Maya authors have been translated from Spanish (which is their second language), and the formal rhetorical style employed by most Maya writers has been left largely intact. To the North American, the Maya style may at first seem a bit pompous: Maya authors write with the authority allowed them by their position as cultural insiders, and thus they often feel justified in making bold statements about the Maya people as a whole. Their ends are, of course, twofold, and the political is at least as important as the poetic. This duality is mirrored in the value of contemporary Maya scholarship: it is at once studied social analysis and primary document, for it tells us about the workings of Guatemalan society while giving us a rare insight into contemporary, urban Maya worldview and philosophy.

While this book examines the particular case of the Maya in Guatemala, the chapters look beyond the specificity of surface events to tease out underlying processes, thus revealing much about the nature of cultural politics in the postmodern world. The post–cold war era ushered in a period of cultural awakening for the many ethnic groups whose interests had been long subjugated to the necessities of fighting Communism or capitalism, as the case may be. Under Soviet rule, ethnic groups throughout the Eastern bloc were denied their own histories as cultural differences were subjugated to Soviet-style nationalism. In Guatemala, the United States and its allies (most notably Israel and Germany), in their battle against international Communism, provided financial and ideological support for ethnocidal campaigns aimed at Guatemala's Maya population in the late 1970s and early 1980s. Carol Smith writes that "one would hardly have expected Maya self-determination to be the rallying cry to rise out of the ashes of Guatemala's holocaust" (1991: 29), and yet that is exactly the case. Maya from all over Guatemala are uniting around a variety of causes. Language, for example, is central to the Maya movement, and treatment of it provides a common thread in the diverse chapters of this book. Language has long been recognized as a powerful political tool (see Fishman 1988), and it is being mobilized by groups around the world, from the Croats (who, in their ethnic cleansing movement, employ historical linguistics to rid their language of Serbian influence) to African Americans (who are creating new personal names based on morphemes borrowed from various African languages). Maya activists seek objective linguistic changes in Guatemala (e.g., co-official status for Mayan languages and the use of the unified alphabet) and also subjective changes in how the linguistic phenomena of Guatemala are understood. For example, the Mayan languages are often criticized in Guatemala as "incomplete" or "defective" because their many loanwords from Spanish—easily recognized by Spanish speakers—are seen as evidence of inferior expressive capacity. However, Maya activists find it empowering to point out that loanwords are the result of cross-linguistic contact present in all languages, and that if Ladinos were to converse in Spanish among Arabic speakers the same supposed lack of expressive capability would be noted in the thousands of Spanish words borrowed from Arabic. The Guatemalan case also demonstrates how seemingly innocuous linguistic issues can provide an effective legislative venue through which subjugated peoples can pursue human rights claims, an issue we take up again below. The Maya movement in Guatemala offers an example for the world of how ethnic claims can be successfully pursued in a nonviolent manner, even in the most extreme of circumstances. The nonviolent—though not pacifistic—strategy of Maya activism is a model worthy of emulation, as the miseries of violent ethnic insurgence of the 1990s make clear.

Guatemala

Guatemala is a country rich in geographic, biological, and cultural diversity. Within its relatively small territory (108,889 square kilometers), Stuart (1956) identifies eight natural regions, each encompassing a number of microclimatic variations (map 1). These may be grouped into three basic zones: a highland area comprising a chain of volcanic mountains cross-cutting the country from west to east, flanked to the north by a large, forest-covered lowland expanse and to the south by a low, narrow strip of Pacific coastline. Ecologists classify the forests of the northern lowlands as quasi rain forest, because although average rainfall is about eighty inches, there is still a pronounced dry season with little or no rain (Morley, Brainerd, and Sharer 1983: 39–40). In this region the Classic Maya (A.D. 250–900) built the famous city-states, where they enjoyed the several hundred years of unparalleled development in political organization, the sciences, and the arts for which they are most remembered today by the rest of the world. To work this fragile environment, the Classic Maya employed a variety of agricultural techniques, ranging from simple slash-and-burn methods to complex systems of irrigated raised fields. Around A.D. 900, due to years of increasing population and overproduction that led to environmental degradation and escalating political tensions between Maya polities, this period of florescence came suddenly to a halt, as one Maya city after another "collapsed" (Culbert 1973).

The Classic Maya are perhaps most famous for their elaborate calendrical system, and several of the chapters that follow give dates in both the Maya and Gregorian calendars. The Classic Maya, as well as some of their predecessors, possessed several systems for naming days and ascribing dates. Of these the most important are the sacred 260-day calendar used for divination (the *tzolkin* or *cholq'ij*), the 365-day solar year (the *haab* or *'ab*), and the Long Count (or Choltun) system, which assigned a unique designation to any given day. The Long Count system fell out of use, as far as we know, around A.D. 909, while use of the 260-day calendar and, to a lesser extent, the 365-day calendar is still maintained by Indian priests in much of Guatemala's western highlands. Today, Maya activists and scholars are resurrecting the Long Count and using it along with the 260-day and solar calendars in their writings.

Map 1. Departments and Major Cities of Guatemala

The Long Count, like the Gregorian calendar, records the number of elapsed periods from a given starting point marking the beginning of the current era. In the Gregorian calendar the starting point for the present (or Christian) era is 1 January of the year A.D. 1. The Maya Long Count begins on a date of unknown importance that corresponds to the Gregorian date 11 August 3114 B.C. The passing of time since that date is counted in the following periods: Q'ij (1 day), Winäq (20 days), Tun (360 days), K'atun (7,200 days), and B'aqtun (144,000 days). These periods are related to the Maya vigesimal system of numeration, which is based on 20 rather than 10, as is our decimal system. The period of the Tun deviates from a purely base-20 count (it is equal to 18 times 20 rather than 20 times 20) so as to more closely align the Tun with the solar year. The other periods, however, are all equal to 20 times the previous period (e.g., 1 K'atun is equal to 20 Tuns, and 1 B'aqtun is equal to 20 K'atuns). Thus, the Maya date 12 B'aqtuns, 19 K'atuns, 1 Tun, 14 Winãqs, 14 Q'ij is equal to 12 x 144,000 + 19 x 7,200 + 1 x 360 + 14 x 20 + 14 x 1 (or 1,865,454) days after 11 August 3114 B.C., which corresponds to 3 July 1994 in the Gregorian calendar. The 260-day count and the 365-day solar calendar mesh to form what is called the Calendar Round, expressing days and months in numerals combined with day and month names (e.g., 5 Ahua 8 Kumku).

A common assumption is that the Spanish encountered in Guatemala culturally pristine societies whose cultures were contaminated and invalidated by their presence. Yet the highland Maya cultures that flourished during the Postclassic period (A.D. 900–1200) had been profoundly affected by repeated invasions from Mexico for at least a thousand years before the Spaniards' arrival. As Lutz observes, the highland Maya had been "Mexicanized and Toltecized before they were ever Hispanicized" (1976: 50). These cultural intrusions would affect most strongly the urban populations, while the rural peasantry would be least affected. This pattern of response to foreign influence continues to modern times.

The material and ceremonial aspects of highland Maya culture were most affected by the repeated invasions, while linguistic behavior remained (relatively) untouched. Suarez remarks that "linguistic contacts were primarily among the upper classes and . . . their potential effects reached lower groups only sparingly" (1982: 92). Hence amid the constant intercultural contact fostered throughout Mesoamerica's history of trade, migrations, and warfare, a large proportion of the lower strata apparently carried on in linguistic isolation. This hypothesis is supported by the linguistic fragmentation found in present-day Mesoamerica.

The late Postclassic period began some ten generations prior to the Spanish invasion when Toltecs from the Tabasco-Veracruz region of Mexico entered Guatemala and eventually controlled large sections of the central highlands (Fox 1978). The Toltecs had a profound influence on their new subjects, who in turn absorbed their new rulers. As Lutz notes, though the Toltecs "introduced many new forms and customs in architecture, secular administration and religious practice . . . they themselves adopted the local Mayan languages" (1976: 50). The Toltec invaders became priests and rulers of many of the highland groups, including the K'iche' and Kaqchikels. The *Popol Wuj* mentions them as founding fathers of the K'iche' kingdom and alludes to their linguistic assimilation:

And then the speech of the tribes changed;
   Their speech became different,
No longer clearly
   Could they understand each other
When they came to Tula,
   And there they separated. (Edmonson 1971: 163)

By A.D. 1250, the highland Maya were organized into five Toltecized groups: the K'iche', Poqomam, Tz'utujil, Mam, and Kaqchikel. The largest and most cohesive of these was the K'iche' polity, whose military expansionism had brought under control many neighboring groups by A.D. 1450 (Carmack 1981). Around 1470, the K'iche' kingdom had grown administratively cumbersome and suffered periodic revolts by its subject peoples. Taking advantage of this growing instability, the western Kaqchikels, formerly K'iche' allies, embarked on their own campaign of military expansion. At the time of European contact, the Kaqchikel rulers of Tecpán controlled over forty surrounding towns and were in military and political ascendance (Fox 1978).

   The Spanish invasion and subsequent European migration superimposed Spanish hegemony on a fluid and complex web of Maya ethnic/linguistic groups, the legacy of which still rules ethnic relations in Guatemala. The country's Maya population comprises twenty-one separate language groups concentrated in the western highlands (map 2).[2] In contrast to official government statistics, most scholars believe that of Guatemala's approximately 10 million inhabitants, between 50 and 60 percent are Maya.[3] Much smaller groups of Garífuna (blacks of African/Caribbean origin), Germans, and other European and Asian immigrants make up less than 1 percent of the total population. Ladinos, most easily defined as everyone else, make up between 39 and 49 percent of the population and dominate national political and economic systems (see Paz 1993).

   While Ladinos consider themselves to be a biologically distinct group and heirs to the Spanish/European cultural tradition brought to the New World by Spanish colonists, the demographics of immigration during the colonial period show that they are mostly of mixed Spanish and Maya blood. Carol Smith writes that "what has distinguished Indians and non-Indians over time has not been biological heritage, but a changing system of social classification, based on ideologies of race, class, language, and culture, which ideologies have also taken on different meanings over time" (1990b: 3). Nonetheless, in Guatemala these ethno-cultural cat-

Map 2. Language Groups of Guatemala

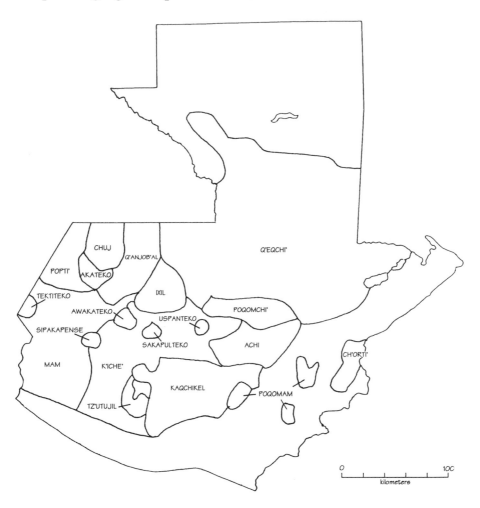

egories are often discussed in terms of race, blood, and biology. Indians are commonly called the "indigenous race," and presumed European blood lines and the accompanying phenotypic features (e.g., light hair and skin, thin lips, narrow nose, etc.) are highly valued by Ladino elites.

The study of ethnic relations in Guatemala has traditionally relied on Fredrik Barth's (1969) concept of ethnic boundaries, seeing a bipolar ethnic landscape in Guatemala in which rigid structural boundaries separate the categories Maya and Ladino. In defining these boundaries, scholars have focused on the distinctiveness of cultural elements unique to each group, going so far as to characterize ethnic categories as "inverse images" of one another (Hawkins 1984). The dominant ideology in Guatemala does indeed define the category Ladino in opposition to Maya ethnic markers: Indians wear typical dress (*traje*), Ladinos do not; Indians speak an indigenous language, Ladinos speak Spanish; Indians practice indigenous New World folkloric culture, Ladinos practice European high culture. Recent research on Guatemalan ethnicity has shifted focus from defining boundaries to recording the fluidity of boundaries and the changing system of meanings assigned to cultural symbols (Warren 1978, 1992, 1993; Watanabe 1992, 1995; Wilson 1995). This new approach recognizes the essential continuity of the Maya cultural tradition while noting that "new criteria of identity gravitate around traditional signs of community, even though at times they may express opposite meanings" (Wilson 1995: 11). A focus on the practice as well as the structure of ethnic identity is especially relevant to the study of the Maya movement. As the chapters that follow make clear, Maya cultural activism is centrally concerned with assigning new meanings to traditional symbols in an attempt to construct a unified, internally defined pan-Maya identity.

Nonetheless, in looking beyond static representations of the diametric opposition between the categories Maya and Ladino, John Watanabe cautions scholars not to forget that "while the subtleties and ambiguities of actual relations between Maya and Ladinos belie such stark oppositions, these racist stereotypes pervade—and shape—Guatemalan life" (1995: 30). Because Guatemalan stereotypes categorize individuals as Maya or Ladino based on a few conspicuous cultural traits (most prominently dress and language), Maya are not naturally (phenotypically) precluded from integrating themselves into the Ladino community. Indeed, the fluidity of Guatemala's ethnic boundaries is perhaps best illustrated by the fact that many Indians have chosen to become Ladinos in an effort to avoid cultural discrimination and to facilitate their integration into the national education system and regional commercial networks controlled by Ladinos. Successful "passing," however, requires not only that Indians adopt Ladino cultural traits and identify themselves as Ladino, but also that others recognize them as Ladino. Thus it is often hard for a Maya to successfully make the transition to being Ladino while living in his home community. If, however, his Spanish is good enough and his adoption of Ladino ways is convincing enough, a Maya may move to another community where he is not well known (ideally a large city) and integrate himself into the Ladino community. The newly ladinized person's upward mobility is nonetheless still limited by a glass (though not completely transparent) ceiling that excludes not only all Indians but also most Ladinos from the close-knit network of elites that effectively controls the upper levels of the Guatemalan government and national economy.

Guatemala's demographic situation and highly unequal distribution of wealth have contributed to the long-standing fear of the country's Ladino elite of an Indian uprising. Sam Colop (chap.6) suggests that this fear results from Ladinos' projecting their own racism onto the Maya people. Regardless of its cause, one concrete result of this fear is that the Guatemalan state has consistently attempted to culturally integrate Indians into Ladino society as an underclass in an ethnically homogeneous, modern nation-state rather than a distinct ethnic group with its own political agenda. Even the casual traveler in Guatemala can see that the government's efforts to eradicate Maya culture have failed. There are twice as many Indians in Guatemala now as at the time of the Spanish invasion (Lovell and Lutz 1992), and the Indian community is ubiquitous throughout the western highlands.

The biggest threat to the status quo in Guatemala for the last three decades has been the country's armed revolutionary movement. Yet this movement has failed to offer a feasible solution to the country's ethnic problems. Like the establishment it seeks to overthrow, the revolutionary leadership sees assimilation as the answer to Guatemala's ethnic conflicts. When it started in the 1960s, Guatemala's guerrilla movement, led by disenfranchised Ladino labor activists and leftist intellectuals, was based in the eastern part of the country, which is mostly populated by Ladino peasants. After suffering a crushing defeat in the late 1960s, the guerrilla movement went into a several-year-long hiatus, reemerging in the early 1970s in the Indian-populated western highlands. While the guerrillas' base of support became largely Indian, their ideology remained firmly rooted in the idea of class struggle, leading them to underestimate the importance of the ethnic/cultural issues. Guerrillas believe that ethnic affiliations disguise exploitative class relations and inhibit the unification of Ladino and Indian peasants and workers, and that ethnic concerns can only be addressed after a class-based revolution (Payeras and Díaz-Polanco 1990; Fernández Fernández 1988). As the guerrillas made inroads in the Indian highlands, the Ladino elites' cold war–inspired fear of Marxist revolutionaries converged with their long-smoldering fear of an Indian uprising, creating an ideological justification for ethnocidal campaigns directed by the military. Ostensibly the military effort aimed to stamp out Marxist revolutionaries, though it targeted not only active subversives but also *potential* subversives, a category often understood to include all Indians.

The military's brutal counterinsurgency campaign reached its height in the early 1980s, leaving tens of thousands dead and hundreds of thousands in exile. In 1986, nominal civil rule was reestablished with the election of Christian Democrat Vinicio Cerezo. In 1991, the presidency was passed between two freely elected civilians for the first time in Guatemalan history when Jorge Serrano Elías took office. In early 1993, Serrano, mimicking Peruvian president Alberto Fujimora, conducted an *autogolpe* in which he disbanded Congress and the Constitutional Court and gave himself broad powers. Serrano, however, seriously misinterpreted the country's political climate, and within two months an unlikely coalition of leftists, unions, businessmen, Maya groups, and the military leadership forced him into exile in Panama, where he is reported to be living a life of luxury after coming into office nearly bankrupt. In an equally surprising turn of events, Ramiro de León Carpio, then the government's human rights ombudsman, was elected by Congress, with the military's explicit blessing, to continue Serrano's term. Contrary to the high hopes that his election raised, reports of human rights violations (to both the government Office of the Human Rights Ombudsman and the Catholic Church's Human Rights Office) sharply increased during de León Carpio's rule. Further, de León Carpio refused to disband the notorious civil patrol system, which the military supports and which de León Carpio himself criticized while he was human rights ombudsman. Throughout these civil governments, the military has kept a tight rein on the government's workings, leading to widespread pessimism among the Guatemalan populace about the prospects for democratic change. This pessimism is reflected in growing voter absenteeism. The 1985 presidential elections had an abstention rate of about 30 percent, in the 1990 election more than 40 percent abstained, and in the 1994 national *consulta popular*, in which voters were asked to approve sweeping constitutional reforms, less than 20 percent of eligible voters cast a ballot.

The Pan-Maya Movement

Current Maya activism seeks a culture-based solution to Guatemala's many problems. The approach is two-pronged: to work for the conservation and resurrection of elements of Maya culture while promoting governmental reform within the framework of the current (1985) Guatemalan constitution and international law. The production and control of history and prehistory are of central importance to the movement's cultural promotion because of the widely held view, found in early Western scholarship and influential today among Maya and non-Maya alike, that "true" Maya culture consists only of those features surviving from the precontact period (see Watanabe [1990] for a review of this view among Western scholars). In this light the centuries of exposure to

European and African culture are seen as "contamination," and the incorporation of non-Maya elements is seen as a weakening or polluting of Maya culture. Consequently, the search for aspects of Maya culture to promote as objects of ethnic pride becomes fueled in part by a craving to establish concrete links with the pre-Hispanic past. For the modern Maya, the most conspicuous link to that past that is indisputably non-Spanish is found in Mayan languages.

The Mayan languages represent a uniquely authentic cultural possession for their speakers. As a banner for ethnic pride, the Mayan languages are appropriate because, unlike many other cultural elements, they have remained largely intact throughout the centuries of foreign incursions and upheaval in Guatemala. In addition, Mayan languages serve as an effective marker of in-group allegiances: one who does not speak a Mayan language cannot participate in discussions in that language and so is excluded from being part of the group. Thus language use, maintenance, revival, and expansion have become a focal point for cultural activism (see the chapters by Brown, England, and Maxwell in this volume). Similarly, the study of ancient Maya hieroglyphic writing and of precontact and early colonial manuscripts written by the Maya is taking on increasing importance in the movement's attempts to revitalize Maya culture. For Maya scholars, hieroglyphs provide concrete data on the workings of precontact Maya society while acting as powerful symbols of the splendor and literacy of that culture (see the articles by Sturm as well as Schele and Grube in this volume). Early colonial documents have likewise become an important source on autochthonous Maya culture and provide the only first-person Maya accounts of the Spanish invasion (see Warren, chap. 5). As Sam Colop (chap. 6) shows, these documents are also used to combat the ethnocentrism inherent in the histories of Guatemala written by Ladinos. Interestingly, other cultural elements unique to Maya culture, such as dress, have not been similarly emphasized among the male leaders of the movement, though they remain a principal symbol of female Maya identity (see Otzoy, chap. 9).

The strategy of the movement differs significantly from other such ethnic movements that appeared around the world in the early 1990s. Like members of these other movements, Maya activists are taking advantage of decreased tensions in current world politics to revive and strengthen their cultural heritage, which has been submerged by centuries of colonialism (external and internal, overt and covert). Their strategy differs from that of, say, the Croats (in the mid-1990s) in that the Maya are seeking a peaceful solution to their problems and trying to work within the framework of the current Guatemalan constitution and international law. In chapter 4 in this volume, Raxche' writes that "integral development of the Maya must be consistent with the constitution of the Republic of Guatemala" (see also Cojtí Cuxil, chap. 2). Maya activists also employ international treaties to justify their agenda, particularly Convention 169 of the International Labor Office and the United Nations Declaration on Indigenous Rights. This strategy of working within the existing legal framework evolved from their experiences during the recent (officially undeclared) civil war between the Guatemalan army and revolutionary groups, in which many Maya leaders were killed because of their perceived sympathies with revolutionary politics.[4]

Focusing first on national recognition and legal change, Maya organizations have been able to carve out a small space in which to work within Guatemala's tangled bureaucracy and legal system. In the last decade, Maya activists have successfully petitioned the government to officialize the unified alphabet for writing Mayan languages proposed by Maya groups; they have been instrumental in working for reform within the structure of the Ministry of Education (Alfredo Tay Tocoy, appointed minister of education in 1993, is the country's first Maya cabinet member); they have participated in presidential election debates; and, perhaps most surprising, they have called for Maya territorial autonomy within the Guatemalan state (see Cojtí Cuxil, chap. 2) without suffering the violent repression that would have answered such a proposal ten years earlier.

The movement is truly a national, at times transnational, phenomenon. This is in sharp contrast to the community-based allegiances that have long characterized Maya social identity (see Tax 1937; Wolf 1957; Warren 1978; Watanabe 1992). The movement promotes association based on linguistic groups and then, building on that base, hopes to foster a pan-Maya, even pan–Native American, identity. By so doing it hopes to peacefully unite Guatemalan Indians into a power base that can exert a proportional influence on Guatemalan politics and so claim social and economic justice for all Maya people.

Accompanying the movement has been a florescence in Maya scholarship in Guatemala over the past ten years. Demetrio Cojtí Cuxil (1984, 1990a, 1990b, 1991) has published several eloquently argued theses on the problem of a Guatemalan national identity, the political implications of linguistic research on Mayan languages, and the faults of Guatemala's national census data. Starting with COCADI's (1985) volume, *El idioma, centro de nuestra cultura* (Language, center of our culture), a number of publications have focused on what can be called "political linguistics." These publications have two goals: first, to produce scholarly linguistic analyses, and second, to use these data to support their political agenda (see López Raquec 1989; Oxlajuuj Keej

1993). Early colonial manuscripts have also received the attention of Maya scholars who are trying to take back control of—or at least have a say in—the production of their history. Sam Colop (1991, chap. 6 this volume) references a number of colonial documents, written by both Maya and Spaniards, to deconstruct the history of contact espoused within the Western tradition in general and by Ladino academics in specific. Alfonso Tzaquitzal Zapeta (1993) has translated the colonial document *Titulo de los señores Coyoy*, giving a contemporary Maya commentary on this early Maya document (see also Warren, chap. 5, for a discussion of Maya translating early documents). Irma Otzoy (1988, chap. 9 this volume) has written on the role of Maya women and their traditional dress in contemporary Guatemalan society and within the context of the Maya movement.

A Note on Editing Conventions Used in This Volume

The spelling of the names of Mayan languages follows the alphabet proposed by the Academia de las Lenguas Mayas de Guatemala and officialized by the Guatemalan government in 1987. The unified alphabet eliminates many of the misleading spellings based on Spanish orthography, changing, for example, the Spanish *qu* and *c* to *k* to represent the phoneme /k/ (see López Raquec 1989 for a complete review of alphabets used to write Mayan languages). As a result, the familiar spelling of the names of some language groups has changed: Quiché is written as K'iche', Cakchiquel as Kaqchikel, Kekchí as Q'eqchi', Acatec as Akateko, Jacaltec as Jakalteko, Teco as Tektiteko, Kanjobal as Q'anjob'al, Uspantec as Uspanteko, Chortí as Chorti', Aguacatec as Awakateko, Uspantec as Uspanteko, Sacapultec as Sakapulteko, Pocomam as Poqomam, Pocomchí as Poqomchi', and Tzutuhil as Tz'utujil. Toponyms derived from Mayan languages have been left in their traditional spellings for clarity. Thus, the department named after the K'iche' nation is written El Quiché. The K'iche' colonial document known as the *Popol Vuh* is written here as *Popol Wuj*, although in chapter 12 Nora England argues for an alternative spelling.

   In translating the articles written in Spanish for this volume we have had to tackle a large number of semantic pitfalls. Our primary desire has been to accurately translate the ideas of native Maya speakers writing in Spanish into fluid English. Toward this end we have decided to leave a few words in Spanish. *Traje*, which in Spanish can mean a man's suit, clothes in general, or a woman's dress, is used here in its most common Guatemalan interpretation: traditional indigenous dress, comprising a *huipil*, or woven blouse, and a *corte*, or thick, woven skirt. Mestizo may be read as a synonym of Ladino; its use accentuates the historical cultural and biological mixing that produced this group. The noun *mestizaje* refers to the crossing of races or cultures, while the verb *ladinize* refers to the unidirectional adoption of Ladino cultural traits by Maya.

Finally, this volume is dedicated to the Maya scholars who grace its pages and the many more like them who have dedicated their lives to the practice of anthropology.

Notes

We would like to thank Steve Elliot, Guisela Arsenio, and the whole staff of the Centro de Investigaciones de Mesoamérica (CIRMA) of Antigua, Guatemala, for their help in putting together this volume as they have helped countless other Maya and foreign scholars over the years; Judith Maxwell, under whose tutelage we happily worked as graduate students and whose profound commitment to the Maya people of Guatemala served as a guidepost for our own research; Victoria Bricker, Demetrio Cojtí, Nora England, Carol Hendrickson, Oxlajuuj Keej Maya' Ajtz'iib', Raxche', and Kay Warren for teaching us, by example and in lively discussions, to eschew simplistic interpretations and look instead for ambiguities and subtleties that are easily overlooked. Fischer would further like to thank Munro Edmonson, Bill Harrison, Pakal B'alam, Mareike Sattler, and Hal and Jane Starratt. His research was funded in part by a grant from the Inter-American Foundation. Brown would further like to thank Arnulfo Simón Sucuc, Martín Chacach, and Narciso Cojtí. We are solely responsible for any errors or omissions.

1. Scholarship on Latin America shows a marked historical bias toward materialistic analyses. Further, European and U.S. scholars of Latin America have been pioneers in the employment of their scholarship for indigenous advocacy (Wright 1988); many Guatemalanists choose to pursue their political agendas through U.S. and European solidarity groups, which are most often aligned with the Guatemalan popular resistance movement, whose ideology is based on classist analyses (cf. Stoll 1993). Thus, it is not surprising that students of Guatemala often question the role of personal advancement in Maya scholarly activism, implying that leaders of the Maya movement are simply ambitious Indians taking advantage of the current international political climate, which is sympathetic to the needs of indigenous peoples, securing for themselves and family members lucrative contracts and employment with national and international agencies.

2. This language map does not reflect levels of bilingualism or density of speakers. In the map it may appear that Mayan languages are predominant in the whole western three-quarters of the country. Ch'orti' and Mopan, however, are spoken only by small and declining numbers of Maya. Q'eqchi' is spoken by a large number of Maya (approximately 361,000) and is indigenous to the area around Cobán, where it remains strongest. In recent years a large number of Q'eqchi' speakers have migrated into the northern lowlands in search of

available land (Pacheco n.d.). Thus, while the distribution of the Q'eqchi' language includes most of the jungle and former jungle of the Petén, the density of Q'eqchi' speakers there is relatively low.

3. The exact demographic profile of Guatemala is unknown due to the lack of reliable census data. Demetrio Cojtí Cuxil has written that the government censuses "do not provide trustworthy data because their goal is not to reflect the demographic reality of the Indian nationalities but rather to produce results that conform to Ladino expectations: hide and minimize the existence of the Indian population" (1990b: 36). Because of the changing definitions of "Indian" and "Ladino" employed in successive censuses (see Maxwell, chap. 13), official figures show a progressive decline in the percentages of Indians since 1870 (Early 1982), dropping below 50 percent of the total population in 1964 (Tzian 1994) and officially reported as being 41.9 percent of the population in 1981 and 41.86 percent in 1987 (INE 1988: 143). Lovell and Lutz (1992), however, present revised data showing the Maya to be 60 percent of the 1991 population, and Tzian (1994) estimates the 1993 Maya population as 61 percent of the total. The latter figures are most often cited by Maya scholars themselves.

4. For further information on the Maya position in Guatemala's internal conflict, see Arias (1990), AVANSCO (1992), Carmack (1988b), Falla (1992), Montejo (1987), Simon (1987), Smith (1990c), and Stoll (1993).

2.
The Politics of Maya Revindication

Demetrio Cojtí Cuxil (UNICEF-Guatemala)

Hidden thoughts of Ladino colonialists:
- Killing an Indian is not the same as killing a man. It is killing a subhuman or an animal.
- It is unfortunate that the Spanish conquistadors and the Guatemalan army have not exterminated the Indians once and for all. Now we have to finish them off using slower, even legal, procedures.
- Oppressing the Indians is not the same as oppressing a people. It is oppressing a degenerate race of disorganized groups incapable of self-government.
- Oppression is necessary for the Indians because it is the only way to make them behave and be useful to the country. Moreover, the Indians have asked to be governed by the Ladinos.
- Assimilating the Maya is not the same as assimilating a civilized people with a vibrant culture. It is assimilating a people without culture or with a dying, residual, and oppressed culture. Ladinization does not harm the Maya, it gives them the opportunity to integrate themselves into a culture.
- Liberating the Indian is dangerous because it liberates a vengeful being. Indians should remain under Ladino control and tutelage, since Ladinos know what is best for Indians.

This chapter is a reworking of a lecture given at the "Forum of the Maya People and the Guatemalan Presidential Candidates," which took place, according to the Gregorian calendar, on 16 October 1990 and, according to the Maya calendar, on 12 B'aqtuns, 18 K'atuns, 17 Tuns, 8 Winäqs, 18 Q'ij (1 Tijax, 11 Yax in the Calendar Round). This event was organized by the Seminario Permanente de Estudios Mayas (SPEM), a private entity made up of professional, student, and self-taught Maya.[1]

In 1991, the Consejo de Organizaciones Mayas de Guatemala (COMG) used this speech as a basis for preparing the document *Rujunamil ri mayab' amaq': Derechos específicos del pueblo maya* (COMG 1991). SPEM, together with the Centro de Documentación e Investigación

Maya (CEDIM), published the complete report from the forum in 1992 (CEDIM 1992).

This chapter's objective is to explore in detail the foundation for each of the Maya demands for revindication. It consists of three parts. In the first, a summary analysis is given of the ethnic reality of Guatemala and the assimilationist and hybridist ideologies that justify the oppression and dismantling of the nations of the Maya people. The second part presents a theoretical framework for revindication that focuses on the autonomist or pluralist model as a solution. The third part develops immediate demands related to diverse aspects of collective life in Maya ethnic communities. In this last part, each demand is accompanied by a brief analysis of the reality to which it responds. While this summary of national demands is comprehensive in neither scope nor depth, it constitutes a starting point for both work and reflection, marking a path for the Maya to follow in the midst of the Guatemalan state. National rights are emphasized over social rights because this chapter seeks to strengthen the positions of Indian rights activists, be they Maya or Ladino.

The Maya People and the Ethnic Reality of Guatemala

Within its jurisdictional space, the Republic of Guatemala contains four peoples of distinct origins: the Maya, the Ladino, the Garífuna, and the Xinca. Each group has its respective language: Spanish of the Indo-European family spoken by the Ladinos; Garífuna of the Carib family spoken by the Afro-Guatemalans; and Xinca of the Pipil family spoken by the Xinca Indians. The Maya, who speak languages of the Mayan family, are divided among thirty ethnic communities or nationalities that define themselves principally by language.[2] Nevertheless, the linguistic criterion is not the only ethnic identifier and definer. History, self-awareness, and the will to be members of each of these nationalities are also important. For example, there are nationalities whose language is almost identical to that of another but who historically have been politically separate, as in the case of the Achi' in relation to the K'iche'.

Of the thirty Maya nationalities, nineteen are located exclusively in either Guatemala or Mexico. Others straddle national borders. Tektiteko speakers are divided between Mexico and Guatemala, Mopan and Q'eqchi' speakers between Guatemala and Belize, Chorti' speakers between Honduras and Guatemala, and Yukatek speakers between Mexico and Belize. Chikomuselteko (a dead or assimilated language) was spoken in both Guatemala and Mexico. The parts of Mexico, Belize, Honduras, and Guatemala that encompass the Maya nations have been called *el mundo maya*, the Maya world.

From a demographic viewpoint, there are approximately 6 million Maya, of which 1 million are in Mexico and 4.5 million are in Guatemala. It is calculated that by the year 2000, the Maya will number close to 10 million.[3] Except where specifically mentioned, this paper refers to the Maya of Guatemala.

Internal Colonialism

The ethnic order that reigns in Guatemala is not one of equal rights for all peoples. The hegemonic Ladino cultural community and its ruling class enjoy many rights, while the subordinate nationalities and peoples have almost no rights. This type of national order may be called internal colonialism,[4] and it exhibits the following characteristics:

A. The Ladino ruling class monopolizes the executive, legislative, and judicial branches of the state. It utilizes these branches to oppress and dismantle the Maya nations.

B. The territories of the Maya nations are annexed by the Guatemalan state and go unrecognized by the current internal political administrative divisions.

C. The nations of the Maya people are fragmented by the current political-administrative divisions within and between the Guatemalan, Mexican, Belizian, and Honduran states.

D. There exists a state language, which is Spanish, and an "official national culture," which is Ladino. The Mayan languages and cultures are treated as folklore.

E. Discrimination and economic exploitation are practiced. The Maya are the major contributors toward the gross national product and the creation of the nation's wealth, but they receive the fewest benefits for their work.

Syncretist and Assimilationist Solutions

Conservative Ladinos address problems arising from internal colonialism through policies designed to maintain subordination, while progressive elements pursue ethnic assimilation and fusion projects. From 1524 (the date of the Spanish invasion) until 1944 (the beginning of democratization), Indian peoples were subordinated because of their supposed inferiority. In the current era of growing concern over human rights, the proposed solution to internal colonialism is ethnic assimilation. Through assimilation the perpetuator of Spanish colonialism (the Ladino) converts the victim (the Maya) into the cause of the colonial dilemma and prescribes the Maya's death in order to solve "the Indian problem" of "the Ladino's" country.

As a foundation for assimilation, the Ladino colonialist cultivates and supports social projects that maintain and take for granted Ladino privilege and hegemony, including the following:

A. Ethnic homogeneity is pursued through the extermination of all non-Ladino nations. The future of the country, as constructed by the Ladino nation, must be based on a sole culture (the Ladino) and a sole language (Spanish).

B. The unity of the Guatemalan state demands the existence of a sole linguistic community. The greater the linguistic heterogeneity, the greater the risks of state fragmentation and treason. Administratively, it is preferable that the governed Indians speak the language of the ruling Ladinos since it facilitates governmental tasks.

C. The development and modernization of Guatemala demands as a prerequisite the death of the Maya cultures since these are the cause of the current underdevelopment of the Maya people and the backwardness of the country.

All Ladinos believe in these dogmas, which are almost five hundred years old. Constitutional changes and international rights have little value before these irrational beliefs. By classifying ethnic struggles as divisionist and retrograde, this line of thought sustains the myth of national unity (which presupposes subordination of the Maya) and the possibility of progress and economic growth (attainable through the ladinization of the Maya).

The Basis and Means of Cultural Assimilation and Syncretism

Ladino colonialism relies on false premises to justify the oppression and dissolution of the nations of the Maya people. Foremost among these are the assimilationist and syncretist fallacies.

The danger of these fallacies is that they are operative. On the one hand, they cause the exterminators of Maya culture to be seen as saviors, the discriminators to be seen as democrats, and the oppressors and exploiters to be seen as liberators and benefactors. On the other hand, they make the Maya who defend the rights of their people appear to be racists, retrogrades, and bad Guatemalans; those who are self-deprecatory and struggle against their culture appear to be "good Indians."

These fallacies have had such a profound effect on the Ladinos that even Ladino organizations and individuals who defend human rights proceed as if the human rights of the Indian peoples did not exist, doubting the legitimacy of the Maya ethnic demands. They qualify such demands as suicidal because they seek self-isolation and self-discrimination or as negative because they seek the establishment of apartheid.

Leftists and progressive Ladinos of all types have difficulty accepting the revindication of Maya nations because their education does not permit them to conceive of a decentralized state composed of delimited ethnic regions enjoying various degrees of autonomy. Moreover, they fear that the Indians will take control of the country and rule over the Ladinos.

Assimilationist fallacies and falsehoods. Assimilationist theories, which posit that the Indians must be absorbed into the Ladino cultural community, have been much criticized. Guzmán Bockler and Herbert show how dominant indigenist ideologies such as *mestizaje*, acculturation, ladinization, and integration conceal the reality of the Indian (1971: 122–164). Elsewhere, I have reviewed various colonialist views of the Indian, including the simplistic assimilationist approach ("the Maya will stop being an Indian immediately after learning Spanish") and the complex assimilationist view ("in time the Maya will stop being an Indian, after he has changed residence and received an education"). None of the colonialist systems of domination and identification address self-determination (see Cojtí Cuxil 1989: 87).

The critiques of assimilation may be summarized as follows:

A. The theses of ladinization hold possible the conversion of the Indian into a Ladino through the change of external ethnic indicators. This is false, because ethnic assimilation cannot be based solely on objective factors but rather must take into account subjective factors such as self-awareness and the will to survive.

B. The paradigm of acculturation maintains that Ladino culture must be given to the Maya because the latter have no culture or have a barbarous one. Yet the Ladinos use the Maya culture to demonstrate the originality of Guatemalan identity to foreigners. Moreover, the Ladinos' characterization of Maya culture as barbarous is based on subjective and prejudicial criteria. Does the Ladino public administra-tion's torture of citizens for political reasons demonstrate civilization?

C. The theory of integration assumes that the Indian is isolated from national life and must be forced to form part of Ladino society. Yet the Maya people are not isolated; they are integrated into the Guatemalan and global labor markets. Ladino colonialism conceives of integration only as assimilation, not as the peaceful coexistence of peoples in a state.

Syncretist falsehoods and fallacies. Policies that promote syncretism have not been widely adopted in Guatemala because they offer solutions that are not beneficial to the Ladinos. They posit the necessity of ethnic and racial fusion between Maya and Ladino, resulting in the elimination of ethnic and racial differences. While the various approaches to syncretism share this common goal, their rhetorical styles differ subtly, as the following examples show:

A. The paradigm of ethnic symbiosis holds that the Guatemalan nations can and must coexist for their mutual benefit. It seeks national unity and is expressed in terms of a "dialogue" between cultures, an interaction and exchange between ethnic communities. This paradigm has positive objectives but is only operative when two peoples coexist voluntarily and under conditions of equality. Currently, there is no such coexistence between Maya and Ladino since the Maya have never been consulted on whether they wish to be Guatemalans or whether they wish to live together with the Ladinos within the framework of a state. What exists today is a manipulation of the Indian people for the benefit of the Ladinos.

B. The theory of biological *mestizaje*, or eugenics, enjoys little favor today (cf. Sam Colop 1988). However, in 1920, Miguel Angel Asturias, a Ladino who won the Nobel Prize for literature, recommended the regeneration of the Indians through biological crossing with the superior European race.[5] Eugenic theory sees the Indians as a degenerate race and a punishment for the country. It favors the Ladino because of his supposedly superior Spanish biological heritage. Yet the classification of specific races of the human species as biologically degenerate is without basis. Furthermore, racial mixing does not produce a superior race but ordinary humans with the same qualities and defects as all mortal beings.

C. Cultural *mestizaje* asserts the possibility of constructing a single national culture from a diversity of cultures. In Guatemala, it is commonly considered that any racial crossing will bring with it a cultural crossing and that this *mestizaje* is good. In effect, the Ladino considers his biological *mestizaje* (Hispanic and Maya roots) as evidence of a cultural *mestizaje*, alleging that his culture is unifying, synthesizing, and thus national. He feels secure in promoting his culture as the only national culture. To derive a cultural blending from a biological mixing is inexact since there is no necessary causal relationship between them, and at present there is no harmonious fusion of the Ladino and Maya cultures. There is, however, an expansion of the Ladino culture to the detriment of the Maya, in effect a cultural genocide. Cultural blending (real as well as imagined, independently developed as well as accompanying biological crossing) is not an indicator of spiritual communion because the similarity of objective features between the Maya and Ladinos does not imply a similarity of subjective components. A Maya can dress and behave like a Ladino without renouncing his loyalty to the Maya people.

Guzmán Bockler and Herbert (1971: 139–142) discuss both racial and cultural *mestizaje* in their chapter dedicated to the ideological expressions of class struggle in Guatemala. They criticize writers who assert that the Ladino embodies the present and future of the country and who claim that Ladinos are a superior race created from two equal races. They also question those who assert that in Latin America there exists a harmonious conjunction of cultures producing cultural *mestizaje*.

Elsewhere I have shown (Cojtí Cuxil 1988) the difficulty in realizing ethnic compromises, above all for colonized peoples. I note that in the absence of equality between languages and cultures in a society seeking to construct a single national culture there cannot be equal contribution to the desired common culture, and therefore the synthesis will consist only of the consolidation of the hegemonic language and culture and the disintegration of the subordinate languages and cultures.

The Ladino Right's Babble on Indian Rights

Guatemala's previous (1965) constitution recognized the material inferiority of the Maya and prescribed their socioeconomic improvement as a condition for achieving their integration into Ladino culture. In practice this pronouncement only served to legitimate the efforts of ethnic assimilation, and the component of socioeconomic improvement was ignored. The state sought to comply only with the goal of the law (cultural integration) and not with the means (the material improvement of the Maya). That the constitution recognized the material plight of the Maya demonstrates the exclusion of and discrimination against the Maya in the Guatemalan state.[6]

In the current constitution, ratified by the National Constituent Assembly on 31 May 1985, the Ladino public administration has taken tentative steps toward the recognition of some cultural and landownership rights of the Maya. Article 66 (Protection of Ethnic Groups) refers specifically to indigenous communities: "Guatemala is formed by diverse ethnic groups among which figure the indigenous groups of Maya descent. The State recognizes, respects, and promotes their lifeways, customs, traditions, forms of social organization, the use of indigenous clothing of men and women, and languages and dialects."

Judicial progress has also been made through the ratification of international agreements and treaties that mention indigenous rights, including the Agreement on the Rights of the Child, which contains certain articles relevant to the rights of Indian children. Advances in the judicial field are due in part to the pronouncements of individuals within and outside of the Constituent Assembly, to indirect pressures brought by Maya (i.e., the enrollment of Indians in guerrilla organizations), and to international protests against the massacres of Maya in the highlands. Thus, this judicial progress has been more a measure of counterinsurgency and a symbolic compensation for the Indian holocaust that began in 1978 than a conceptual and political advance of Ladino rulers. For that reason, the 1985 constitution continues to prescribe Spanish as the only official language and Ladino culture as the national culture (Article 72).

The Christian Democratic administration, in power from 1986 to 1991, the first democratic government after thirty years of military rule, did little to comply with these constitutional proclamations. The only relevant legal statutes enacted during this time are Government Accord 1046-87 of 23 November 1987, which instituted the unified system of writing the Mayan languages, and the Legislative Accord, approved on 18 October 1990, which created the Academia de las Lenguas Mayas de Guatemala. Both cases suggest at best a tentative willingness of the Ladino administration to equip the Maya people with the technical instruments and institutions to strengthen and revitalize their languages and cultures.

Nonetheless, the 1985 constitution makes no allusion to political, territorial, or economic rights. Nor has judicial progress led to the adoption of more complete international agreements developed specifically to recognize the rights of indigenous peoples, such as the International Labor Organization's Convention 169 on Indigenous and Tribal Peoples in Independent Countries. The Guatemalan state's refusal to ratify Convention 169 may also signal its future response to the United Nations Declaration of the Rights of Indigenous Peoples, which will be submitted for ratification in 1996.

The Concept of the Maya People and Their Rights
The Nature of the Maya People

The constitution of Guatemala recognizes the "groups of Maya descent" as ethnic minorities, not as a group of nations defined by kinship, historical origins, and worldview. It barely mentions Indian rights and does not fully recognize ethnic communities as subjects with rights.

For the United Nations, "minorities" are distinct cultural groups that are legally and politically integrated into larger nations and have the right to protection against discrimination by members of the majority culture(s) (see United Nations 1987). These "minorities" may include immigrant groups who cannot exercise the right to govern themselves or decide their political and legal relation to other peoples.

International law has difficulty in recognizing indigenous nations because, if it were to do so, it would have to acknowledge their right to self-determination. While this right is recognized by the charter of the UN (see United Nations 1978), its application is problematic since it would dismember many existing nation-states. For that reason, and because it is composed of representatives of the hegemonic social groups of each state, the UN tends to recognize ethnic, linguistic, and religious minorities while not giving them the status of a distinct people.

The Maya consider the thirty Maya nations/linguistic communities to be a common people. They define the Maya people (*pueblo*) in almost the same way as the International Court of Justice:[7]

> a group of persons who live in a given country or locality; who possess their own race, religion, language, and traditions; and who are united by an identity of race, religion, language, and tradition in a sense of solidarity, with the purpose of preserving their traditions, of maintaining their religion, of assuring the education of their children in accordance with the spirit and traditions of their race to help themselves. (Indian Law Resource Center 1984: 20–24)

As a people, the Maya nations are entitled to certain rights, including the right of self-determination, which may be exercised within the framework of the Guatemalan state (internal self-determination) or outside of it (external self-determination). The United Nations Charter and its International Human Rights Covenants clearly apply to the Maya. They establish the following:

> 1. All peoples possess the right to self-determination. By virtue of this right, they can freely determine their political status and act freely to pursue their economic, social, and cultural development.
> 2. All peoples can, for their own ends, freely dispose of their natural wealth and resources. . . . in no case may a people be deprived of its own means of subsistence.
> 3. The states forming part of this pact . . . must promote the pursuit of the right to self-determination and must respect that right in keeping with the revisions of the Charter of the United Nations. (United Nations 1978: 23–28)

These directives of self-determination are applicable to the Maya, yet their status as a distinct people is not recognized either by the constitution of the Guatemalan state or by the United Nations. The implementation of Maya human rights is contingent on the recognition of the Maya's right to self-determination, which must be advanced through formal rulings at the international level, as well as through changes in Guatemalan society.

Autonomy as a Solution to Internal Colonialism

Under conditions of internal colonialism, peoples must seek their human rights through autonomy, pluralism, and decentralization. The monolithic structure of the Guatemalan state reflects the absence of an ethnic pact between the Maya and Ladino.

Autonomous solutions should not be confused with mere technocratic concessions that eventually promote the maintenance of a strongly centralized state. Autonomy supposes the exercise of legislative powers. With autonomy, territories can legislate terms of their existence in a manner that is definitive (they cannot be revoked by the central power) and independent (their content is not determined by a state law).

Autonomy involves complete decentralization. Autonomous internal organization of states is associated with democracy because the local autonomous agencies must be freely elected by their constituents. While there are varying degrees of autonomy, the historic model of a politically decentralized government would be the federal state. The scope of autonomy reflects the degree of decentralization in autonomous communities (see Celaya Ibarra and Celaya Ulibarri 1992: 35–45).

Autonomous solutions seek equality among nations and peoples at the most elementary levels (protection for minorities against discrimination by the majority) as well as the most integral levels (rights of internal and external self-determination). The search for national or ethnic equality is accompanied by a search for social equality, which in the case of the Maya includes the following demands:

A. Social and economic equality between Maya and Ladinos must be sought more through integration and leveling than through separatism. Ethnic equality must be achieved through respect of differences and mutual autonomy. Both peoples should have equal opportunities to reproduce and ethnically perpetuate themselves. This is not a matter of giving Maya the opportunity to turn themselves into Ladinos but rather to continue as Maya and progress economically.

B. The right to ethnic difference must not be confused with the maintenance of social inequality. Social and ethnic equality must recognize and satisfy both ethnic aspirations and vital material needs.

C. Legal norms should remedy the unjust distribution of duties and benefits between Maya and Ladino. For example, a disproportionate majority of military draftees are Indian, while the majority of public posts are held by Ladinos.

D. Laws should seek a compensatory justice to achieve equality between Maya and Ladino. Differential treatment in the past served to marginalize and colonize the Maya; it should now be used to decolonize and compensate them for their social disadvantages.

E. The Maya must be permitted to create a balance between traditional and modern as they modernize their cultures.

Human Rights of the Maya People

In 1976, the International Conference on the Rights and Liberation of Peoples took place in Algeria. Its principal task was drawing up a

Universal Declaration of the Rights of Peoples because the various declarations of human rights and codes for the rights of states had yet to be integrated into an overarching declaration.[8]

The Algeria declaration addresses the right to exist, the right to political self-determination, and the cultural and economic rights of peoples. While it is difficult to apply the Algeria declaration as a whole to the case of the Maya, among the applicable rights are:

A. The right to exist as a people: The Maya have the right to respect for their cultural and ethnic identity. They have the right to recuperate and conserve their original ethnic territories. They have the right not to be objects of massacres, persecutions, and living conditions that impede the manifestation and development of their identity and integrity as a people.

B. The right to ethnic and cultural differences: The Maya have the right to use, preserve, and develop their cultures and languages. They have proprietary rights to the cultural, artistic, and historic wealth of their people. Further, they have the right to defend themselves against any cultural impositions that are foreign to them.

C. The right to political self-determination and limited self-government: The Maya have the right to determine their political and cultural destiny. They also have the right to free themselves from all forms of colonial domination, internal or external, direct or indirect.

D. The right to a relative economic autonomy: The Maya have proprietary rights to their wealth and natural resources as well as the right to recuperate them and to be indemnified for their expropriation. They have the right to be fairly compensated for their work and to equitable conditions in their dealings with Ladinos. They have the right to participate in the scientific and technical progress which forms part of humanity's common heritage. (Casalis 1978: 47–52)

The Immediate Demands of the Nations of the Maya People

The demands of the Maya set forth here correspond to their status as ethnic "minorities," or nations constituting a political minority. These are the most urgent demands since they seek to resolve the most pressing problems of Maya nations, some of which are battling imminent demise.

These rights have been called "specific rights" because they seek to enable the Maya to achieve equality with Ladinos. Specificity should not be understood as rights that only the Maya can enjoy, since the Ladinos (at least the ruling class) already hold them.

Current Maya revindication seeks a multiethnic Guatemala through the recognition of equal rights for all ethnic communities. These demands cannot be satisfied by the limited rights accorded Indians in the current constitution. Neither can they be fulfilled through Ladino nationalism, which either consecrates Ladino domination over Maya or proposes Maya assimilation.

Territorial Demands

Territorial rights for each Maya nation.   The territorial rights of each nation must be recognized since the Maya were the first to discover and populate the territory that the Guatemalan state now occupies.

International law recognizes territorial rights of ethnic minorities and peoples when they fulfill two requisites: the claimants (1) discovered and (2) still inhabit the land in question. The Maya case fulfills both conditions.

Currently, the territories of the nations of the Maya people are permanently expropriated by the colonialist Guatemalan state. Independence from Spain in 1821 did not return political or territorial sovereignty to the Indian nations. Rather, it brought the perpetuation of colonialism under successive masters: Spaniards from 1524 to 1821, Creoles from 1821 to 1871, and Ladinos from 1871 to the present.

Territorial rights in Guatemala are "forgotten" rights since they are rarely mentioned by human rights defenders. The Guatemalan state currently administers territorial space that does not belong to it, and it exercises sovereignty that belongs to the pre-Alvarado Maya nations. This fact must not be merely recognized; territories that have been unduly expropriated must be returned.

Political-administrative divisions based on ethnicity.   Guatemala's current political-administrative divisions should be restructured to respect ethnic and linguistic borders.

At present, the political-administrative division sanctions the fragmentation of ethnic communities initiated by Pedro de Alvarado. The Spanish invaders divided Maya territory into administrative units that did not correspond to ethnolinguistic regions in order to fragment nations and isolate them from one another. The Catholic Church did the same. This colonial division contributed to the development of local allegiances and the loss of ethnic unity, as well as increased dialectal divergence in languages.

In 1986 the Preliminary Law of Administrative Regionalization of the Republic (Decree Number 70-86 of the Congress of the Republic) continued the colonial strategy of administratively dividing Maya ethnicities, though ostensibly to aid development and decentralization.

It institutionalized at the national level fragmentation that had already existed at the local level.

As a consequence, there are quatrilingual departments and multilingual regions. For example, administrative Region VI includes the departments of San Marcos, Quetzaltenango, Sololá, Totonicapán, Suchitepéquez, and Retalhuleu and is inhabited by Mams, K'iche's, Kaqchikels, and Ladinos. Such fragmentation impedes regional officialization of Mayan languages and cultures and the delimitation of the jurisdictional spaces of autonomous ethnic governments.

Territorial autonomy.   The return of ethnic autonomies must be accompanied by the reestablishment of territories resembling as closely as possible those that had been in place for thousands of years before the Spanish invasion. Should this be impossible, each ethnic group should be guaranteed control over a sufficient extension of land to permit a viable economic existence in keeping with its culture and its pace of development.

Ethnic-based territorial autonomy should entail the right of each nation to exercise control over cultural domains and to legislate public order in its jurisdictional space. Autonomy means that each nation will have its own birthplace and resting place.

Within multiethnic societies, there can exist two types of autonomy for nations: a cultural autonomy, with the members of each ethnic community dispersed in different places, and a territorial autonomy, with the members of ethnic communities concentrated in a given location. Currently, the majority of Maya nations (or linguistic communities) are concentrated in geographically delimited areas, which facilitates the recognition and exercise of territorial autonomy. Since linguistic regions already exist, all that is needed is a formal recognition and legalization of their borders.

Private and collective landownership.   The current constitution (1985, Article 67) recognizes the Indians' right to practice special forms of land tenure such as collective possession of land (i.e., communal holdings). Legal mechanisms to apply this right are now needed. Further, the government must guarantee the Maya's natural and inalienable right to recover lands that have been expropriated and to freely determine their use. It should be kept in mind that for the Maya, land is not merely an object of possession and means of production but also an important element in their beliefs, customs, and culture. Therein lies the importance of land.

The dispossession and expropriation of Maya land has been a permanent feature of colonial rule, particularly prevalent during three periods: the expropriations in 1524 by Spanish invaders, those in 1871 by liberals working for then-president Justo Rufino Barrios to privatize and reduce the communal Indian lands, and those in 1980, which employed supplementary titles to take possession of lands throughout the departments of Izabal and the Petén.

At present there are collective and individual landholders who lack proper titles. Some place their faith in the oral transactions through which their land was obtained; others cannot afford to obtain titles because of the costly and time-consuming legal process involved. For these landowners, obtaining titles is crucial to avoid expropriation, and their claims to ownership by possession must be recognized.

Control and utilization of natural resources.   The Maya should be guaranteed the right to control and use the resources that their lands contain and should be given the technical and financial assistance necessary for their conservation and renovation. The soil and subsoil resources of Maya territory belong to the indigenous people, and only they have the right to decide the manner and scale in which these resources will be exploited.

Currently, such rights are unknown in Guatemala, especially in regard to the use and control of subterranean resources such as petroleum and minerals. The exploitation of these resources is accepted only within the framework of private property. The current constitution mentions the protection of indigenous lands and agricultural cooperatives (Article 67) and the provision of state lands to indigenous communities that need them for development (Article 68), but it does not discuss control and exploitation of natural resources.

Political Demands

Political autonomy.   The Maya right to political autonomy must be recognized. The Maya should have the right to decide their national destinies through regional governments that conform to Maya modes of administration (e.g., through the councils of elders).

Currently, no Maya nation enjoys autonomy. I refer here to ethnic autonomy, not to autonomy at lower governmental levels. There have always been Indian mayors in hamlets and villages, and there is a growing number of Maya mayors at the municipal level: of all the mayorships in the highlands, 20 percent are in Maya hands. Nevertheless, there is no autonomous Maya polity, and the higher levels of government, such as departmental and regional administrations, remain totally in the hands of Ladinos, who generally promulgate and apply colonialist laws.

Maya representation in Congress.   It is necessary to establish Maya representation in the Congress of the Republic and in all elected assemblies of autonomous and semi-autonomous, national and international organizations. This will permit the Maya to participate in the Guatemalan state and to have legislators defend their ethnic interests.

Representation should be realized through ethnic regions and not through the current electoral districts. Representation should reflect the density and numerical importance of each Maya ethnic community. If the Maya constitute 60 percent of the Guatemalan population, then 60 percent of congressional representatives and 60 percent of those representing Guatemala in international organizations should be Maya. Furthermore, if the K'iche' constitute 20 percent of the Maya population, then 20 percent of the Maya representatives should be K'iche'. The smallest Maya nations should be allocated at least one congressional representative.

Article 157 of the current constitution stipulates that legislative power belongs to the Congress of the Republic, which is composed of deputies elected directly by the people through universal suffrage in electoral districts. Congressional deputies represent the divisions of the state which hold administrative, fiscal, and geopolitical significance for the Ladino government. However, for the civilian population, especially for the Maya nations, these divisions do not represent historic or political boundaries. Congressional deputies represent districts developed to restrain the civilian population, not to express political and ethnic unity.

The Maya have participated in Ladino political parties, but their participation has always been marginal, accidental, and hardly representative: in 1974 two Maya were elected as congressional deputies; in 1982 ten Maya were nominated to participate in the Council of State; in 1985 eight indigenous deputies were elected (constituting 8 percent of the Congress); and in 1990 five Maya deputies were elected (constituting 5 percent of the current Congress).[9]

Maya participation in public planning. All state organizations that deal with cultural conservation or Maya development (e.g., the general secretary of economic planning, the Sectorial Units of Planning and Research, multipartite national commissions, and technical assistance councils) must enlist the participation of Maya representatives committed to the interests of their ethnic communities.

Maya organizations should also be consulted about programs that have an impact on the Maya people. Nonetheless, consultation, in itself, allows only marginal participation and at times can be converted into an act of political demagoguery. Consultation is not a substitute for representation.

Currently, Ladino bureaucrats formulate development policies for the Maya without consulting them. The majority of these bureaucrats, due to their colonialist indoctrination, conceive of Maya development only in material terms or in terms of integrating the Maya into Ladino culture. The colonialist beliefs held by state technocrats influence the distribution of departmental budgets and reproduce the state's ideology of Ladino colonialism. This situation would be solved in part if the ethnic composition of the state reflected the ethnic composition of the civilian society that it serves.

The appointment of public functionaries based on ethnicity.   Members of Maya communities must be appointed as public functionaries of the state dependencies operating in their territories. This will permit the Maya to address state administrative and jurisdictional entities in their own languages. At the regional level, public posts should be reserved for the members of each Maya nation.

Local functionaries should not be transferred outside of their ethnic community without their consent. Further, functionaries who do not belong to the ethnic community they serve should be fluent in the regional language.

Today, the public functionaries who serve the Maya are either Ladinos from the capital being punished for failings in their work or Ladinos from other parts of the country. Neither type of public employee speaks the language of the population it serves, and worse, they have no intention of learning it no matter how many years they spend in their post. Their patriotic task is to ignore or disdain the Indians and to maintain oppression by treating them as second-class citizens.

There are indigenous public employees, but their numbers are minimal, their rank is low, they work outside their ethnic territory, and they are discouraged from identifying themselves as Indians.

Jurisdictional Demands

Preeminence of international law.   Article 46 of the constitution, which establishes the preeminence of international law over internal law in regard to human rights, must be put into operation.

Guatemala is a signatory to several international agreements and treaties that favor the nations of the Maya people, including (1) the Agreement on the Rights of the Child, signed by Congress in 1990; (2) the International Convention on the Elimination of All Forms of Racial Discrimination, ratified in 1983; and (3) the Convention for the Prevention and Sanction of the Crime of Genocide, ratified in 1952. Nonetheless, due to a lack of awareness, the Maya, as well as other sectors of the population, have not demanded compliance with these treaties.

Ratifying international agreements on indigenous rights.   Pending international agreements and treaties on the rights of indigenous and national minorities must be ratified.

These agreements are often more progressive than the current constitution of Guatemala in terms of Indian rights. For example, the International Labor Organization's Convention 169 on Indigenous and Tribal Peoples in Independent Countries is still not ratified by Guatemala. This agreement has two objectives: to enable tribal and indigenous peoples to enjoy the same elemental human rights as the rest of the populations of the states they inhabit; and to safeguard the vital rights and interests of these peoples.

Because the current constitution does not specifically address discrimination against the Maya, discrimination in Guatemala exists not de jure but de facto through sociopolitical and economic systems that are inherently discriminatory. This de facto discrimination denies the Maya fundamental human rights and freedoms enjoyed by Ladinos (Stavenhagen 1988: 271).

Autonomy of the Maya nations. It is necessary to constitutionally recognize the autonomy of Maya linguistic communities. This may be achieved through adoption of certain international agreements and treaties or through internal state legislation. Such autonomy may be understood as regional, ethnic self-government, in contrast to the current centralized government. The responsibilities of these regional governments would include law enforcement, education, sanitation, industry, commerce, agriculture, and social services. The central government would concern itself with diplomatic relations, state defense, maritime issues, and macroeconomic policy.

There is no better model for the autonomy of the Maya people than the United Nations Declaration of the Rights of Indigenous Peoples. Article 3 of this declaration establishes that "indigenous peoples have the right to free determination. In virtue of this right they may freely determine their political condition and freely pursue their own economic, social, and cultural development."

Reforming the current political-administrative divisions of the country. The current administrative regions and departments of the country must be changed to correspond to the country's twenty-three ethnic regions. In cases of extensive and demographically dense regions, such as that of the K'iche', internal departments may be formed. Municipal autonomy would not be affected by the administrative restructuring.

The Preliminary Law of Administrative Regionalization of the Republic is founded on Articles 224, 225, 226, 231, and other declarations of the Guatemalan constitution. These articles and declarations, as well as the content of the preliminary law, should be revised.

Making official or co-official the Mayan languages. National languages should be officialized (or at least co-officialized with Spanish) by region so that Indians have the option of using their native language when dealing with the public administration and justice system. The status of each Mayan language should correspond to the numerical importance of its speakers but never be lower than that of auxiliary language in public education. Once officialized, Mayan languages could be used in judicial tribunals and in written legal documents such as land titles, birth certificates, and identification cards.

Constitutional Article 143 (which establishes Spanish as the only official language) must be modified. At present it treats Indian languages as folklore and relegates them to household usage.

Officializing and operationalizing Maya law. The right of the Maya to use and promote Maya law must be recognized, since it establishes the rules of behavior and interaction for the majority of Indians. Maya channels of authority such as councils of elders and leaders of *cofradías* should be accorded a legal status. When demanded by the circumstances of given cases, Maya law should be used in Ladino courts as a supplementary or alternative law, and it should be presented by indigenous co-judges.

Currently, Maya law is not recognized by the constitution or the justice system, and so the Maya are judged under the norms of Roman law as adapted by Ladinos.

Linguistic Revindication

The development of Mayan languages. Before 1990, there were no laws dealing with the development and promotion of indigenous languages (Stavenhagen 1988: 273–274). On 9 October 1986 the Academia de las Lenguas Mayas de Guatemala (ALMG) was founded by eleven entities committed to codifying the writing of Mayan languages. On 3 March 1987 the Congress of the Republic was pressured to pass legislation approving the creation of the ALMG, and in 1990 Congress authorized its creation as an instrument for the development and promotion of indigenous languages (Legislative Decree 65-90).

Nevertheless, the state, through its Ministry of Finance, has not complied with the annual budgetary assignment to the ALMG of 5 million quetzales as legislated in 1990. The state must not only fulfill its commitments to this Maya-controlled entity, it must increase the annual budget, because 5 million quetzales is insufficient to revitalize twenty-three subordinated linguistic communities. Furthermore, the ALMG must use the funds it receives more effectively if it is to make real progress in standardizing the Mayan languages.

Emergency programs to rescue linguistic communities in danger of extinction. Emergency programs to help rescue the Indian languages,

Mayan and non-Mayan, that are becoming extinct (i.e., Xinca, Itzaj, and Teko) must be implemented by all institutions concerned with human rights and cultural heritage. Among the entities obligated to carry out this task are the ALMG, the Ministry of Education, the Ministry of Culture, and international organizations such as the United Nations Educational, Scientific, and Cultural Organization (UNESCO).

It is ironic that during the UN International Decade of Indigenous Peoples, Maya ethnic communities are suffering linguistic and cultural genocide. State agencies responsible for rescuing and protecting endangered languages remain indifferent to their death. The state does not comply with its constitutional mandate to recognize, respect, and promote the lifeways and languages and dialects of the ethnic groups of Maya descent (Article 66).

The development and use of the Mayan languages in education. At the elementary school level, the language used for teaching should be the student's mother tongue. Elementary education as well as literacy training must employ additive models that promote stable bilingualism rather than subtractive models that encourage the transition from speaking a Mayan language to speaking only Spanish.

Currently, Maya students do not have the opportunity to use or to study their mother tongues in school. Maya students are thus ignorant of the grammar of their languages, and most do not know how to write them. The current methods of bilingual education and literacy training, based on assimilationist models that support transitory bilingualism, produce Hispanicized Indians and not Mayan-Spanish bilinguals.

The development and use of Mayan languages in public offices. Learning and using regional Indian languages should be made obligatory for public functionaries, Maya and non-Maya. Moreover, in all state activities the use of the Indian language of the area should be obligatory, whether directly by the authorities and subalterns or through interpreters and translators. The use of Mayan languages in all departments of the state protects the fundamental human right of monolingual Maya to participate in their government.

Public functionaries do not at present serve the Maya in their Mayan languages. They believe the ruled should adapt to the language of the rulers, and not vice versa. Thus, the linguistic organization of the country is still colonial: the vanquished must speak the language of the conqueror, or of the conqueror's descendants.

The development and use of Mayan languages in the courts of justice. Justice must be imparted in the Mayan language of those concerned. Procedural norms should authorize any member of a Maya community to use his or her mother tongue. If a particular Indian language is not officialized as a judicial language, then a translator should be provided. It is important that the judge, the lawyer for the defense, and the defendant all clearly understand one another.

The Maya are judged in a language that is not their own and that often they barely understand, making the dispensation of justice itself a violation of human rights. The penal code is based on the fiction that all Guatemalan citizens are equal, while placing the Maya at a clear disadvantage compared to their Ladino countrymen. Indeed, many Maya do not speak the official language of their country, are illiterate, and lack the economic means to pay for professional services, all of which diminish their ability to exercise their procedural rights and fundamental liberties (Stavenhagen 1988: 273).

The development and use of the Mayan languages in the mass media. The Maya must be guaranteed access to the media to promote their culture, traditions, and institutions and to permit participation in the cultural life of their country. The Mayan languages should be used in all forms of media, preferably by the Maya themselves. In magazines and newspapers, articles and whole sections should be written in Mayan languages.

In the regions of Guatemala populated by Maya majorities, mass media are almost nonexistent, and the few that do exist rarely broadcast or publish in Mayan languages. Rural radio programs, for example, use Mayan languages mostly to broadcast evangelical sermons, to advertise commercial products, or to promote political candidates. They almost never broadcast informational or educational programming.

Expulsion of the Summer Institute of Linguistics. Permission for the Summer Institute of Linguistics (SIL) to stay in Guatemala should be revoked, because the institute's purpose has been to plant and promote divisions in Maya communities.

This evangelical institution (also known in the United States as the Wycliffe Bible Translators) practices ethnocide under the guise of research and evangelism. For that reason it has been expelled from countries such as Mexico and Ecuador. It employs technical linguistic data in translating the Bible into Indian languages and thus for converting Indians to fundamental evangelical sects. Institute members interpret Maya art and dances as manifestations of devil worship. In Guatemala the SIL did all it could to block the creation of the Academia de las Lenguas Mayas de Guatemala and the unification of the alphabets used to write the Mayan languages. Under the administration of now-deposed president Serrano Elías, it worked with pastors and evangelical Indian deputies in an attempt to destroy the government accord on the unified alphabet.

The SIL's new directors are trying to switch from a hostile posture to one of possible cooperation, or at least of pacific coexistence, with the Academia de las Lenguas Mayas. Yet while they are initiating a rapprochement with the ALMG, their literacy training program in Mayan languages persists in using an alphabet based on Spanish orthography.

Educational Demands

Restructuring of the Ministry of Education. The Ministry of Education must be budgetarily and structurally redesigned to develop the following subprograms: Ladino Education, Maya Education, Garífuna Education, and Xinca Education. This restructuring would necessarily correspond to the number of Guatemalan peoples since each people has the right to freely organize the education and professional formation of its population. Thus each people would be able to autonomously administer the budget it is given for its education. Clearly, the Maya educational subsystem would have to possess its own authorities and its own schools at the various teaching levels, including teacher-training schools. Political and cultural autonomy must be based on Maya control over its own educational system.

Currently, there is a single Ministry of Education (controlled by Ladino technocrats), and its vice ministries obey its criteria in pedagogical and administrative matters and not the criteria of the peoples that they should serve. From a pedagogical point of view, the ministry acts as if all the students in the country were urban and Ladino. Bilingual education and literacy training are still in the pilot stage, and there are no consolidated models of mass Indian education.

Mayanizing the form and content of school teaching. School subjects should include the language, science, technology, history, civilization, culture, arts, literature, and regional economy of the ethnic community to which Maya students belong. This implies the development of educational materials and the use of innovative methodologies generated by the Maya themselves. Teaching students about the culture of their community contextualizes their identity while protecting them from alienating cultural intrusions.

Maya students must know their ethnic coordinates and not just those of the hegemonic peoples and current nation-state. Nonetheless, this communion of students with their own culture must not impede them from learning what they need to know in order to interact with the dominant culture. Neither isolation nor assimilation can be the currency of indigenous education.

At present Maya culture, history, art, and grammar are proscribed from school teaching. The educational system still denies the Maya knowledge of their own history and ethnic reality as well as grammatical knowledge of their own mother tongue. Schools thus operate as a state organ par excellence, carrying out the ethnocide of the Maya in the interest of the state.

Providing Maya public schools for the formation of bilingual teachers. The state must recognize the right of the Maya people to have their own schools to train teachers for primary and secondary education, both rural and urban. If the Maya are not permitted to have their own public schools, then the Regional Public School System (which was created to train Maya bilingual teachers) should be reinvigorated.

Government Accord 185 of 1945 indicates that the first regional rural public school (the Alameda) had as its objective the instruction of agricultural production, natural resources, industrial development, housing conditions, dialects, and other characteristics of the departments of Sacatepéquez, Chimaltenango, and Sololá (Carrillo Ramírez 1971: 283–285). Government Accord 58 of 12 March 1953, referring to Rural Public School Number 2, indicates that such schools are for training teachers for the rural schools of the Republic, preferably in the Quiché region (see Carrillo Ramírez 1971:298).

These schools have not achieved their goals, due to both internal and external factors: some of their Maya graduates do not identify themselves as Maya, and, further, their knowledge of Maya issues is no different from that of graduates of ordinary public schools.

Educational grants and credit programs specifically for Maya. Study grants and educational credit programs for Maya students should be established at the primary, secondary, and postsecondary levels. Compensation should cover tuition subsidies, lodging, transportation, and clothing so that Maya students might compete on an equal level with their Ladino counterparts. While these programs should be available only to Maya, the Ministry of Education's grant program as a whole should be fairly distributed among Maya and Ladinos.

A study carried out by Alfredo Tay (1993) confirmed that Maya receive fewer educational services from the state than do Ladinos. Thus in 1988, at the primary level, only 33 out of every 100 Maya children had access to schooling, while 74 of every 100 Ladino children had access; at the middle or secondary level, 7 of every 100 Maya adolescents had access to schooling, while 27 of every 100 Ladino adolescents had access; at the upper level, the situation is graver, with only 1 of every 100 university-age Maya having access to schooling.[10]

Supporting the formation of Maya study centers. Because Guatemalan universities operate more as colonial rather than multinational centers of higher education (hence ignoring colonial problems in their major programs of study), it is necessary to support the creation and maintenance of specialized Maya study centers that could be either independent of or adjunct to universities and colleges. The existence of these centers would give Maya and Ladinos the opportunity to specialize in particular aspects of Maya culture and civilization. The creation of a Maya university is also necessary, since it would act as an expression of sovereignty and a means of ethnic reproduction.

Currently, most Guatemalan universities act to reproduce colonial ideology and its practice over the Maya. Thus, in the only public university, the University of San Carlos, one finds the following anomalies: (1) the marginal and insignificant presence of Maya as students, teachers, and authorities, despite the university's obligation to contribute to solving the "Indian problem" and having a scholarship program; (2) a colonial structure in the sense that the university cannot be called bilingual or multilingual (even its regional campuses do not teach aspects of the Maya culture of the communities among which they are set); and (3) a marginal or nonexistent treatment of Maya issues, ranging from pure and simple blockades and omissions to peripheral inclusion among common subjects. The University of San Carlos started a Center for Ethnic Studies in 1992, but its orientation and effects have yet to be seen. At the beginning of this century San Carlos offered various classes and degrees in Mayan languages, but now such studies are relegated to the peripheral Language Learning Center.

Reorienting the formal and informal education of the Ladino. Maya and Ladinos cannot learn to coexist harmoniously as long as the educational system remains a vehicle for reproducing ignorance of and disdain for the Maya and their culture. For that reason, it is necessary to reorient Ladino educational materials, teacher attitudes, and curriculum content, eliminating prejudices and erroneous attitudes and ideas about Indians.

The official educational system transmits erroneous and distorted facts and prejudices about Maya history, culture, civilization, art, and sciences which are often insulting and offensive. It thus creates and practices aggressive ethnocentrism and racism. Teaching materials do not point out Maya contributions to the region, to the country, and to humanity, nor do they teach features of Maya daily life that could be usefully adopted by all, such as relations to the environment and the capacity for physical and cultural survival. Without the above changes, one cannot speak of tolerance within the education system, much less brotherhood between Maya and Ladinos.

Cultural Demands

Reorienting the cultural policies of the Guatemalan state. State cultural policies must be reoriented to recognize the existence and development of the cultures of the Maya people. This recognition involves making Maya cultures official at the regional level and co-official at the state level, thus giving Maya culture the same legitimacy and legality as Ladino culture enjoys.

At present, in law and in fact, the national culture is Ladino culture; Maya cultures are only rural, domestic cultures, part of Guatemalan folklore. The commercial exploitation of Maya cultures for the tourist industry demonstrates the moral cynicism of Ladino leaders, who deprecate and exterminate Maya cultures, on the one hand, while selectively utilizing and exploiting them at the political level (as symbols of Guatemalan identity) and at the commercial level (in the tourism industry), on the other.

Recognizing the cultural autonomy of the Maya. The Maya people must be able to freely organize and administer their own cultural, athletic, social, and religious institutions. As noted, Ladinos control the cultural destiny of the Indians, be it directly through the Ministry of Culture or indirectly through ownership of the media and control of universities, churches, governmental and nongovernmental organizations, cooperatives, and sports groups. These entities follow the cultural philosophy of their proprietors and leaders, generally Ladinos brought up in the tradition of the Ladino fatherland.

Cultural autonomy must be understood as an expression of sovereignty and as a means of exercising the right to be different. When ethnic difference is freely chosen, it is neither apartheid nor suicidal isolation: autonomy is a voluntary option of the colonized, while apartheid is one imposed on the part of the colonizer.

Restructuring the Ministry of Culture and Sports. The Ministry of Culture must be restructured so as to serve the needs of both the Ladino and Maya peoples. There should be a public agency to exclusively serve the Maya people, whose cultural needs are, because of the marginalization and persecution to which they have been subjected, more numerous, urgent, and acute than those of Ladinos.

At present, the Ministry of Culture acts as if there existed only one ethnic group in the country, the Ladinos. Its actions that favor the Indian people are circumstantial, responding to immediate pressures. It has even supported ethnocide through implicit and explicit condemnations and colonialist reproductions of Maya culture. It has done very little to alleviate the alienation seen in sectors of both the Maya and Ladino cultures.

Providing each ethnic community with its own radio station. Each ethnic community must be given at least one radio transmitter to serve as a means of ethnic expression and reproduction. In exercising cultural autonomy, each Maya ethnic community must be able to freely organize its own radio stations and participate in television production.

Maya nations currently depend on state functionaries and media owners to obtain air time. These media outlets follow the dictates of a free market economy, which does not take into account a population without buying power such as the Maya in Guatemala. For this reason, Guatemalan ethnic groups almost never express themselves in the mass media. Even Guatemalan Ladinos do not dominate mass media since 84 percent of the televised programs are imported (UNESCO 1976: 13).

Compensating for the disadvantage of the Maya people in the media. Urgent and exceptional steps must be taken to promote the publication of books, journals, and periodicals in Mayan languages. The development of film and recording industries, libraries, museums, and all forms of cultural expression should also be promoted. These forms of expression could be traditional as well as modern and used by the Maya both as a means of obtaining their goals and as ends in themselves.

At present, not even the Ladino culture receives attention from the Ladino administration. Archives, libraries, and cultural centers all suffer from the state's neglect, while the recording and publishing industries are monopolized by private enterprise. While this neglect takes place in the small-scale media market of the urban Ladino culture, it is much more acute in the rural Maya sectors.

Recognizing the value of Maya ceremonial centers. Ceremonial centers of religious significance to the Maya should be preserved and recognized as public resources. Ceremonial centers, be they on public or private land, should be conserved in their original state and should remain open to the Maya free of charge.

At present, Maya altars, no matter how historic, are subject to changes of ownership according to the free play of supply and demand. Moreover, the lack of protection leaves them vulnerable to vandalism. Maya have to pay an entrance fee to see the archaeological centers of their ancestors and then are treated like third-class citizens by the staff. This is further proof that the Maya are foreigners not only in their own country but also in their own homes.

Civil and Military Revindication

Abolishing military solutions to social and ethnic conflicts. The usual practice of solving social and ethnic problems through military means must be brought to an end and replaced by democratic processes. Military solutions inevitably involve violations of human rights and do not resolve problems because of the attitude of revindication they generate in the losers.

Consequently, the current military conflict that has lasted thirty years must be brought to an end. Civilians must lead society and seek solutions to the problems generated by the conflict. Civil society must be demilitarized through the elimination of civil defense patrols, the network of military commissioners, paramilitary groups, model villages, and development poles. The unremunerated military service that Maya civilians perform in the so-called civil patrols and the forced concentration of Maya peasants in strategic villages constitute grave restrictions of fundamental liberties as well as violations of human rights (Stavenhagen 1988: 275). The role of the army must be redefined in a democratic society, especially as stipulated in Article 244 of the constitution, in which the army is described as an institution destined to maintain "peace and internal security."

The usual practice of Guatemalan leaders has been to resolve social conflicts through military means (militarization of civilians, population concentrations, disappearings, summary and selective executions, and massacres). In these military solutions, the Maya are the most affected: since they suffer the most injustices, they are most involved in protests and rebellions. When the Maya lift their heads and demand their rights, massacres are the usual response. Their colonial history is also a history of massacres.[11]

Enforcing equal distribution of military obligations between Maya and Ladinos. Once the need to maintain a national army has been established, and once the obligation for Guatemalans to voluntarily serve in it has further been established, then care must be taken that all able citizens of any social class and ethnic community fulfill this duty. Consequently, the forced, discriminatory recruitment of Maya must end. Indian recruitment has been carried out through surprise abductions that violate human rights and provoke injustices.

The constitution establishes that among the civic duties and rights of Guatemalans is "serving and defending the Fatherland" through "performing military and social service" (Article 135). The army distributes fliers saying that "it is the duty of every Guatemalan to serve the fatherland in the ranks of its army," a duty corresponding to "all Guatemalans as they reach legal age." Nevertheless, the army has selected only Maya, principally illiterate Indian peasants, to fulfill this citizenly duty. While the law equally distributes military duties among Maya and Ladinos, its unequal application harms Indians and favors Ladinos.

Consequently, the ethnic composition and hierarchy of the army is typically colonial: officers are mostly Ladinos, and the troops are mostly Indians. Since Maya constitute the majority of the troops they are used as cannon fodder and bait in warfare. Whenever Ladinos seek military solutions, Maya end up getting killed: the recent conflict that started in 1978 with the massacre at Panzós and subsided around 1985 was fought by Maya combatants on both sides.

Restructuring the national army. The internal structure and geographic allocation of army units and bases should be revised so that members of each ethnic community serve in their own ethnic region and in units whose official language is their own. This restructuring would support Article 244 of the constitution, which establishes the army as "unique and indivisible," since the command unit would be appropriate to the ethnic reality.

Shielded by a belief in the civilizing effect of military service, the army carries out cultural ethnocide among Maya recruits by placing them in units where their mother tongue is not spoken. Recruits are forcibly taught Spanish. This often physically violent process generates traumas in young Indian veterans, producing symptoms of ethnic self-loathing and social maladaption: alcoholism, unstable family life, rural delinquency, and becoming part of an urban lumpenproletariat.

The size of the army must be reduced with the goal of liberating resources and using them to satisfy vital needs of Guatemalans, such as education, health, and housing. Assigning enormous amounts of state resources to maintain a large army cannot be justified while more than 70 percent of Guatemalans live in extreme poverty and do not receive basic public services.

Economic Demands

Reducing the discrepancy in material development between regions. Economic reforms must be carried out to end the disparity in development between administrative regions. The state must promote economic development in all regions, instead of favoring the capital and other Ladino-populated areas. Preferential policies are needed to support the development of poorer regions, such as providing concessions to firms that locate in rural areas. The poorest regions are precisely those where the majority of the Maya live, such as El Quiché, Huehuetenango, Alta and Baja Verapaz, Sololá, and Totonicapán.

Income disparities indicate the economic inequality among regions. During the period 1986–87, the country's lowest incomes were reported in the northwestern areas, mostly populated by Maya (INE 1988). Average monthly income in the indigenous northwest was 98.74 quetzales, while in the Ladino southeast it was 186.00 quetzales and in the metropolitan region it was 244.95 quetzales. Further, in 1984 the life expectancy of Ladinos was longer than that of Indians (Ghelert Mata 1984: 27–28). Ladino men had an average life expectancy of fifty-six years and Ladino women of sixty-four years. Maya men had a life expectancy of forty-eight years and Maya women of barely forty-seven years. This situation remains unchanged.

Reducing social inequalities generated by the state.   The state must change the way it distributes resources among regions and departments. Each administration favors those regions that are home to its supporters or that are mostly inhabited by Ladinos. This leaves marginalized regions with little infrastructure and few public services, making it difficult for them to attract investors. The state must execute development programs favoring the most needy regions. If the state is not capable of enacting such compensatory justice, it should at least strive toward a fair geographic distribution of public resources.

Data support claims of unfair government spending. In 1976 the state invested more in the residents of the capital than in the residents of rural areas; in rural areas it invested more among Ladinos than among Maya. Thus for each inhabitant of the rural Ladino areas of Jalapa, Jutiapa, and Chiquimula, the state spent an average of 7.22 quetzales, while for each inhabitant of the capital it spent an average of 28.27 quetzales. On the other hand, for each inhabitant of the Indian departments of Huehuetenango, Totonicapán, and El Quiché, the state spent an average of only 2.5 quetzales. Unequal state investment also causes higher infant mortality rates among Maya than Ladinos. In 1990, of every 1,000 Maya live births, 77 died, while for every 1,000 Ladino live births, only 70 died.

Humanizing the free market economy.   The philosophy and practice of the free market economy must be humanized to seek a common good, not just growth in the already privileged sectors. The pursuit of profits must not be an end in itself, nor should it employ unscrupulous means. The free market economy should not subordinate human interests to market interests, nor should it exploit Indian culture and relinquish national identity. Part of the profits earned through the sale of Indian culture to tourists should be reinvested to improve the material and spiritual life of the Maya.

Guatemala's free market economy is still brutal, because powerful elites have never been forced to change their anachronistic feudal thinking regarding labor practices, which is manifested in the following ways: (1) the discriminatory use of Indian labor, in which contracts are not honored; (2) the legislation of a minimum wage for only certain sectors of the economy (and the lack of enforcement of the same in the areas of agro-exportation and domestic help, where Maya labor predominates); (3) the small amount of taxes paid to the state by privileged sectors and the large amount paid by the popular sector; (4) the tourism industry's exploitation of the vitality and cultural diversity of the Maya, from which the Maya do not benefit directly or indirectly.

Establishing policies favoring the semi-autonomous material development of the Maya.   Economic dependence triggers disintegration and internal division of social classes in each ethnic community. Thus, the

Guatemalan state should take measures to favor the semi-autonomous development of the Maya's economy.

The Maya demand the following rights: to control their wealth and natural resources, to participate in scientific and technical progress, to take what they deserve from the economic and social systems, and to follow their own path in economic development. The state must also protect Indian lands from usurpation, respect the intellectual property rights of artisans, and promote the conservation of authentic craft production.

The Guatemalan state promotes only European and North American cultural values and models of development under the guise of liberal and neoliberal policies: individualism is imposed on communalism, productivity and profitability are imposed on balance with and adaptation to nature. These development models violate the Indians' rights of identity by usurping their authority over their own territory. As a result, Indians lack self-determination in their development. For now, there is no ethnodevelopment.[12]

The capitalist development model has positive aspects (satisfaction of certain basic needs) and negative aspects (acute social stratification, destruction of the environment, commodification of humans, and alienation). Alternatives to the shortcomings of capitalism may well be found in Maya culture, which contextualizes economic growth in terms of social and environmental balance.

Social Demands

Nondiscriminatory application of constitutional rights. The state and its repressive agencies must respect the exercise of constitutional rights by the Maya. It is discriminatory to permit the Ladinos the exercise of certain rights that the Maya are denied.

Article 136 of the constitution gives Guatemalan citizens the right "to elect and be elected," "to opt for public office," and to participate in "political activities." Articles 33 and 34 establish the rights to associate freely and to gather and demonstrate. Finally, Article 223 guarantees the free formation and functioning of political organizations. Nevertheless, when the Maya attempt to organize themselves, they are thwarted by the repressive forces of the state (e.g., the courts, police, and military), which accuse them of racism, divisionism, and unconstitutional behavior. A purely Ladino political party is not called racist, though a purely Maya one is. For example, when the Frente Indígena "Patinamit" entered the 1978 elections, Ladino representatives accused it of being racist and fomenting racial struggles, forcing it to change its name to the Frente de Integración Nacional.

Supporting the Maya's right of resistance.   The state must no longer interpret Maya cultural and political resistance as subversive and anti-Guatemalan and must stop oppressing it. Article 45 of the constitution recognizes that "resistance by the people for the protection and defense of constitutional rights is legitimate."

Since Articles 58 and 66 guarantee the right to cultural identity as well as obligate the state to recognize, respect, and promote the lifeways of the Maya, Maya resistance to the Ladino government and its cultural impositions is constitutional. Therefore, the right of the Maya to organize in any way to defend their culture, development, and vitality must be respected.

Promoting the struggle against racism and colonialism.   Finally, the democratic and anticolonialist forces of Guatemalan society must support the struggle against racism and internal colonialism. Racism, already common currency within powerful Ladino circles, is gaining ground. It appears that the more educated a person is, the more racist and intolerant he or she becomes toward the Maya (see Casaus Arzú 1992: 191–206). Racism and colonialism manifest themselves in daily life as moral and psychological violence, which in turn engender illicit forms of political conduct, such as authoritarianism and paternalism, humiliation and discrimination. Thus, racism must be overcome before effective government reforms can be enacted.

Notes

1. Due to the collective nature of the forum, a specific commission requested and approved the content of this talk. I remain, however, the sole author of this document. An earlier version of this chapter was published in Cojtí Cuxil (1994). This article was translated from Spanish by R. McKenna Brown and Edward F. Fischer; helpful comments on the translation were provided by Andrés López of the Mayan Indian Support Group.

2.   Ethnicity and nation are used here synonymously. According to the French tradition, an ethnic group is a collection of people who possess certain common features, above all language and culture. While the basic defining criterion of ethnicity or nation is language, other criteria include religion, art, self-awareness, a will to live together, and history (see Héraud 1963).

Mayan languages are subdivided into families according to their historical divergence. Basically, the Mayan languages are grouped into four divisions: Yukatekan, Wastekan, Western, and Eastern. These families have been further subdivided through genetic analyses focusing on grammar and vocabulary (see England 1992b).

3. The Guatemalan census of 1981 indicates that speakers of Mayan languages were 35.92 percent of the total population, while Maya as a whole made up 43 percent of the population. These data are not reliable, however, because they consider only very traditional Indians as Maya and count only those individuals who do not speak Spanish as Mayan speakers. These same problems

hold true for the censuses of Mexico and Belize. Almost all the Central American countries practice such "statistical ethnocide" by negating and minimizing the existence and number of Indians.

4. Michael Hechter, in analyzing English domination over the Scots, Welsh, and Irish within the framework of Great Britain, defines "internal colonialism" as the economic exploitation and cultural discrimination of one people over another within a single state. George Balandier has defined "colonial situation" as the domination that a people suffers at the hands of a conquering, foreign people that is culturally and racially different. In colonial situations the dominant group keeps the dominated in a position of material inferiority (see the chapter "What Is Colonial?" in Neuberger 1986).

While the Ladinos may not be foreign in Guatemala, they are direct descendants of the foreign Spaniards. Moreover, they are culturally different from the Maya and are reproducers and benefactors of the internal colonialism initiated by the Spanish.

5. Sam Colop (1988: 2) gives an example of eugenics found in the now infamous thesis of Miguel Angel Asturias: "do with the Indian what you do with other animal species when they show symptoms of degeneration: new blood, that's the answer!"

Asturias's thesis, which was presented to the Faculty of Law, Notary, Political, and Social Sciences of the National University of Guatemala in 1923, was titled "Sociología guatemalteca: El problema social del indio." Chapters 5 and 6 outline the author's biological solution to the Indian problem, including a section on the degenerative physical and psychological features of the Indian. Chapter 6 euphemistically describes a program of "social therapy" to destroy these degenerative features which includes encouraging European immigration and ladinization "to transfuse new blood into their veins" (Asturias 1923).

6. In the conclusion to his chapter on Indian discrimination in Guatemala, Stavenhagen (1988) states that the discrimination Indian citizens suffer stems from a system of historical domination that articulates with the system of domination that world capitalism now exercises over Guatemala. Discrimination in Guatemala is a social phenomenon that involves political, judicial, socioeconomic, and cultural exceptions, restrictions, and preferences which limit the Indians' exercise of human rights and fundamental liberties (Stavenhagen 1988: 271–298).

7. The International Commission of Jurists defines a people as a group with the following characteristics: "(1) a common history, (2) racial or ethnic ties, (3) cultural or linguistic ties, (4) religious or ideological ties, (5) a common territory or a common geographic location, (6) a common economic base, and (7) a sufficient number of people" (Indian Law Resource Center 1984: 20–24).

8. In the United Nations Declaration of the Rights of Indigenous Peoples, passed in Algeria on 4 July 1976, participants gave the following guidelines to define a people:

1. A people is a human community distinguished by differences that are sufficiently meaningful in relation to other peoples. (Between the Maya people and the Ladino people, meaningful differences exist such as culture, history, and religion.)

2. A people is a group which has to submit to the power of the majority

group in a state. (In Guatemala, the Maya are the demographic majority, but they are dominated by the demographic minority Ladinos, principally the Ladino ruling class.)

3. A people may itself comprise a homogeneous state, or it may be a minority nation whose collective rights are recognized within the state. (In Guatemala, the Maya people are negated in their existence and have almost no collective rights within the state.) (Casalis 1978: 469–475)

9. The number of Indian candidates for political office has always been insignificant compared to the number of Ladino candidates. In the 1985 elections, political parties in the nine departments with a majority of Indian inhabitants put forth 326 candidates, of which 44 (13.5 percent) were Maya. Moreover, political parties often place their Indian candidates in races that they expect to lose (Paz 1993: 19–29).

10. The study ("Análisis de situación de la educación maya de Guatemala") was directed by Dr. Alfredo Tay Coyoy for UNICEF and is currently in press. In it Tay cites a study carried out in 1985 by the Asociación para el Desarrollo Educativo (ADE) which found that of 57,432 university students in the country, only 3,551 (6.19 percent) were Maya.

11. George Lovell (1988) shows that the Maya have survived three holocausts:

1. the holocaust of the Spanish invasion of 1524 led by Pedro de Alvarado in what is today Guatemala, in which 2 million Maya were killed and the survivors were concentrated in *congregaciones, encomiendas,* and *pueblos de indios;*
2. the holocaust of the invasion of international capitalism in 1871 under Justo Rufino Barrios, in which rural Ladinos appropriated up to 70 percent of Maya communal lands and one to two thousand Indians were abducted each year to perform forced labor in coffee plantations on the south coast. Scorched earth campaigns were targeted at those areas where the Maya rebelled against this return to slavery and militarization; and
3. the holocaust of state terrorism initiated in 1978 by Eugenio Kjell Laugerud and Romeo Lucas García that resulted in the forced migration of approximately 100,000 Maya political refugees, the internal dislocation of more than 1 million refugees, and the death of tens of thousands of other Indians. This period also saw the return of scorched earth policies and the concentration and militarization of the civil population in model villages and development poles.

12. Ethnodevelopment is an inalienable right of Indian peoples that promotes the expansion and consolidation of native culture through encouraging autonomous decision making. Ethnodevelopment gives cultures the right to guide their own development, to exercise self-determination at all levels, and to have their own egalitarian organization and power structure (Camacho et al. 1982).

3.
Induced Culture Change as a Strategy for Socioeconomic Development: The Pan-Maya Movement in Guatemala

Edward F. Fischer (Vanderbilt University)

Over the last few decades scholars and practitioners of development have broadened their concern with macrolevel structural adjustments in the economies of developing countries to stress the concomitant necessity of enhancing the dignity, self-respect, and self-determination of the poor (Worsley 1984; Ghai 1988; Cernea 1991). Albert O. Hirschman (1983), realizing the need not only to integrate such cultural elements into development strategies but to make them the basis of development, introduced the concept of the "conservation and mutation of social energy." According to Hirschman, social energy is the key to stimulate active participation in development projects and to overcome the fragmentation that often hinders collective action. Expanding upon this idea, Charles Kleymeyer (1992) uses the term "cultural energy" to denote a force that acts to revitalize a cultural tradition as well as stimulate collective action and in so doing affects the motivations and behavior not only of a select group but of all the members of a culture. As a result of such theoretical developments, the idea of harnessing local cultural traditions for grass-roots development projects is now being espoused within the World Bank, the United Nations Research Institute for Social Development, the Inter-American Foundation, and the Ford Foundation; indeed, the United Nations Educational, Scientific, and Cultural Organization (UNESCO) has declared 1988 to 1997 the World Decade for Cultural Development. Despite this growing interest, Kleymeyer writes that recent initiatives in culture-based development suggest "two things—a growing realization of the need for a new development paradigm and the general lack of knowledge about which combination of techniques might make a workable model" (1992: 29).

This chapter addresses the shortcomings Kleymeyer points out by presenting data from recent culture-based development initiatives taken by a group of Maya scholars working in Guatemala. Rejecting the idea of cultural assimilation implicit in the development strategy of the Guatemalan state, these scholars are constructing a model in which a revalued

Maya culture provides the foundation for long-term, sustainable development. Their efforts, which I collectively term the pan-Maya movement, seek no less than a major redefinition of Maya identity through subsuming traditional community-based allegiances to a unified pan-Maya culture.[1] By mobilizing certain common elements of indigenous culture, they hope to unify Guatemala's fragmented Maya groups and empower them to take a more active role in Guatemalan political and economic systems, a necessary precursor for equitable economic growth and democratization in Guatemala, as elsewhere.

I begin by reviewing Guatemala's economic development policies. As will become apparent, the common theme of these policies has been the assimilation of the Maya population into a Western-style national economy. I then trace the roots of the pan-Maya movement, showing how native activists have employed cultural traditions to resist the assimilationist policies of the state since 1940. I conclude by examining the current pan-Maya movement in terms of an emerging indigenously produced development paradigm, offering a critique of its present strategy and its potential as an alternative to failed development projects of the past.

State and Development in Guatemala

Starting with the debate over indigenous rights between Fray Bartolomé de Las Casas and Juan Jinés Sepúlveda in the sixteenth century, the so-called Indian problem has dominated the non-Indian (Ladino) national political dialogue in Guatemala. The problem, as framed by Ladino scholars and politicians, is that the culture of the Maya, who make up a majority of the country's population, represents the antithesis of what they aspire to, namely, a unified, thoroughly modern, Western-based nation-state. While popular ideologies have waxed and waned over the years, the Guatemalan government has consistently pursued policies that encourage, even force, the Maya to give up their "primitive" culture for more civilized European lifeways in the hope that this will lead to economic integration and growth (see Otzoy and Sam Colop 1990; Raxche', chap. 4).

Ironically, many of these ideas have been presented as *indigenista* (indigenist) policies. While the philosophy of *indigenismo* dates to the work of Las Casas, non-Indian politicians resurrected it as a formal political policy during a series of Inter-American Indigenism Congresses begun in 1940. Bonfil Batalla identifies three central tenets of the modern Latin American *indigenista* philosophy developed in these congresses: the recognition of Indians as economically and socially weak, the need to integrate Indians into national culture, and the need to develop those aspects of Indian culture perceived as positive (1981: 14). Despite this last goal and the general rhetoric of cultural sensitivity, *indigenista* policies sought to eliminate intrastate cultural barriers by integrating Indians into homogeneous, non-Indian national societies (Barre 1982). Thus, the use of the term *indigenista* is misleading, because the *indigenista* policies of Ladino governments actually exclude Indian voices and agendas in their practice.

In Guatemala current arguments supporting ladinization (the adoption of non-Indian culture) as a catalyst for development took shape following the Second World War. In the late 1940s the Guatemalan government was searching for a way to capitalize on the worldwide, postwar economic boom, and its economic policymakers turned to a theory of economic growth associated with Raúl Prebisch and the United Nations Economic Commission for Latin America (UNECLA), which saw agricultural modernization as the key to industrialization and development (Grindle 1986: 47). Even the revolutionary governments of 1945 to 1954, commonly viewed in the United States and Guatemala as socialist or Communist (a perception that ultimately led to their downfall), subscribed to these ideas of capitalist economic growth. Jim Handy writes that the presidents during this period, Juan José Arévalo and Jacobo Arbenz, "were determined to create within Guatemala a modern capitalist economy, breaking down what they perceived to be the lingering remnants of feudalism" (1984: 103).

Arbenz, who assumed office in 1951, borrowed many of his economic policies from a report produced by George Britnell for the International Bank for Reconstruction and Development (IBRD) (Handy 1984: 115).[2] In that report, Britnell made specific suggestions for Guatemala based on the UNECLA plan, calling for agricultural modernization to increase output and for diversification of crops in the highland areas (IBRD 1951). Britnell believed that "the cultural isolation and defensive attitude of the Indians, products of their hard experience in centuries past, constitute perhaps Guatemala's basic national problem" (ibid.: 469), because such a culture resists innovation, specifically agricultural modernization. He also noted that "the basic poverty of Indian highland agriculture permanently hampers not only any agricultural progress but the whole economic growth of Guatemala" (ibid.: 35).

After a U.S.-backed coup in 1954 that installed a more business-friendly leadership, the Guatemalan government continued with the economic course charted by the previous administrations (with the notable exception of the agrarian reform program) by removing export taxes for certain agricultural crops and instigating an import substitution plan that gave tax credits for the importation of capital equipment (Porras Castejón 1978). Rewarding these legislative initiatives, the

World Bank, the U.S. Agency for International Development (USAID), and other international donor agencies injected a large amount of capital into the Guatemalan economy in the late 1950s. During this period there was a marked diversification in export crops, many infrastructural improvements, and an increase in manufacturing. The incentives paid off, and between 1960 and 1974 Guatemala experienced an unparalleled agro-export boom, with the export earnings of the top five crops increasing in value more than 300 percent to $368 million, all the while maintaining the quetzal's value on par with the U.S. dollar. Steady growth continued throughout the 1970s, with the gross national product (GNP) increasing by an average of over 5 percent per year, and, taking into account population growth, GNP per person averaging growth of 2.5 percent annually (Davis 1988: 15; Poitevin 1993: 41). The benefits of this bull economy, however, were largely restricted to a small elite of Ladinos who controlled large tracts of land, while the production of staple crops intended for internal consumption actually fell in relation to population growth (Adams 1970; Fletcher et al. 1970).

A worldwide decline in commodity prices at the end of the 1970s brought to a close this period of booming growth. Economic indicators from the early 1980s paint a gloomy picture: foreign reserves, at $800 million in 1979, had completely disappeared by the end of 1981 (Handy 1984: 202–203); and GNP growth fell to under 1 percent in 1980, which, coupled with population growth, resulted in a 2 percent decline in the GNP per person (Poitevin 1993: 41). This period of financial crisis in the early 1980s led to rapid growth in the ranks of Marxist insurgents who operated in poverty-stricken rural Indian areas and in turn to a succession of brutal military rulers in Guatemala who were bent on destroying Communist sympathies and integrating the Indian population once and for all into the national economy.

In 1982 the military regime of General Efraín Ríos Montt adopted the Plan Nacional de Seguridad y Desarrollo (National Plan for Security and Development), which included four key areas of concern: political stability, economic stability, psycho-social stability, and military stability (AVANSCO 1988: 4). Under this plan the army first instigated a system of civil self-defense patrols in rural areas which they claimed would create "the conditions of peace basic to the integrated development of these communities" (Ejército de Guatemala, quoted in Krueger and Enge 1985: 23). Then, in 1984, the army began congregating villagers displaced by the violence into *polos de desarrollo* (development poles comprising one or more model villages) in a plan reminiscent of the Spanish colonial policies of *congregaciones* and *reducciones*. It was believed that the model villages could integrate Indians both culturally and physically into the Guatemalan nation, thus eliminating a base of support for Communist groups and laying the foundation for economic development. An ambitious program of infrastructural projects within the new villages was proposed to stimulate economic growth: building new roads, adequate housing, schools, and crop storage facilities; providing electricity and potable water; modernizing agricultural production with inputs of new machinery and greater access to outside markets; and instigating accessible credit programs (Krueger and Enge 1985: 29). Most of these programs were never instigated, however, and in practice the model villages served more as vehicles for ideological indoctrination than as incubators for development projects (Simon 1987).

By 1986, as civilian rule was reestablished in Guatemala, the economic situation began to improve, although structural inequalities in the system persisted. In 1985 GNP growth declined -0.6 percent but increased to 0.1 percent in 1986 and 3.9 percent in 1989 (Poitevin 1993: 39). Though this modest growth continued in 1990, it was offset by a high inflation rate, which reached its highest point ever in December 1990 at 60.6 percent. Through an economic austerity program, inflation was brought under control in 1991, and by December of that year it was down to 9.2 percent. With inflation under control and GNP growth continuing at a modest rate, Guatemala enjoyed a period of economic stability in 1991–92, threatened only by the high population growth rate of 2.9 percent (Guatemala News Watch 1992). By mid-1993 inflation had once again begun to creep up, GNP growth was expected to fall by almost 1 percent for the year, and foreign reserves were rapidly diminishing.

On the international level, the late 1980s witnessed the much-touted end of the cold war and the resulting shift in the strategic priorities of the world's more developed countries. Because of these revolutionary changes, Western superpowers were no longer able to define themselves in opposition to the specter of Communism; and, with the decline in this perceived threat, they began to withdraw financial and ideological support for Guatemalan military action against left-wing insurgents, especially when it involved blatant abuses of human rights. After steadily increasing during the late 1980s, reaching an all-time high of $9 million in 1989, U.S. military aid to Guatemala was slashed in the early 1990s, as well as being suspended several times by the U.S. Congress because of human rights violations. Despite these suspensions of military aid, it should be noted that the CIA's annual budget of approximately $10 million for Guatemalan operations continued to be disbursed during these periods (Weiner and Dillon 1995).

After the 1989 fall of the Berlin Wall and the subsequent political changes throughout Eastern Europe, Western powers began to feel an obligation to support the ideological conversion of their former Eastern bloc enemies, while facing the necessity for greater fiscal responsibility at home and a growing discontent with foreign aid programs. As a result, the early 1990s saw international aid channeled away from Guatemala and other Latin American countries to support new programs in Eastern Europe. In addition, the World Bank, the Inter-American Development Bank, and USAID made it clear to the Guatemalan government that future funding would depend on improving the human rights situation and liberalizing trade policies (Economist Intelligence Unit 1992: 21). In 1992 Guatemalan officials signed a Standby Agreement with the International Monetary Fund in which they promised to eliminate state subsidies and promptly began to privatize several national enterprises, including the national airline, Aviateca. Both the Guatemalan government and its foreign funders hoped that by increasing political stability and opening markets, private equity investment would replace foreign aid.

These shifts in international power relations and their impact on Guatemala have resulted in a period of redefinition for the Guatemalan state: its raison d'être can no longer be to hold the front line in a hemispheric battle against Communism; it is being forcibly weaned from foreign aid; and it is trying to work through a fledgling democratic system in a period of economic, political, and social instability. It is in this context that the pan-Maya movement has been able to create a space for itself within the Guatemalan national political arena.

Maya Development Alternatives

For their part, Maya leaders, largely excluded from the national debate over the role of their people in the Guatemalan political economy, have pursued their own policies of development. Such policies, presented in terms of cultural issues, began to be articulated on a national level during the 1944 to 1954 revolutionary governments of Arévalo and Arbenz, due, no doubt, to the political space opened by the liberal reforms of these two administrations. Richard Adams writes that for the Indians, "the real significance of the events of 1944–1954 lies in this: it was the period when Guatemala's indigenous peoples, because they were given access to new rights as campesinos by a reform government, began to recognize that social change was possible" (1990: 158).

The history of Maya cultural activism is closely tied to the study of native languages, and in the mid-1940s language began to be mobilized as an important political symbol of Indian self-identity. Linguistic issues have been a focal point for cultural activists, because speaking a Mayan language is the predominant marker of Maya ethnicity, one that has been relatively conservative during the last five hundred years of Spanish contact; it thus represents the antithesis of the dominant, Spanish-speaking Ladino culture. Demetrio Cojtí Cuxil writes that "Maya people exist because they have and speak their own languages" (1990a: 12).

The importance of the tripartite relationship between language, culture, and politics was first clearly expounded by the intellectual father of the current ideas of pan-Mayanism, Adrián Inés Chávez (1904–1987), an indigenous scholar of K'iche' language and culture. In June 1945 at the Primera Convención de Maestros Indígenas de Guatemala in Cobán, Chávez unveiled a new alphabet for the K'iche' language (which he spelled Kí-chè).[3] He argued that orthographic revision was necessary to create a set of truly indigenous symbols that would reveal the beauty of the language as well as act as a catalyst for development by promoting literacy and disseminating contemporary scientific knowledge (Chávez 1974: 65; Lima 1992). Chávez developed the alphabet so that it could be used to write not just K'iche' but all Mayan languages, stressing linguistic and thus ethnic unity, so that "a Mam person could read Kaqchikel without knowing the language, or a Kekchí could read Kí-chè without knowing that language" (Chávez 1974: 16). The new alphabet consisted of twenty-seven letters (twenty from Spanish that retained their Spanish phonetic values), two tildes, and a circumflex. The practicalities of printing in this new alphabet plagued Chávez for another twenty-two years, until 1967. In September of that year the German embassy in Guatemala presented him with a Kí-chè typewriter manufactured by Triumph Werke Nürnberg and a corresponding set of type produced by a Costa Rican university with German funding.

Though the Chávez alphabet is little used today, his legacy continues to underwrite Maya cultural activism. The I Congreso Lingüístico Nacional he envisioned in 1949 as an ongoing forum for linguistic debates was resurrected in 1984, and the Academia de la Lengua Maya Kí-chè (ALMK) he founded in 1959 continues to be an important national player in the promotion of Maya culture (Chávez 1984).

During the 1950s a major program of research on Mayan languages was begun by the Summer Institute of Linguistics (SIL), an evangelical group of Bible translators. The SIL arrived in Guatemala in 1952, working under a contract for the Instituto Indigenista Nacional (IIN) to supply schoolbooks and train teachers in Indian areas. The joint IIN/SIL venture was aimed at incorporating Maya children into the national education system, thereby laying the foundation for cultural integration so important to the Guatemalan state. The SIL's goals, however, did not stop there, for their ultimate aim was and is to erode the strong position of Maya religion and Catholicism and promote Protestantism through translations of the Bible. (Many SIL missionaries believe that after the New Testament is translated into all the languages of the world Jesus will return to earth [Stoll 1982: 22–23].) SIL linguists developed distinct alphabets for each language which were based on Spanish orthography to facilitate comprehension by those already familiar with Spanish (and, conversely, to facilitate learning Spanish for those illiterate in that language). They also tailored their publications to community-specific dialects, leading to accusations that they encouraged linguistic fragmentation within the Maya population (Herrera 1990a). Most Maya leaders are highly critical of the SIL because of that group's opposition to the unified alphabet for writing Mayan languages proposed by the Academia de las Lenguas Mayas de Guatemala (ALMG) and their exclusion of Maya from policy-making positions (see Cojtí Cuxil 1990a: 20–23). Nonetheless, their programs helped foster the growing interest among young Maya in their native languages, and a number of contemporary cultural activists trace their involvement in linguistic issues to SIL programs. They also helped to found Guatemala's first organization dedicated to the promotion of indigenous literature, the Asociación de Escritores Mayences de Guatemala (AEMG) (García Hernández 1986).

Certain Catholic groups have also acted to stimulate a mobilization of the Indian population around economic and political issues. Prominent among these is the Catholic Action movement (Acción Católica), established in Guatemala in 1948. The conservative national hierarchy of the Catholic Church hoped that Catholic Action would help combat radical, Communist politics on a local level by providing an acceptable outlet for Indian frustration with social inequality in the country (Warren 1978: 88–93; cf. Miller 1990). The Catholic Action program was built around a system of training native catechists introduced by Maryknoll missionaries of the Catholic Foreign Mission Society of America. In the program, parish priests trained Indian catechists from outlying areas who then returned to their villages to give classes in contemporary Catholic doctrine and prepare people to take the sacraments. Their focus on contemporary theology was aimed at battling syncretistic forms of Catholicism developed in the colonial period, especially the *cofradía* system of religious brotherhoods (Falla 1978a; Berryman 1984). Following the Second Vatican Council (1962–1965) and the Medellín Conference of the Latin American Episcopal Council (1968), there was a marked shift in Catholic Action programs from theological to social issues. Out of these meetings emerged a consensus among a large number of progressive priests that the Church must concern itself with improving the material conditions of its followers, raising the consciousness of the poor, and enabling them to become the authors of their own destiny (Berryman 1984: 27–29). This progressive element within the Church became heavily involved with the formation of cooperatives, schools, and health services (Calder 1970; Berryman

1984). Many of the young catechists trained in these programs became community leaders and activists and propelled what Shelton Davis calls a "'sociological awakening' of the Guatemalan Indian population" (Davis 1988: 16; cf. Berryman 1984; Falla 1978a, 1988).

In the early 1970s the role of language as a focal point for Maya cultural activism was reinforced by the work of the Proyecto Lingüístico Francisco Marroquín (PLFM). In 1971 Jo Froman, Robert P. Gersony, and Anthony M. Jackson took over the direction of the PLFM, which had been previously run by a group of Benedictine monks, and instigated an intensive program of secular research on Mayan languages in which Maya were trained as linguists. In a highly unusual arrangement, the PLFM obtained funding from the U.S. Peace Corps, the Ford Foundation, and OXFAM to pay U.S. linguists to train groups of young, rural, and poorly educated Guatemalan Maya in technical linguistics. Terrence Kaufman, in his role as chief linguistic consultant to the PLFM, encouraged the creation of a new orthography for Mayan languages, arguing that those developed by foreign missionaries and used by the government were inaccurate and ethnocentric because they relied on Spanish characters to represent Maya phonemes (Kaufman 1976a). The SIL alphabets were accused of fostering intercommunity divisions within language groups. SIL leaders responded by sending out a call to supporters in the United States for "prayers that the proposal [of the PLFM alphabet] either be dropped or turned down" (quoted in Stoll 1982: 268). The more than eighty Maya associates of the PLFM, working with the U.S. linguists, carried out linguistic studies of their home communities, producing dictionaries and grammars that followed Kaufman's strategy by employing an orthographic system that highlighted similarities between languages and dialects (Cojtí Macario 1984), thus emphasizing Maya cultural unity. Direction of the PLFM was turned over to native linguists in 1975, a long-standing goal of the project (PLFM 1993).

While Guatemala's rapid economic growth in the 1960s, fueled by agricultural exports, enriched already wealthy Ladino plantation owners, it also produced a relatively well-off class of Indians, some of whom became active in cultural preservation issues. As a result, the early 1970s saw a flurry of cultural, as well as linguistic, activism centered in the K'iche' region. Between 1970 and 1972 the Asociación Indígena Pro Cultura Maya-Quiché, the Asociación de Forjadores de Ideales Quichelenses, and the Asociación de Escritores Mayances de Guatemala (AEMG) were all established in Quetzaltenango to promote Maya culture (Arias 1990). Beginning in 1972 a series of meetings, or Seminarios Indígenas, began to facilitate national contact between local Maya leaders. One participant in the meetings states that these were great enough events, with sufficient characteristics to call them national in that there was a level of representation of ethnic groups, villages, not in that it was a large, transcendental movement for the popular organizations of those times. Those seminars were propelled by Indians who were professionals in some manner—teachers, university students, or former teachers. They were sufficiently radicalized and believed that, in order to develop an Indian struggle and to resolve the country's situation, it was necessary to form Indian organizations. (Quoted in Arias 1990: 240)

One organization formed in the wake of these meetings was Patinamit.[4] Founded in 1974 by Professor Fernando Tezahuic Tohón of Tecpán, Patinamit acted as a de facto political party supporting Tezahuic's bid for a seat in Congress. Tezahuic won the 1974 election as a candidate of the Partido Revolucionario (PR), as did another Kaqchikel leader, Pedro Verona Cúmez of Comalapa, a Christian Democrat. Although these were not the first Maya congressional deputies, the significance of their election stems from the fact that they were the first to "identify themselves as Indians at this level of power" (Falla 1978b: 440; see also Paz 1993: 27–28).[5]

Unfortunately, personal feuds between the two deputies, fueled by sensationalized press reporting, hindered their ability to effect change in the national government. In June 1976 Tezahuic was accused of selling his vote in an important election in exchange for the position of fourth secretary of the Congress. In response, Tezahuic called a meeting of Patinamit on 10 July to let his constituents decide whether or not he should resign as the fourth secretary. In its edition the following day, the daily newspaper *La Nación* reported that "representatives of a majority of the country's indigenous communities" met and voiced their support for Tezahuic.[6] The size and nature of this apparent national-level political mobilization of Maya was called into question by writers of the more conservative *El Imparcial*. They wrote of the participants in the Patinamit meeting: "we do not know from where they came or by what manner they represented themselves as 'a majority of the indigenous communities of the country,' but they supported [Tezahuic] simply by bringing with them indigenous surnames."[7] In an interview published in *La Nación*, deputy Pedro Verona Cúmez stated that Patinamit had no more than two hundred members and that neither he nor Tezahuic were worthy to speak in the name of the country's Maya population because "indigenous peoples have been the most honest, true, and sincere of all Guatemalans. . . . their name is sacred." In the same interview, Verona stated that Tezahuic's plan to create an indigenous interest group in Congress was racist, and he called into question Tezahuic's Indianness:

"I am 100 percent indigenous, which I can prove with documents. . . . in contrast, Tezahuic does not even have a desire to have his own Maya-style clothing, and the Maya-style outfit he occasionally wears [in Congress] is borrowed."[8]

While this political infighting between Indian deputies was going on in the national Congress, community-based activists throughout the highlands were attempting to mobilize the Maya population at local and regional levels. Notable among these were the young K'iche' professionals who formed the group Xel-hú, named after the K'iche' toponym for their home city, Quetzaltenango, Guatemala's second largest city. Xel-hú's leaders stressed the need for national pan-Maya unity, but they opted for a grass-roots approach and so focused their efforts on getting Indians elected to local offices in a few towns in the Quetzaltenango region. Though they failed in their attempt to gain control of Quetzaltenango's city government (in fact, none of their candidates were elected there), they were influential in electing San Juan Ostuncalco's first Indian mayor in 1976 (Ebel 1988: 177–178).

Eventually, several members of Patinamit decided to expand the focus of their organization, distancing themselves from Tezahuic's problems and highlighting the connection between the preservation of Maya culture and the political future of the Maya people. As a first step, Celia Chet, Pedro Siquinajay, Jesús Chacach, and Juan Tuy Bozel organized a ceremony in San Francisco El Alto, Totonicapán, in 1976 to award Adrián Chávez a jade necklace and bestow upon him the title Great Teacher (Ri Nimalej Etamanel). In the declaration read at the ceremony, the leaders of Patinamit stated that the jade necklace was a symbol of their cultural identity and a remembrance of their ancestors, who were the "creators of grand cities that overshadowed those of Europe, creators of systems of mathematics and astronomy that have yet to be surpassed . . . , and the driving force of one of the most brilliant epochs of mankind."[9] By honoring both Chávez and his cultural heritage, the members of Patinamit were celebrating a "new type of Indian," a professional who had suffered through the pressure to assimilate into Ladino culture and yet continued to reaffirm his maternal culture (Falla 1978b: 445).

Realizing the political importance of cultural issues, a group of Maya professionals launched a monthly magazine entitled *Ixim* (Corn) in 1977 as an alternative to Ladino-controlled national media outlets. The editorial intent of *Ixim* was to raise the collective consciousness of the Maya people by covering issues such as ethnocide, economic exploitation, and cultural discrimination in such a way that the common plight of Maya people was made apparent (Coj Ajbalam 1981). Since nothing binds people together like a threat from a common enemy, *Ixim*'s often inflammatory discourse highlighted cultural differences between the Maya and their ethically degenerate Other, the Ladinos. Publishing articles in a number of Mayan languages as well as Spanish, the editors of *Ixim* also made a valiant attempt to establish a journalistic/literary tradition in indigenous languages. Though the publication of *Ixim* lasted only a little over a year, its sophisticated and scathing critiques of neocolonialism foreshadowed the work of the current generation of Maya cultural activists.[10]

As members of Patinamit and the founders of *Ixim* were beginning to stress the importance of the relationship between cultural and political issues, some Maya leaders believed that the time had come to organize an indigenous political movement to make explicit their political aims. In November 1976 a committee was formed to organize an official indigenous political party for the 1978 elections. The committee (Marcial Maxía of Santa Cruz Balanyá, Jesús Chacach of San José Poaquil, José Lino Xoyón Camargo of Chimaltenango, and Patricio Ortiz of San Ildefonso Ixtahuacán) founded the Partido Indígena de Guatemala "as subjects seeking our own history and destiny" (quoted in Falla 1978b: 447). Reaction from the national press to the new party was quick and devastating, accusing the group of racism and of attempting to destroy efforts toward national unity. As a result, within three weeks the name of the party had been changed from the Partido Indígena de Guatemala to the Frente de Integración Nacional (FIN), and leaders began to speak more of national unity than ethnic differences.[11] Initially, the party aligned itself with the Christian Democrats, but by early 1978 it had joined with the PR, which had been courting its endorsement, and gave its support to the candidacies of General Romeo Lucas García for president and Dr. Villagrán Kramer for vice president (Falla 1978b: 454–455). After his inaugural address, partially delivered in Q'eqchi' Maya, it became apparent that the many campaign promises made by Lucas to win Maya support were hollow, and the fledgling pan-Maya movement went into a hiatus during his administration and throughout the early 1980s, when government repression against all forms of popular resistance increased sharply.[12]

After the Nicaraguan revolution in 1979 and the growing power of rebels in El Salvador, Guatemala's role in the hemispheric battle against Communism took on new importance and greater urgency. Benedicto Lucas García, the brother of the president, was appointed minister of defense in October 1981 and began a massive counterinsurgency campaign against rural villages (overwhelmingly populated by Maya) that were suspected of collaborating with the Marxist guerrillas simply because they were located in regions in which the guerrillas operated.

In March 1982 a military coup took control of the government and instated as president General Efraín Ríos Montt, who since his exile in 1977 had become a fervent born-again evangelical Christian (Stoll 1988: 95). Under Ríos Montt's rule, Guatemala saw a rapid acceleration of the war between the military and Marxist insurgents, whose philosophy found increasing support among members of the rural population who were suffering because of the collapse of the agricultural export market and the general deterioration of the Guatemalan economy. Through the campaigns Victoria 82 (Victory 82), Firmeza 83 (Firmness 83), and the infamous policy of "frijoles y fusiles" (beans and bullets), Ríos Montt maintained the military philosophy of the Lucas García administration: the native populace either could accept humanitarian aid and ideological indoctrination by government forces or be subject to extermination as accessories to treason. Thus in Guatemala, as in much of the world, native peoples were unwillingly pulled into an ideological battle between two competing Western political philosophies. The non-Indian population of Guatemala, heirs to a long tradition of fear of a "caste war," were taking no chances with the hearts and minds of their Indian subjects and so supported the military's counterinsurgency campaign.

Ríos Montt's reign was ended by another coup in August 1983 after eighteen long and bloody months. He was succeeded by General Oscar Mejía Víctores, who presided over the election of a constituent assembly in 1984 and the writing of a new constitution in 1984 and 1985. He handed over power to the democratically elected Marco Vinicio Cerezo of the Christian Democratic Party in January 1986 (Davis 1988: 10).[13]

During the height of the violence, Maya groups were forced into a ten-year hiatus. With the democratic opening in 1985 and the concurrent scaling down of the violent counterinsurgency campaigns, Maya cultural activists once again began to pursue their agendas with renewed vigor. The collective efforts I have termed the pan-Maya movement took shape after the II Congreso Lingüístico Nacional in 1984, at which time a resolution was passed calling for the creation of an institution to preside over the creation of a unified alphabet for writing Mayan languages. Toward this end a meeting was held in October 1986 of all the groups working on Maya linguistics in the country: the Asociación de Escritores Mayances de Guatemala (AEMG), the Proyecto Lingüístico Francisco Marroquín (PLFM), the Programa Nacional de Educación Bilingüe (PRONEBI), the Centro de Investigaciones Regionales de Mesoamérica (CIRMA), the Instituto Indigenista Nacional (IIN), the Instituto Lingüístico de Verano (ILV, the Spanish name of the SIL), the Centro de Aprendizaje de Lenguas de la Universidad de San Carlos (CALUSAC), the Instituto Guatemalteco de Escuelas Radiofónicas del Quiché (IGERQ), and the Proyecto de Desarrollo Integral del Pueblo Maya de la Universidad Rafael Landívar (PRODIPMA). At this meeting the Academia de las Lenguas Mayas de Guatemala (ALMG) was founded to promote a new unified alphabet for Mayan languages (based on the one developed by the PLFM and strongly opposed by the ILV) and to coordinate linguistic conservation efforts (see López Raquec 1989). The ALMG quickly rose to the forefront of the revitalization movement. The prominence of the ALMG reflected an overwhelming emphasis on linguistic issues, but over the last few years cultural organizations have appeared that focus on topics ranging from economic development to Maya religion.

The movement is being led by a young and active group of Maya intellectuals, the first generation of Maya Mayanists, pioneers of what Kay Warren calls "the new academic discipline of Maya studies" (1992: 192). Most of these individuals pursue studies at the university level. Programs in linguistics at the Universidad San Rafael Landívar (funded through USAID) and the Universidad Mariano Gálvez (funded by the SIL) are aimed specifically at young Maya scholars, and the Centro de Documentación e Investigación Maya (CEDIM) has a grant program for Maya women to study in national universities. Informal ties with foreign scholars have enabled a small but prominent group of Maya to study at universities in North America and Europe. In addition, a growing number of foreign scholars, subscribing to an ideology of empowerment and standing accused of academic imperialism, support revitalization efforts by training Maya in the techniques of their respective disciplines. Forums such as the annual Taller Maya, sponsored by the ALMG, and the Oxlajuj Aj Summer Program in Kaqchikel, sponsored by Tulane University, allow foreign and indigenous scholars to exchange recent work and research perspectives.

The initial efforts of the pan-Maya movement have concentrated on reappropriating (from Western academia) and reinterpreting (from an indigenous perspective) research on the ancient and modern Maya. Maya leaders are using the information they gather to develop an ideology that emphasizes self-determination, cultural pride, and pan-Maya unity. They believe that a rejuvenated Maya culture can peacefully lead Guatemala into a situation of cultural pluralism and thus allow the indigenous peoples greater access to economic and political institutions. In seeking a model for the future, many Maya scholars produce social analyses in the essentialist tradition, seeking that which is wholly and truly Maya, untainted by Spanish introductions. They base their interpretations on ethnographies, colonial Maya documents (primarily the *Popol Wuj*), and critiques of histories written by non-Indians. Maya scholars stress that they must first regain control over their past (i.e., the production of their history) before they can start to build their future.

The first step in building this future is the promotion of the pan-Maya ideology and mobilization of markers of Mayaness within Indian communities. Maya scholars take a strong Whorfian view of language and culture, asserting that only by speaking a Mayan language can one understand Maya culture and worldview.[14] Cojtí Cuxil writes that "for the Indians of Guatemala, apart from Mayan languages there is no authentic and complete expression of their sentiments" (1990a: 12). Activists have thus focused on language conservation and revival, hoping to reverse the trend toward Spanish monolingualism (R. M. Brown 1991). At the same time Maya linguists are constructing linguistic markers of cultural awareness and standardizing Maya lexicons and grammars. For many, the best linguistic forms are the most ancient. Q'ulq'ulkan, a Maya student of linguistics, states that "the old way is the correct way. I desire to reconstruct the correct way so that we can use the term better. What we want is purity of language." Native linguists such as Pakal B'alam incorporate historical linguistics into prescriptive grammars, giving stylistic preference to the forms that are "oldest" or most widely used, especially across dialect and language boundaries (B'alam n.d.; Oxlajuuj Keej Maya' Ajtz'iib 1993: 124).[15]

In their search for elements from autochthonous Maya culture, activists have also turned to Maya hieroglyphic, numerical, and calendric systems, salient symbols of the grandeur (and literacy) of precontact Maya culture that are now used to mark cultural awareness. Likewise, female activists stress the antiquity of the designs and techniques used in Maya textile manufacture. Many weavers are even reviving older designs and styles (Hendrickson 1986, 1991, 1995). For example, master weaver Ix Ey conducts research at the Museo Ixil in Guatemala City to record patterns in antique textiles that have fallen out of use. She then uses the older, more "authentic" designs and colors in her own work. Such efforts at cultural revitalization in the material arts often converge with marketing strategies, with weavers capitalizing on tourists' desire for authentic souvenirs.[16]

Several Maya organizations are also implementing culture-based programs aimed specifically at helping poor Maya farmers. The Coordinadora Cakchiquel de Desarrollo Integral (COCADI), for example, patents natural pesticides used by Maya farmers in the hope that they can eventually be marketed commercially. Through their educational extension program, COCADI also teaches Maya farmers how to use these natural products in place of the expensive chemical agents on which many have become dependent. Such work is stimulating the production of organic agricultural products, which command a premium in the U.S. market. COCADI also runs a nonprofit hardware and farm-supply store, Ru Kux Samaj (The Heart of Work) in Tecpán. The Q'eqchi' group Qawa Quk'a likewise focuses on agricultural economics. Wilson writes that "they exalt all that is 'traditional,' linking their dependence on the market to the demise of their traditional culture" (1993: 125). The group encourages Q'eqchi' farmers to stop buying factory-made goods and use locally produced items instead. They also discourage the use of chemical fertilizers and pesticides, which in turn lessens the debt burden of poor farmers.

While undertaking such grass-roots efforts, Maya groups promote their agenda on a national level, lobbying political leaders to instigate programs that encourage linguistic and cultural pluralism. In October 1990 the Seminario Permanente de Estudios Mayas (SPEM) organized a public meeting between Maya leaders and presidential candidates to discuss government policies toward the Maya population. At this historic meeting Dr. Alfredo Tay Coyoy and Dr. Demetrio Cojtí Cuxil presented a number of specific demands in regard to ethnic politics in Guatemala, and the presidential candidates were asked to respond based on their respective party policies. Disputes over terminology (e.g., race versus ethnicity) and whether or not programs aimed exclusively at Maya discriminated against the Ladino population precluded any fruitful discussion, leading Ricardo Cajas Mejía to conclude that "none of the candidates present has clearly stated what plan of government they have, what their policy of ethnodevelopment is, and none has expressed a specific plan of governance that benefits the Maya people" (CEDIM 1992: 67–68). Nonetheless, that such a meeting even took place attests to the growing importance of Maya in national politics.

The legal basis for many of the political demands of Maya groups comes from the 1985 constitution, which ensures the right of individuals and communities to have their own customs and languages (Article 58), promises to protect the cultures of native ethnic groups, especially the Maya (Article 66), and notes that while Spanish is the official language of the country, indigenous languages are part of the cultural patrimony of the nation (Article 143) and should be taught in schools in areas populated mostly by Maya (Article 76). Focusing on these constitutional rights, the ALMG has been instrumental in gaining concessions from the government. In 1988 it successfully petitioned the legislature to adopt the unified alphabet promoted by the ALMG. In late 1990 then-president Vinicio Cerezo signed into law a bill that grants the ALMG 5 million quetzales a year to support its programs in cultural conservation.[17] Despite the binding nature of the legislation, the government has been hesitant to fully implement the law, and as of August 1993 the ALMG had received only 2 million quetzales from the fiscal year 1992 budget. With the money that it has received, the ALMG has opened branch offices in each of the linguistic communities it represents and has begun outreach programs in each community to educate the Maya population about their cultural and linguistic rights. Although it receives its funding from the government, the ALMG retains a semi-autonomous status. As a result of its association with the government and the increasing number of bureaucratic tangles that this involves, the ALMG has retreated from the vanguard of the pan-Maya movement.[18]

The ALMG's previous role as the organizational coordinator of the movement has been taken over by the Consejo de Organizaciones Mayas de Guatemala (COMG), formed in 1990. The COMG is an umbrella group made up of fifteen organizational members.[19] Its purpose is to unite the many Maya organizations, relating their often disparate projects to a common set of goals as outlined in *Rujunamil ri mayab' amaq': Derechos específicos del pueblo maya* (Specific rights of the Maya people) (COMG 1991; see also Cojtí Cuxil, chap.2). The organization also encourages work in vital, yet untouched, areas of concern, for example, in the areas of women's rights and Maya religion. The former concern led to the formation of the Consejo de Mujeres Mayas de Guatemala (CMMG). The COMG also acts as the Guatemalan liaison with the Coordinadora de Organizaciones y Naciones Indígena del Continente (CONIC).

The Maya groups discussed above have resisted association with organizations of the popular sector whose philosophies are based on the Marxist concept of class relations. Maya cultural activists contend that popular groups have underestimated the importance of the ethnic/cultural aspect of the problems in Guatemalan society. Indeed, many leaders of the popular movement believe that ethnic affiliations disguise exploitative class relations and inhibit the unification of Ladino and Indian peasants and workers. Others claim that ethnic concerns can be addressed only after a class-based revolution (Payeras and Díaz-Polanco 1990; Fernández Fernández 1988). Nonetheless, Maya constitute a major base of support for popular groups such as the Comité de Unidad Campesina (CUC), the Coordinadora Nacional de Viudas de Guatemala (CONAVIGUA), and the Grupo de Apoyo Mutuo (GAM), and in 1990 a number of popular groups formed the Coordinadora Maya "Majawil Q'ij" to tap into the growing concern among Maya with cultural issues. Majawil Q'ij has sponsored several public Maya ceremonies and produced brochures on cultural conservation, yet its goal remains to mobilize Maya to participate in a class struggle (Bastos and Camus 1993: 95–98).

While distancing themselves from the leftist political opposition, the organizations involved in cultural revitalization have also by and large maintained autonomy from the government. Benefiting from a trend of the 1980s in international funding to bypass governments and directly support nongovernmental organizations (NGOs), Maya groups have obtained funds from agencies such as the Inter-American Foundation, UNESCO, the Fundación Friedrich-Naumann, and the Spanish embassy. By establishing contacts directly with international organizations and individual foreign scholars, Maya culture organizations have bypassed the need for government funding and support, while gaining some insurance—in the form of increased international recognition—against physical violence by reactionary groups.[20]

These projects, however, employ only a small number of individuals, and a growing problem for Maya activists is finding employment in which they can pursue their goals. Playing on the entrepreneurial spirit of their families, some have started businesses such as bookstores and publishing houses to serve the needs of Maya research institutes. Others teach in universities or work as consultants for the United Nations and other international organizations. Still, the greatest number of Maya activists are employed by governmental organizations, especially the Programa Nacional de Educación Bilingüe (PRONEBI) (CECMA 1992; Herrera 1990a). If the pan-Maya movement continues to inspire young Indians to pursue studies in the social sciences, competition for scarce professional jobs can be expected to increase.

Indigenous Development and the Western Tradition

Ostensibly, the ideology of the pan-Maya movement rejects the Western cultural tradition (Bonfil Batalla 1981: 36–37). Yet the particular form of pan-Maya cultural identity that Maya leaders are promoting and the historical justifications of that identity are being constructed in the present and so are clouded by present situations. For the Maya cultural tradition, which has long existed under Western-based Euramerican cultural hegemony and which is reasserting itself in the context of postcolonialism, the construction of a viable cultural identity involves the hybridization of Western and indigenous traditions (Friedman 1992).

For example, Raxche', in his chapter in this volume, attacks aspects of the Western tradition that have not allowed elements of Maya culture to be employed toward socioeconomic development. But one must not forget that the very idea of socioeconomic development is a quintessential modernist concept developed out of Western colonial situations. Maya cultural activists overwhelmingly accept a generic Western view of material progress, as well as funds from development agencies in the United States and Western Europe. By so appropriating elements of Western culture and reappropriating elements of their own history,

Maya leaders want to create a cultural identity that is viable in the global political economy as well as uniquely theirs. For better or worse, this identity rests on many assumptions about the world that were developed in Western Europe and the United States.

Maya scholars also employ specific schemes developed in the Western European tradition to further their own agenda. For example, their most radical proposals call for the creation of (semi-)autonomous Maya nations within the framework of the Guatemalan state (COMG 1991). Such calls to nationalism, however, presuppose ideas about nationhood that were developed in the West during the first quarter of this century (Hobsbawm 1983: 14), and the Maya do not ignore this connection, often citing systems of federal government developed in Belgium, Switzerland, France, and Spain as models for a future Guatemala (Sam Colop 1992; Experiencias 1990; COMG 1991). Likewise, as noted above, academic disciplines developed in Western Europe and the United States such as anthropology and linguistics are employed by Maya activists to record, preserve, and revive Maya lifeways.

Conclusion

Through its unique synthesis of Western and Maya traditions the pan-Maya movement has accomplished a number of things: producing indigenous scholarship (as witnessed in the growing body of works published by Maya research organizations such as CEDIM and Cholsamaj), mobilizing ethnic markers (such as the use of hieroglyphs, neologisms, and traditional clothing designs), implementing agricultural extension programs (as seen in the programs of COCADI and Qawa Quk'a), and obtaining cultural rights legislation (mostly notably the officialization of the unified alphabet and the funding of the ALMG). In the past, such forms of cultural resistance have met with extreme, often violent, opposition from the Guatemalan government. Why, then, has the pan-Maya movement remained largely unscathed by political repression?

The answer lies in part with the moderate message of Maya activists and their use of savvy diplomacy when presenting it. Maya leaders stress that they are primarily working to preserve Mayan languages and culture. Because of this strategic emphasis on cultural issues, their demands fall outside the historical political confrontations between the Guatemalan Left and Right, and they are not inherently antagonistic to either side. Andrés Cuz, former president of the ALMG, states that Maya groups are not looking for confrontations with other groups but are trying to find common ground. They have succeeded to an extent. Segments of the elite sector are ready and willing to grant demands for cultural and linguistic rights, allowing them to demonstrate their progressiveness to the rest of the world in this period of increasing concern over indigenous rights.[21] Such concessions are also timely, given that foreign assistance is being tied closely to Guatemala's human rights record.

The cultural promotion work of the pan-Maya movement is an important first step toward rectifying structural inequalities in Guatemalan society that have impeded balanced economic growth. Maya leaders repeatedly stress that culturally appropriate and sustainable development for the Maya of Guatemala must originate with initiatives coming from within Maya culture. Only after the Maya population at large has been culturally empowered can they begin to effect substantive changes in a truly pluralistic national Guatemalan society: the realization of the value and power of their own culture, and the concomitant increase in self-respect and confidence, will eliminate any self-imposed obstacles to active participation in national economic and political systems and will lower entrance barriers to those systems. In this light, cultural promotion projects, which are far removed from the technocratic tradition of economic development efforts, are laying the groundwork for long-term, sustainable socioeconomic development.

With a number of obstacles yet to be overcome, it is premature to claim success for the pan-Maya movement's strategy of development. Active participation in the movement is limited to a small, urban, geographically restricted, relatively affluent, and well-educated sector of the Maya population; indeed, it seems that around the world grass-roots organizations, economic innovations, and even revolutions most often originate with demographically similar groups (Geertz 1963; Wolf 1969; Scott 1976). The challenge of Maya activists now is to expand their base of support to include subsistence farmers, petty commodity producers, and housewives as well as university students and urban elites from all of Guatemala's Maya groups.

In addition, the military and extreme right-wing factions within the government remain real threats to the success of the pan-Maya movement. As the events surrounding Jorge Serrano's *autogolpe* in 1993 demonstrated, the military still holds the power to decide the outcome of national political events. But, as the coup also showed, segments of civil society are beginning to exert their power more effectively in support of moderate policies. If this trend toward moderation continues and if the pan-Maya movement can maintain and expand its base of support, it will be in a position to correct the inequities in Guatemalan society that have restricted the fruits of economic growth to a small group of Ladino elites for almost five centuries.

Notes

Portions of this essay were presented at the XVII International Congress of the Latin American Studies Association, the 1992 annual meeting of the American Anthropological Association, and the 1993 annual meeting of the Society for Applied Anthropology. The essay has benefited substantially from the comments and criticisms of Pakal B'alam, R. McKenna Brown, Demetrio Cojtí Cuxil, Andrés Cuz Mucu, Nora England, Todd Little-Siebold, Judith M. Maxwell, Raxche', Mareike Sattler, Shana Walton, Kay B. Warren, and an anonymous reviewer. All errors remain my own.

1. Starting with Tax's (1937) declaration that the *municipio* is the most appropriate unit of social analysis for studies of Guatemala, anthropologists have repeatedly noted that communities are the primary locus of Maya cultural allegiances. Current nomenclature derives from a seminal essay by Wolf (1957), in which he argues that social equalizing mechanisms that inhibit upward mobility are a central feature of such "closed corporate communities." The persistence of community traditions is variously explained as providing an outlet for the social ambitions of those excluded from national institutions (Smith 1977), as the creation of non-Indian elites to facilitate exploitation of native labor (Martínez Peláez 1970), as an effective strategy to resist the hegemony of the Guatemalan state (Smith 1990a), as a reaction to colonial oppression (Hawkins 1984), and as an ancient form of social organization that has survived to the present (Hill and Monaghan 1987; Tedlock 1992). Wantanabe (1990, 1992) refers to the latter approach as "cultural essentialism." In their efforts to reclaim their past, many contemporary Maya scholars have adopted the essentialist approach, an issue that I address in this paper.

2. Part of this report was published in Guatemala in the volume *Economía de Guatemala* published by the Seminario de Integración Social Guatemalteca (Britnell 1958b). Many of the ideas presented in the IBRD report are developed in an earlier work (Britnell 1951) also published in *Economía de Guatemala* (Britnell 1958a).

3. In this paper I employ the unified alphabet for writing Mayan languages discussed below.

4. The Comité de Unidad Campesina (CUC) was also formed at this time. One of the founders of CUC, Pablo Ceto, an Ixil agricultural engineer, described the group's beginnings as follows: "Besides our group the Asociación Pro-Cultura Maya Quiché, I was aware of other groups of young Christians, nativists, pastors, etc. And we also began to encounter the aspirations of religious people and students who were disposed to join with the campesinos and Indians in the search for a different future" (quoted in Fernández Fernández 1988: 4). The CUC, however, explicitly rejected the position of *indianistas* who promoted cultural and ethnic awareness, basing their struggle in a Marxist conception of class relations. In a sympathetic history of CUC, Fernández Fernández (1988: 10) characterizes the indigenous movement as being led by a privileged group of Indians attempting to gain power by claiming to represent their ethnic group.

5. In this election the Christian Democratic candidate for president, General

Efraín Ríos Montt, won but "was denied office by the army, and driven into exile in Spain" (Carmack 1988a: 51).

6. "Comunidades indígenas se rebelen contra el PR," *La Nación*, 11 July 1976, 2.

7. "Hacañas del PR discriman al indígena mañosamente," *El Imparcial*, 11 July 1976, 1, 4.

8. "Idea de crear 'bancada indígena' en el Congreso ya es adversada por uno de los diputados indígenas," *La Nación*, 12 July 1976, 6.

9. "Organización indígena rinde homenaje a un viejo maestro," *El Gráfico*, 26 September 1976, 3.

10. Although *Ixim* went out of print in 1979, the Centro de Documentación e Investigación Maya (CEDIM) resurrected the publication in 1993 (CEDIM 1993).

11. "Tezahuic: 'El partido que nos proponemos crear suprimirá la discriminación racial,'" *El Gráfico*, 18 December 1976, 8.

12. By stating that the movement went into hiatus during the period of intense violence should not imply that the Indians remained silent, for they did not. The Centro de Estudios de la Cultura Maya (CECMA) was founded soon after the election of Lucas in 1979 and has survived to this day. In the early 1980s the Movimiento Indio Tojil emerged, calling for the formation of autonomous Maya nations within the framework of a new Federal Republic (Fernández Fernández 1988: 11; Bastos and Camus 1993: 31–32). Robert Carmack (1988a: 68–69) notes that during the violence a number of K'iche' Maya turned to their cultural heritage for inspiration. They claim that readings from the *Popol Wuj* warned them about specific traps set by the army and made explicit an analogy between the ancient K'iche' gods of the underworld (Xibalbá) and contemporary soldiers. One Maya priest claimed that Tecum Uman, prince of the K'iche' nation who died fighting the conquistador Pedro de Alvarado, had returned with 2 million warriors "to bring justice to Guatemala" (quoted in Carmack 1988a: 69). See Warren (1993) and Wilson (1991) for other Maya representations of the violence. Further, Indian participation in popular, class-based resistance increased during the violence. In February 1980, a group of indigenous leaders associated with CUC met at Iximche', the site of the Kaqchikel capital outside of Tecpán, and issued a declaration condemning the recent government attacks on Indian communities and detailing the series of massacres suffered by Maya peoples starting in 1524 (Declaración de los Pueblos Indígenas Reunidos en Iximche', reprinted in Fernández Fernández 1988: 49–55).

13. In this election nine Maya won seats in the Congress, which holds a total of ninety-six deputies (Bastos and Camus 1993: 54).

14. Shana Walton (personal communication) first pointed out to me this connection between Mayanist writings and Benjamin Whorf's theory of linguistic determination.

15. For example, there are four primary variants of the first-person subject pronoun in Kaqchikel-Maya: *in re'*, *yin*, *yïn*, and *rin*. All of these forms are historically derived from a contraction of *ri in*, with *rin* being the first derivation and the others following. Maya linguists working to standardize the language have thus chosen *rin* as the preferred form because of its etymological primacy,

even though most of these same linguists are from areas that use *yin*.

16. In an informal survey of women marketing traditional clothing in Antigua, Guatemala, in 1993, I found that virtually all stressed the antiquity of their products as a main selling point. It is reported that weavers often wear new pieces for several months before attempting to sell them as antiques.

17. In September 1993 the exchange rate was 5.8 quetzales to 1 U.S. dollar.

18. Interestingly, a fear that this would happen was voiced by leaders of the ALMG before the 1990 law was passed (Quemé et al. 1990).

19. These are the Academia de las Lenguas Mayas de Guatemala (ALMG), the Asociación de Desarrollo, Servicios y Educación Integral Comunitaria (ADSEIC), the Asociación de Escritores Mayances de Guatemala (AEMG), the Centro Cultural y Asistencia Maya (CCAM), the Centro de Documentación e Investigación Maya (CEDIM), the Centro de Estudios de la Cultura Maya (CECMA), the Consejo de Mujeres Mayas de Guatemala (CMMG), Cooperación Indígena para el Desarrollo Integral (COINDI), the Coordinadora Cakchiquel de Desarrollo Integral (COCADI), the Coordinadora de Desarrollo y Formación Integral (CODEFIM), Fundación Metodista de Desarrollo Integral (FUMEDI), the Fundación para el Desarrollo Educativo, Social y Económico (FUNDADESE), the Fundación Agropecuaria Uleu, Mayab' Nimajay Cholsamaj, and Saqb'e Mayab' Moloj.

20. Social research in Guatemala continues to be a dangerous endeavor if it delves into issues that the military would prefer to be left unexamined: Myrna Mack Chang, an anthropologist studying refugees displaced by the country's violence, was brutally murdered by government security forces in 1990, and in 1993 military officials searched the house of Ricardo Falla, a Jesuit priest and anthropologist well known for his work documenting military massacres, confiscating his field notes and forcing him to flee the country. Although I am not aware that any of the current generation of Maya scholars has been killed, such violence remains a very real possibility. One prominent Maya social scientist recently told me that he believes he is occasionally followed and his telephone is tapped.

21. I am not implying that the Ladino elite is a thoroughly homogeneous group that consistently opposes the interests of the Maya population. There are a few prominent Ladino liberals who actively support the goals of the pan-Maya movement and many more who take issue with only the most radical Maya proposals. Nonetheless, the vast majority of members of the Ladino elite harbor a deep suspicion of all Maya organizations, believing them to be fronts for unnamed (though presumably Communist) foreign interests.

4.
Maya Culture and the Politics of Development

Raxche' (Demetrio Rodríguez Guaján)
(Comunidad Lingüística Kaqchikel)

To better understand Maya culture and the politics of development it is first necessary to clarify certain issues: What is culture? What is Maya culture? Who are the Maya? What is development? What are the political principles involved in development work? Finally, what is the point of reference for Maya development in Guatemala?

What Is Culture?

Culture is the set of beliefs, sentiments, technology, language, social organization, and worldview created, learned, and transmitted by a group. Culture consists of material goods as well as spiritual goods that groups of people generate as part of their reproduction and development strategies. The process that gives birth to the unique culture of a people takes place over hundreds or thousands of years, creating deep roots difficult to remove in a short time.

Culture is dynamic. It constantly evolves. In spite of constant evolution, the culture of a people maintains an essential sameness, and therein lies a group's capacity to identify itself as distinct. During its history, a culture leaves behind a variety of remains, all of which constitute the cultural patrimony of its members and of all humanity.

What Is Maya Culture?

The cultural development of the Maya people began more than five thousand years ago. It developed in what is today the south of Mexico, all of Belize and Guatemala, and parts of Honduras and El Salvador, an area of approximately 325,000 square kilometers (or the size of El Salvador, Honduras, Nicaragua, and Costa Rica combined). Maya civilization left written records of its past dating back to at least the beginning of the Christian era (two thousand years ago).

In its long history, Maya culture has had epochs of brilliance. To illustrate some of its most salient achievements, I cite the following:

1. The Maya invented the mathematical concept of zero at least five hundred years before the people of India (Ivanof, cited in COCADI 1987: 8). This brilliant invention permitted the development of Maya mathematics and other sciences such as astronomy, history, and arithmetic. The concept of zero was invented only twice in human history, by the Maya and by the people of India, independently of each other.

2. The Maya developed mankind's first positional system of numeration and have used this system for approximately 2,300 years. In Europe the concept of zero and the positional system of numbers were only fully introduced in the fifteenth century.

3. Maya astronomers developed the most exact calendar in existence before the advent of modern astronomy. Comparing the length of the year calculated by different calendars illustrates the advance of Maya astronomy (Morley 1989: 217):

ancient Julian year	365.2500 days
present Gregorian calendar	365.2425 days
Maya astronomy	365.2420 days
modern astronomy	365.2422 days

The Maya calendar can firmly place any date in its chronology "with a precision so great that it cannot be repeated until a lapse of 374,440 days has transpired, an admirable feat in any chronological system" (Morley 1989: 259–260). Today, elder Ixil and Q'anjob'al Maya still use this calendar (Colby and Colby 1986: 59–60), albeit modified by the systematic policy of cultural extermination that the Maya have endured for the past five hundred years.

4. The Dresden Codex, one of the few Maya books to escape the Spaniards' indiscriminate destruction, presents a table of 69 dates in which solar eclipses occur at 33-year intervals (every 11,960 days). This table accurately predicts eclipses to this day. Since just one Maya astronomer, or even one generation of astronomers, could not calculate such large periods of time, we must assume a constant accumulation of notes, studies, and observations over several generations (Thompson 1984: 207–209).

5. The Maya domesticated corn, an advance in alimentary genetics that they shared with all of the native American peoples living in the region known today as Mesoamerica. Today, corn is widely cultivated on every continent. The Maya also contributed rubber, chocolate, and other products to world agriculture.

Maya civilization achieved numerous other advances in medicine, odontology, mathematics, astronomy, engineering, and architecture.

Likewise, the Maya distinguished themselves in the arts of sculpture, painting, weaving, and carving. One example of their carving mastery was their ability to work jade, an extremely hard mineral (according to comparisons of hardness, where the diamond has a hardness index of 10, jade falls between 6.5 and 6.8). Such cultural achievements are even more surprising when compared with the resources available to achieve them: stone tools, no pack animals, and without using the principle of the wheel to build transport vehicles.

Who Are the Maya?

Maya culture has been shaped by the favorable and unfavorable circumstances under which we Maya have lived throughout our history, yet it remains the same culture developed over thousands of years by our ancestors in the territory that is today Guatemala. The form of our culture has changed, but not its essence.

Because of this cultural continuity, we—the more than 5 million Guatemalans who speak a Mayan language—are Maya; we who conserve the worldview that propitiates harmonic coexistence with our Mother Nature are Maya; and those of us who conserve the fundamental roots of the Maya culture are Maya. The sisters and brothers who, due to adverse circumstances, have lost part or almost all of their cultural identity but who are enthusiastically working to recover their culture and their identity are also Maya. Above all, we who identify ourselves, before ourselves and the world, as Maya (*roj, qawinaq, qawinaqil qi'*) and fight for the revitalization of our culture are Maya. For all Maya, the recovery and development of our own languages is our principal immediate objective.

What Is Development?

The dictionary describes development as the action and effect of developing, as growth, and as the qualitative and lasting economic growth of a country. Most definitions conceive of development as an improvement in the standard of living of individuals, families, and communities, including positive changes in their material and spiritual life.

The unity of spiritual and material development must be kept in mind so that development is not misunderstood as simply an augmentation in consumption, which is often irrational. It is important to see cultures as groups of people with human dignity, not simply as masses of consumers and producers of profit for industry and commerce. Thinking of development as only promoting consumerism endangers ecological equilibrium and propitiates the loss of natural resources. Development should not be understood as only building bridges and roads, which are a means to and not the end of development. While we must pursue our own material development, we must also give particular attention to developing the potential of all peoples and their respective cultures so that we may coexist in harmony with our Mother Earth and at the same time improve human coexistence on the face of the planet.

While substantial differences of opinion about the definition of development are few, most theorists fail to address the type of cultural diversity extant in Guatemala, which is characterized by colonial relations between the Ladinos and the Maya.[1] Most development theories refer only to the development of monocultural societies (or multicultural societies with deeply rooted policies of assimilation), because they are formulated by members of hegemonic cultural communities. In Guatemala development plans are complicated by the existence of two major peoples, markedly different in history, language, and culture and with a history of unequal relations. In this context, growth, advancement, excellence, improvement, and change are relative: what direction does "development" have to take in order to qualify as advancement, positive change, or improvement if what the Ladino cultural community considers advancement is the continuation of colonial subjugation and domination of the Maya cultural community? Development philosophies are not formulated by the Maya, who, because of the cultural oppression they have suffered for five hundred years, have their own concept of the type of development that the country needs.

Because of the distinct interests of the Maya and Ladino peoples, there are different opinions on how best to manage Guatemala's diversity of cultures. On the one hand, there are those who want to continue the social model inherited from Spanish colonialism because it permits them numerous economic, political, psychological, and cultural advantages at the expense of the Maya. They do not consider Maya culture as a resource for development, nor do they consider the Maya capable of being active subjects of their own development and the development of the country. On the contrary, they hold that the Maya are obstacles to the development of Guatemalan society and are better off becoming Ladinos. On the other hand, there are the Maya and those who respect the rights of peoples wanting to maintain and develop a multicultural Guatemala. This growing current of thought considers the attempt to ladinize the Maya counterproductive, because it obliges them to renounce their culture—a culture that can furnish varied and creative answers to the challenges of development. This line of thought maintains that the extermination of Maya culture is not advancement, progress, or favorable change, and it recognizes forced change of a culture as a violation of human rights. Moreover, it believes in the possibility of a unified state comprising Maya Guatemalans and Ladino Guatemalans, without the necessity of cultural uniformity: not ladinizing the Maya nor mayanizing the Ladinos. This line of thought considers Maya culture one of the most valuable resources for the independent development of the country. Like climatic diversity, which permits diverse crops, Maya culture (technology, forms of social organization, a worldview that seeks to maintain ecological equilibrium, and so on) is a fundamental and indispensable resource for our development. Yet to date it has not been used to our benefit; on the contrary, it has been maligned and exterminated.

Approaches to Development in Guatemala

Approaches to development in Guatemala fall into one of three categories depending on the role they assign to the Maya population: assimilationist, integrationist, and pluralistic. While the assimilationist and integrationist positions have similar ends, they differ in their means, and pluralistic development is opposed to both.

The Assimilationist Approach

Assimilation is the process by which the dominant culture of a given society deprives of influence and eliminates, by direct and brutal means, the culture(s) of the other people(s) in the name of a single state. This approach is generally employed in the subjugation of colonized peoples.

The process of assimilation in Guatemala was initiated five hundred years ago, and through it Maya culture has been persecuted by and absorbed into the dominant culture. It is motivated and practiced by direct and violent means. It is the policy followed first by the Spanish (1524–1821), then by the Creoles (1821–1871), and today by the Ladinos (since 1871) in their relations with the Maya.

Assimilationists believe that the cultural annihilation of Maya Guatemalans constitutes advancement because it civilizes and integrates them into a national culture (read: Ladino culture). Its strategy is to import cultural resources and impose them on the Maya, without considering that such measures further the country's external dependence while exterminating the cultural resources of the Maya. Maya cultural resources represent the independence and personality of the Maya community in particular and Guatemala in general.

Assimilationists consider the vigorous permanency, or even the precarious survival, of Maya culture an obstacle to the country's development, and they seek instead a culturally unified, Ladino Guatemalan society through the extermination of Maya culture. Assimilationists want to *resolve*, through the death of Maya culture, the prevailing colonial situation that provokes so many negative statements by the international community. Every day it becomes clearer that Guatemala is the South Africa of Central America. The U.S. State Department, Amnesty International, Americas Watch, and the Catholic Church, as well as numerous peasant, academic, student, and cultural organizations that represent the Maya, have documented and denounced the oppression that Maya suffer under the rule of the Guatemalan state.

Assimilation attempts to make us "new Ladinos" in our forms of dress, consumption, thinking, and speaking. Yet it converts us into poorly ladinized Guatemalans, poorly ladinized because a people such as ourselves who have millennia of history and who have resisted five hundred years of systematic cultural annihilation cannot be completely exterminated.

Assimilationists constantly speak of change, meaning transition of Maya culture (classified as inferior) to Ladino culture (considered superior), as an indispensable condition to obtain development in Guatemala. Below are some examples of assimilationist actions in our communities:

1. Assimilationists want to eliminate what we are able to produce, distribute, and utilize and make us consume that which we do not. For example, in medical treatments they indiscriminately push us toward greater dependency on laboratory products (thereby increasing our economic and cultural dependence) instead of promoting our own medicine. In other countries, university programs study indigenous medicine, while in Guatemala it is deprecated because it is only used by herbalists, curers, traditionalists, and other Indians.

2. Assimilationists vigilantly follow a policy of dividing and minimizing in order to finally exterminate our languages, which are the *center of our culture*. Guatemala recognizes only one official language (Spanish) in spite of its being a multilingual country, with Maya constituting approximately 60 percent of the population. The majority of the country's schools teach only in Spanish and offer only English as a second language. The Programa Nacional de Educación Bilingüe (PRONEBI) is insufficient to counter the assimilationist impact of the national educational system.

3. Assimilationists seek to replace our forms of social organization. Because of the five hundred years of extermination of Maya culture,

most organizations extant in our communities are not characteristically Maya: they are not based on leadership defined by service to the community, they are not governed by age, and they are not structured in our own forms. Within the few towns (e.g., Santa Catarina Ixtahuacán and Nahualá) that maintain an organization of their own (mainly at the level of the municipality) through the councils of leaders (*k'amol taq b'e*), there exist systematic forces that denigrate, marginalize, and ignore them.

4. Assimilation promotes the loss of our distinctive dress. Most Maya males from the central part of the country have lost their distinctive dress. In the northwest, men better maintain the use of their dress, though centuries-old policies of assimilation are changing this. Maya women, despite the strong pressure of cultural discrimination, vigorously maintain their dress. With the exception of the two largest cities (Guatemala City and Quetzaltenango), there are relatively few regions of the Republic where Maya women have abandoned traditional dress on a wide scale.

5. Assimilationists seek to eliminate our distinctive worldview. Our Maya worldview was assaulted in the first years of the European invasion because it was considered to be satanic. After five hundred years of aggression the effects can still be felt: each day we lose more of our profound respect toward Mother Nature, respect toward our elders, and reverence toward our dead. Each day we dehumanize ourselves more, a result of alienation from our worldview.

Assimilationist policies stand in opposition to the legitimate right of all peoples, no matter how large or small they may be, to maintain, develop, and enjoy their own culture. Social conflicts usually exist in societies where cultural assimilation is practiced, such as between Irish and English in Great Britain and between Basques and Castilians in Spain. Assimilation and cultural oppression of distinct peoples is not the best way to unify multicultural societies, as demonstrated by the examples of Lebanon, England, Spain, Yugoslavia, the former U.S.S.R., India, South Africa, and Ecuador.

The model of development generated by assimilationist policies may be called ethnocidal development (or, in Guatemala, ladinizing development). It is a form of colonial development that accompanies colonial situations such as that experienced by the Maya living in the Guatemalan state.

The Integrationist Approach

This approach stems from the theoretical assumption that the Maya are segregated from the political, economic, and cultural life of Guatemala and therefore must be integrated into national life—must be ladinized—in a gradual but sure manner.

In reality, the Maya are completely meshed with the gears of production of Guatemalan society: they supply the largest quantity of manual labor to produce export crops such as coffee and sugar; they produce the largest portion of food for internal consumption, such as basic grains and vegetables; and in addition, through their heritage in arts and culture, they largely support the tourist industry, which is the second largest earner of foreign currency. Likewise, the glorious Maya past is utilized by the Ladino community to present a unique image of Guatemala to the world. Thus, the Maya are a fundamental part of the generation of Guatemala's riches, and they supply essential elements for Guatemala's unique national image. The integration that has not been allowed the Maya is access to the economic, political, and cultural rights that would support the work they perform that serves to generate the country's wealth.

The integrationists propose using elements of the Maya's own culture to integrate them more rapidly into the Guatemalan nation (of Ladino culture). In attempting the partial and temporary integration of certain characteristics of Maya culture within Guatemalaness, the following has occurred:

1. Mayan languages are utilized only to teach the contents of Ladino culture and only while Maya students are learning Spanish. Once Spanish is learned, Mayan languages are relegated to a secondary role in schools, in daily life, in relations with the state, and in the majority of the acts of Guatemalan society. Currently, Mayan languages only have space in the intimacy of the home and in isolated hamlets, and only for as long as radio and television do not also expel them from there. In 1992 PRONEBI served the four largest Mayan language groups and several small but linguistically vigorous language groups such as the Q'anjob'al. Languages in imminent danger of disappearing, such as Poqomam, do not receive attention, even despite their speakers' initiatives to create bilingual schools to prevent language death. Further, PRONEBI currently serves only kindergarten through the first four years of primary school. Its educational coverage is far from reaching the 60 percent of the country's student population who are Maya. It is far from preparing 60 percent of all teachers and support personnel that work in the Ministry of Education. It is far from using 60 percent of the state funds designated for classroom and extracurricular education. It is far from producing 60 percent of the educational material produced in the country in bilingual editions. It is far from serving the needs of the Maya in middle and secondary levels. As Guillermina Herrera (1990b) states, "This is not due to chance, because PRONEBI is immersed in an assimilationist society."

A broad state policy that respects the cultural rights of the Maya is needed, not isolated programs such as PRONEBI that conform to the colonial vocation of the Guatemalan state and society.

2. Maya clothing is conserved only for folkloric and touristic ends, while its use is prohibited, directly or subtly, in centers of study, at work, and in social and official meetings. Maya dress is used in commercial advertisements (for alcoholic drinks, tourist promotions, and so on) but not to promote the idea that distinctive dress is an important element of the material culture of the Maya.

3. Marimba music is used to introduce foreign ideas to the Maya people by means of advertisements accompanied by arrangements with Maya songs and rhythms.

4. Our aesthetic models are used in the industrial production of commodities (e.g., textiles) that then bankrupt our own production and distribution systems, leaving us to be merely consumers.

Integrationism, like assimilationism, ignores the survival, development, and florescence of Maya culture and the people who carry and reproduce it. Clearly, the Maya, as the subjects of the country's and their own development, have no role in this approach.

Integrationism in Guatemala seeks only a one-way integration, where the Maya are forced to renounce their fundamental cultural values and adopt the values of Ladino culture, while the culture of the Ladino community is protected, fomented, and sustained by the state. Ladinos maintain the development of their culture (within the general limitations presented by the organization of Guatemalan society, where 87 percent of the population lives below the poverty level) without any economic, legal, or moral necessity to know or adopt aspects of Maya culture. In order to live in Guatemala, Ladinos do not need to know one word in a Mayan language (most do not even know how to say thank you); in contrast, the Maya who do not speak Spanish cannot even exercise their most elemental rights as citizens because these rights can only be exercised in Spanish. The state and society do not give incentives for the Ladino community to learn aspects of our culture, for this might result in intercultural exchange, respect, and coexistence with their fellow Maya citizens. Guatemalan anthropologists do not learn Mayan languages, not even as research tools and less still to demonstrate support of the right of the Maya to maintain and develop their languages. Thus, there are very few Ladinos bilingual in Spanish and Mayan, but many know English, French, German, Portuguese, Italian, or another European language.

Integrationism is a variant of the assimilationist approach, though it is more technical and perhaps more effective in minimizing, debilitating, and finally extinguishing Maya culture.

The Pluralist Approach

The pluralist approach seeks the coexistence and mutual enrichment of culturally diverse peoples within a single state and the respect of internationally recognized human and cultural rights. Cultural pluralism promotes the use of a culture's own resources, such as social organization, technology, worldview, and language. It protects and values the cultural identity of peoples so that each group may promote the development appropriate to its needs. Thus, the pluralist approach seeks cooperation and unity through diversity.

In opting for pluralist development, one may no longer speak of a single national culture. To speak of the Guatemalan culture or Guatemalaness would be to refer to certain common elements capable of agglutinating the diverse cultural communities within Guatemala, such as the common state, common citizenship, common territory, and certain cultural elements unique to each cultural community that in time would be freely adopted by all (e.g., culinary preferences and technology). A pluralistic Guatemalan culture would be a space for encounter and dialogue with conditions of equality between the different peoples that exist in the country.

To achieve a truly democratic society in Guatemala, development must be pluralistic in form and essence. Adopting such a stance means, among other things:

1. modifying the unequal economic and political relations that exist between the Maya and Ladino peoples;
2. breaking the cultural domination that the Ladino community has maintained over the Maya, starting with the officialization of Mayan languages in their respective regions;
3. decentralizing services and decision-making power, enabling each cultural community to pursue its own integral development, starting with the regulation of its judicial and political order at a local as well as regional level;
4. opening, amplifying, and finally returning the control that each group should exercise over its own culture;
5. combatting the simplistic thought that the Maya do not have culture—it must be accepted that the basis of the country's development is located in Maya culture, a culture that permits the Maya to identify their problems and seek solutions based, principally, on their own resources; and
6. complying with the territorial, political, judicial, linguistic, educational, cultural, civil, military, economic, and social demands of the Maya people as outlined in the document *Rujunamil ri mayab' amaq'* (COMG 1991; see also Cojtí Cuxil, chap. 2).

Within a multicultural state such as Guatemala, pluralistic development may also be called complete democracy, ethnic democracy, ethnodevelopment, self-determination, integrated development, differentiated development, or federalism.

The Social Context of Maya Development

The social and political situation of the Maya is misunderstood in
Guatemala. To promote the development of the Maya and of all Guatemala, one must understand Guatemalan politics and international
human rights laws as well as follow the spirit of the articles that deal
with cultural development in the Guatemalan constitution. Development programs must be contextualized within the global tendency to
value diverse cultures. Above all, the desire of the Maya to maintain and
develop their culture, clearly seen in the endurance of their cultural
identity under extremely adverse conditions, must be recognized (see
López Raquec 1989: 99–100).

The Cultural and Political Situation of the Maya

To set forth the political and cultural situation of the Maya, I quote
Demetrio Cojtí Cuxil on Guatemala's ethnic stratification:

> Guatemala is a multinational society administered by a state.
> Critical analyses of the ethnic-political reality and of the concrete
> functioning of nationality inevitably lead to the same conclusion:
> there are various nations because there are various ethnic identi-
> ties. Consequently there cannot exist a nation-state. Within the
> multiple communities that comprise Guatemalan society there is
> one that controls the state and utilizes it to guarantee its hege-
> mony over the others, stifling cultural evolution and survival. This
> is the Ladino community, which subjugates, through the state, the
> Maya ethnicities. This is done because the state functions as a
> colonial state (and not as a multinational state) and the Ladino
> community functions as the governing ethnicity. (1984: 17–21)

The situation described by Dr. Cojtí has its origin in the abolition of
the independence of the Maya initiated in 1524; this process was finished
with the total destruction of the Itzaj Maya state in 1699 (Villagutierre
Soto-Mayor 1933: xxix–xxv). Not one historical event since, not even the
creation of the Guatemalan state in 1821 by the Creoles or the taking of
power by the Ladino Justo Rufino Barrios in 1871, has restored the
independence of the Maya. In 1995 the Maya remain politically and
culturally colonized. The political and cultural reality of the Maya

cannot be ignored, and the integrated development that the Maya aspire to within the framework of the current Guatemalan state must be realized.

Viewing Cultural Diversity as Positive

In the last few years, the global tendency to consider multicultural societies as potentially better endowed to seek the path of their own development has become more explicit. Multicultural societies with pluralistic policies are better situated to achieve development because of the multiplicity of solutions that diverse cultures can offer to development problems. Ethnodevelopment (in our case, Maya development) can achieve the well-being of the Maya while giving them greater economic and cultural independence.

An example of the potential contribution by our people to the well-being of society is Maya medicine. The government of Vinicio Cerezo (1986–91), in collaboration with foreign technicians, inventoried the medicinal plants of Guatemala with an eye to their future use in commercial drugs. The Maya did not participate in this study, yet those who best know the names and medicinal properties of plants in Guatemala are the Maya. Likewise, the Maya have made advances in hydrotherapy with the *tuj* (similar to a European sauna bath) and its use in both preventive and curative medicine. There exist incipient efforts to record these aspects of Maya culture by nongovernmental organizations (NGOs) as well as by the Folklore Center of the University of San Carlos. Lamentably, because of the myopia of those who direct higher education in Guatemala, it will still be many years before this knowledge can be acquired in university classrooms.

The worldwide appreciation of cultural diversity and the increasingly systematic revindication of the Maya are so encouraging that many NGOs, and a few decentralized state entities, are opting for pluralistic models of development; NGOs directed by Maya as well as by Ladinos are starting to support the development of the peoples that constitute Guatemala, for practical ends and as a matter of principle.

Human Rights

Various international agreements exist on the economic, social, and cultural rights of peoples. For example, Article 27 of the International Agreement of Civil and Political Rights guarantees the rights of ethnic, religious, and linguistic minorities to have their own cultural life, to profess and practice their own religion, and to employ their own language. Likewise, the first article of the International Agreement on Economic, Social, and Cultural Rights, as well as the first article of the

International Agreement on Civil and Political Rights, gives the right of free self-determination to all peoples so that they may pursue their economic, social, and cultural development. In Guatemala the Maya are a majority of the population, yet they do not enjoy the rights established by these international agreements for minorities.

The constitution of the Republic, in Article 46, establishes the preeminence of international law over internal law in regard to human rights as set forth in those treaties and conventions accepted and ratified by Guatemala. Yet Guatemala has not accepted or ratified the agreements mentioned above, some in force since 1976 in other countries. It must do so if it is to have a true democracy and integrate itself into the international community of democratic states.

Since 1991 diverse Maya organizations, such as the Consejo de Organizaciones Mayas de Guatemala (COMG), and international organizations, such as the International Labor Organization (ILO) of the United Nations, have encouraged Guatemala to ratify Convention 169 on Indigenous and Tribal Peoples in Independent Countries, which it has yet to do. Nonetheless, the United Nations is currently in the process of producing the final version of the Universal Declaration of the Rights of Indigenous Peoples, which will be the supreme law of human rights, individual as well as collective, of all indigenous peoples, including the Maya. If adhered to, this accord will guarantee fundamental rights that the Maya do not presently have in Guatemala.

In conclusion, NGOs and those interested in development in Guatemala must respect international laws dealing with the human, cultural, economic, and political rights of peoples. Doing so will foster a pacific and mutually enriching coexistence between Maya and Ladinos in Guatemala and thus the pluralistic and truly democratic development of our society.

The Constitution of the Republic

Integral development of the Maya must be consistent with the constitution of the Republic of Guatemala. The principal articles to be considered are:

Article 58: The right of people and communities to their cultural identity in accord with their values, language, and customs is recognized.

Article 66: Guatemala is made up of diverse ethnic groups, among which are the indigenous groups of Maya descent. The state recognizes, respects, and promotes their forms of living, customs, traditions, forms of social organization, the use of indigenous dress by men and women, languages, and dialects.

Article 67: The lands of cooperatives, indigenous communities, or whatever other form of communal holding or collective agrarian property, the same as familial patrimony and popular dwellings, shall enjoy the special protection of the state, of credit assistance, and of preferential techniques that guarantee their possession and development with the end of assuring all inhabitants a better quality of life. Indigenous and other communities holding lands that historically belong to them and traditionally have been administered in a special way shall maintain this system.

Article 68: Through special programs and adequate legislation, the state shall provide state lands to indigenous communities that need them for their development.

Article 70: A law shall regulate that which is relative to this section. (This refers to the obligation of the state to implement a specific law to regulate the protection that indigenous communities should have from the state.)

These articles show progress toward Maya development and a departure from the neglect and total marginalization of previous constitutions. However, nine years after adopting these articles, the state has yet to emit specific laws and put into practice the details of Maya development. Indeed, the effects of this new constitution on the Maya are no different from those of previous constitutions, which did not even attempt to respect and support our cultural identity.

The Fortitude of the Identity of the Maya

During the last 469 years the Maya in Guatemala have managed to maintain their cultures under the most adverse circumstances. Today, Maya identity and culture remain strong. The Maya maintain in large part their worldview and technology, their spirit of service toward community, and, above all, their languages, which are unmistakable symbols of their identity and existence. The Maya maintain their ethnic loyalty, and the current awakening of the more educated Maya has greatly strengthened the resistance of peasant and other Maya. But we cannot ignore the enormous weight of five centuries of continuous assimilationist and integrationist policies that we have suffered.

The Maya's maintenance of their culture has been realized without the help of the state and without resources that could have facilitated its development. The very least that organizations interested in Guatemalan development can do now is support the right of the Maya people to strengthen and develop their culture.

Through the encouraging trends discussed, and with the endorsement of a growing number of pluralistically minded development institutions, we hope for a creative reflorescence of the cultures of the Maya and, with it, pluralistic development and true democracy in our country, Guatemala, of which we Maya form the largest part.

Notes

An earlier version of this article was published in Spanish as the introduction to *Cultura maya y políticas de desarrollo* (Raxche' 1992). This chapter was translated from Spanish by Edward F. Fischer and R. McKenna Brown.

1. When I mention Ladinos, I am referring mainly to the leaders of this cultural community.

5.
Reading History as Resistance: Maya Public Intellectuals in Guatemala

Kay B. Warren (Princeton University)

Todorov (1984), Sahlins (1981, 1985), and Obeyesekere (1992) have framed key debates concerning indigenous interpretations of Europeans at first contact. Given their historicist preoccupations, however, none of these authors asks about the stakes twentieth-century indigenous activists might find in these arguments, or the very different interests indigenous readers currently bring to the colonial frontier.[1] This essay deals with Maya intellectuals, with their practice of reading history, the political issues they find riveting in ancient texts, and the significance of history for their current struggles. Taussig's (1993) tactic of tacking back and forth between historicist and presentist perspectives inspires this inquiry. There are echoes as well of Tedlock's (1983) ethnopaleography. Yet my approach is more ethnographic than either Taussig or Tedlock, more concerned with community building and cultural context, with mimetic moments Maya find important at this political juncture. The project takes on special importance in Guatemala, where Maya intellectuals have become the architects of a national movement for ethnic revindication.

This essay traces the work of a group of prominent linguists from Oxlajuuj Keej Maya' Ajtz'iib' and the Rafael Landívar Instituto de Lingüística as they spent a week in 1992 studying the famous *Annals of the Kaqchikels*, which were written at the time of the first contact between Maya and Spaniards in 1524.[2] These linguists are involved in a wide variety of community education projects as teachers and producers of nationally distributed educational materials. They read, translated, and later published excerpts from the *Annals* for use in nonformal education programs. The group's engagement—what I would describe as a Talmudic sense of the text's complexity—is central to my analysis. My focus will be on issues they found compelling in this eyewitness portrayal of Maya life before and after the Spanish invasion. Maya culturalists see these chronicles as vital windows on the past and as useful guides for a variety of difficult projects in the present. Following the Maya stress on the multiple layering of meaning, my analysis finds the history work group revealing in their explicit agenda for the meeting and their hidden transcript of cultural preoccupations.[3] I conclude the essay with a consideration of the practice and politics of our anthropological readings of Maya cultural resurgence.

Maya History Workshops

Each year, culturalists host hundreds of informal meetings, lectures, workshops, conferences, and short courses for activists and community members. Whatever their format, these events are opportunities to contest the representation of Maya in national culture, to imagine a Mayacentric history, and to reveal the paradoxes of the movement. Maya intellectuals active in culturalist networks now meet in small informal study groups, where they read Maya chronicles dating from the sixteenth to nineteenth centuries and discuss advances in the decipherment of ancient glyphs. Chronicles and legal documents called *títulos* were written in indigenous languages such as K'iche' or Kaqchikel with sixteenth-century innovations to represent sounds foreign to Spanish. These documents are now considered sacred, in some cases biblical, texts.

To read a Maya chronicle is to confront its plurality. Chronicles often include transliterations of pre-Hispanic glyphic and pictorial texts, oral histories, and eyewitness observations. Documents were copied and recopied at various times, and "originals" were lost, hidden, and sometimes destroyed. Subsequent generations inserted marginal annotations, addendums, updated histories, and new introductions or dropped sections they found uninteresting (or perhaps too interesting). In Guatemala most are known only through Spanish translations. In many cases the originals are not accessible to native speakers because of differences between ancient and modern forms of the languages and because so few people are literate in indigenous languages.

Why is this project important to the very busy public intellectuals of the Maya movement? Pakal B'alam, an intense, fast-speaking *ch'ip* (youngest son) from one of the most nationally prominent culturalist families with roots in Tecpán, observed that origins are important, because, "true 'history' or not, they show the Kaqchikels have their own origin."[4] The *Annals* are consulted to answer the question, "From what point [in history] did we exist as Kaqchikels, who said we were Kaqchikels?" The chronicle is also seen as having wider lessons about the depth and genesis of Maya culture, which few Guatemalans know in any detail. As a non-Kaqchikel participant from Palín, Waykan added:

"We are studying the chronicles, the *Popol Wuj, Annals of the Kaqchikels,* and *Rabinal Achi.* They will teach us a great deal, more still since we are so locally oriented and study localized languages. They will teach us not only other means of expression but how to relate to others in general, how people related before and how they relate now. This can help us a lot." Given the number of Mayan languages in Guatemala, the long-range goal is to produce modernized versions of the chronicles in their original language and to disseminate Spanish translations that will reach wider audiences. The linguists see the project as one of creating larger identifications and counterhistories which, as Pakal B'alam put it, "do not argue the opposite of official histories for their own sake but rather seek truths that have not been fully aired."

Reading the *Annals of the Kaqchikels*

In the spring of 1992 a small group of Maya linguists met for a week to study the sixteenth-century version of the *Annals* and its nineteenth- and twentieth-century Spanish translations. Kab'lajuj Tijax, a highly respected professional and elder in Maya linguistics originally from Comalapa, talked about the substance of the text in the following terms. This masterwork depicts "official Maya history," a view from the past of the origins of a major indigenous people, their common cosmology, their experiences of armed European invasion, and, critically, their genealogical continuity and survival over the centuries. These are the truths that need airing. Official state histories in the schools and beyond allude to this chronicle, but most often just to tell of the defeat of the Maya at the conquest. Tellingly, none of its official translators has been a native speaker of Kaqchikel.

The *Annals* manuscript represents a distillation of ancient cosmogonic knowledge and of first-person accounts that span the years A.D. 1510 to 1604. Compiled first by Francisco Hernández Arana, who witnessed the Spanish invasion in 1524, and, after 1583, by Francisco Díaz, who added a running account of important events in Sololá (known as Tzolola in pre-Hispanic times), the manuscript was recopied in the mid–seventeenth century by a professional scribe.

The original historians were members of the Xajila family, direct descendants of early Kaqchikel rulers and at different times mayors of Sololá during the early colonial period (Recinos and Goetz 1953: 13–14). At the end of the manuscript, five additional short narratives appear, composed between 1550 and 1590 by Diego López. The additions describe the genealogy of the Pakal lineage, its connection to the governing Xajil political-descent group, as well as specifics on land rights, political offices, and rights to succession.

History and Self-Discovery

The study group highlighted worldview, or *cosmovisión*, as a fundamental philosophical and aesthetic element of the chronicles. As Pakal B'alam observed, "Myths don't just relate the history of a people but their way of thinking." The group decided to focus on specific topics since it was not feasible to do a careful reading of the entire chronicle in the time that was available. In a quick consensus, the group agreed on the mythic origins of the Kaqchikels, the indigenous rebellion at the pre-Hispanic capital Iximche', the Spanish invasion, and the Pakal B'alam genealogy.[5] These eclectic choices reveal important subthemes in Maya revitalization.

Origins and the Tulan Diaspora

The work group began with the Maya genesis, with the chronicle's portrayal of the origins of divine ancestors, the physical world, and humanity. Creation does not begin from nothingness in Maya cosmogonies. Inevitably, there are plural formative beings before pivotal moments of origin and an interplay of creations, some successful, others failed.[6] In the *Annals*, the narrator addresses his readers, the children of Tulan and members of the Xajila lineage, telling them of their mythistory in distant times, places, and generations:[7]

1 Behold, I will write part of the history of our first fathers, our
      grandfathers,
   those who engendered people in the past
   when the hills and valleys had not yet been created,
   when there was only the rabbit, the bird,
      they say.
   Then the hills and valleys were in fact created;
   they are our fathers, our grandfathers,
      my children of Tulan.[8]

The history then becomes genealogical, tracing the ancestors Q'aq'awitz and Saqtekaw and their relation to the founders of the four Kaqchikel lineages from the distant Tulan.

After the genealogies, the *Annals* speak in a series of spatial metaphors about Kaqchikel ethnogenesis. The chronicle narrates the foundational migration from Tulan and describes interdependent cycles of creation for humans and corn. The failed creations on the way to a new ordering are another signature of Maya cosmogony.

4 These are the words of Q'aq'awitz and Saqtekaw.
    This is the true origin of the words that Q'aqawitz and Saqtekaw
        tell.
    From the four directions came the people of Tulan.
    There is a Tulan in the east,
    another in the south,
    one out in the west from whence we came,
    another in the north.
    These are four Tulans,
        you, our children,
            they say.
    From the west we came from Tulan to the other side of the
        sea. . . .

5 Soon came Chay Ab'aj[9] created
    by Raxaxib'alb'ay, Q'anaxib'alb'ay.
    Soon man was created by Tz'aqol B'itol;[10]
    he who feeds the obsidian stone.
    It was hard to create mankind,
    to finish mankind.
    He was made of wood,
    he was made only of earth.
    He did not speak,
    he did not walk.
    What was made had neither blood nor flesh
        they say, our first fathers, grandfathers,
            you, our children.
    They did not find the right element for his creation,
    finally they found the element:
    only two animals knew where it was
    in the mountain called Paxil.
    These animals were the coyote and the raven.
    It was found in the intestines
    of the coyote when it was killed,
    was cut open.
    Corn sprang from his insides. . . .

    The entrance to Tulan was closed.
    The place from whence we came was in the form of a bat
    which enclosed the entrance to Tulan
    the place where we were born
    and were engendered;

there we were given our responsibility
in the darkness, in the night,
  you, our children.
That which Q'aqa'witz, Saqtekaw said,
  you our children,
has not been forgotten.
There have been many generations
  which nourished themselves with these words in the past.

The passages evoked strong visual images for the linguists. They circulated a drawing of the walled city of their origin with its totemic main gate that had been done by a student of Linda Schele. There the bat (*sotz'*) portal was pictured with massive doors and an indecipherable greeting traced in glyphs. The linguists discussed the autochthonous writing system, created by their ancestors and never understood by the colonizers. "They nourished themselves with their words" takes on another layer of meaning in the drawing. I can only add that this is doubly interesting given the possible existence of the *Annals* mythistory in codex form, as Carmack (1973) speculates.

The linguists also drew a geometric illustration to represent the abstract spatial imagery underlying the origins narrative. Their four-cornered universe highlighted the underworld (not hell), overworld, cardinal directions, and central axis. Creation unfolded on a cosmic stage, marked in numerous subtle ways, such as the mention of Raxaxib'albay (*rax* = green) and Q'anaxib'albay (*q'an* = yellow), yet elusive to many students of the text. Translators frequently passed by oblique references to this spatial imagery, apparently because they were unimpressed with the nuances of origins symbolism. The veiled language reminded earlier audiences of the cosmic stage on which human history unfolded in cyclic time.

When Maya cosmology was translated into Spanish and given greater scholarly attention in the nineteenth and twentieth centuries, it was incorporated into Christian categories. Intensifying the tendencies of colonial transcribers, who had been trained by Catholic priests, later translators equated the Maya underworld (*xib'alb'ay*) with hell, Maya divinities with the devil, Spaniards with gods, and Maya with pagans. It has always been a temptation to translate the Maya worldview, with its abundant twins and dualisms, into the good/evil dichotomies common to Christianity. This is a chronic problem, something that culturalists currently fight in their own discussions as they attempt to purge the Maya worldview from its encounter with various historical waves of European religion.

Rebellion at the Ancient Capital, Iximche'

The group turned next to the ancient political intrigues through which the Kaqchikels emerged as an autonomous indigenous state capable of jockeying with other Maya states for territory and dominance. The rebellion occurred after the Kaqchikel separation from its political progenitor, the ever-dominant K'iche' state. A pivotal event in early Kaqchikel history was the struggle between rival ruling lineages that culminated with a rebellion of the Tuquche' political-descent group at the Kaqchikel capital, Iximche'. As leaders strategized to amass power, the envious Tuquche' leader, Kai'Junapu, confronted the leaders Oxlajuuj Tz'ii' and Kab'lajuj Tijax, "who did not want war / their daughters and sons suffered" (passage 100). The battle began in classical form with the amassing of Tuquche' forces. Among other combatants, four women fought with lances and bows and arrows:

> 102 Four women were prepared.
>   They carried double-bladed lances,
>   their bows and arrows.
>   They found themselves in battle,
>   always the four daughters. . . .
>   Their arrows reached the shield of Chukuyb'atz'in.[11]
>   For this reason the men were frightened
>   because of the great battle the old leaders gave them.
>   Once again the war leaders showed the bodies of the
>   women. . . .
>   Our grandparents Oxlajuj Tz'ii' and Kab'lajuj Tijax dispersed the
>   Tuquche'.

The political history at the Kaqchikel capital was absorbing. As the group reviewed this passage, linguist Kab'lajuj Tijax followed the victory of his namesake, who as it turned out was one of the last rulers independently chosen by the Kaqchikels. The victory over the Tuquche' people marked the emergence of the Kaqchikels as an expansive state force.

There was one puzzle in the study group's work on early political history. Why, in the midst of studying Kaqchikel political emergence, was the group interested in a passage describing women warriors? No one in the group seemed particularly concerned with women's issues as defined by current social movements. Later, I had a chance to pursue the question. As is common knowledge, gender has become increasingly politicized by feminist groups in Latin America and the United States.

It is now an important consideration in development programming by agencies such as USAID and European foundations and is routinely raised by activists as an issue at international rights conferences. Maya women, especially professionals, feel they are under pressure to see women as exploited by men; the male leadership worries about being portrayed as sexist in what remains a decidedly androcentric cultural system.

Members of the group explained that the idea of women warriors, even if mentioned only in passing, is appealing because it demonstrates that women were held in respect and occupied positions of prestige in the original cultural system. Thus, Maya women would be right in opting to join with men, as they did at Iximche', stressing joint ethnic goals over their personal struggles. For today's readers, this image is not one of Amazon independence, as the well-known translator Recinos had speculated (1950: 112n.205), but rather a hopeful rationale for common purpose across social cleavages. It is interesting how often the gender issue bubbles up at culturalists' meetings. This momentary taming of the suppressed was more easily accomplished than at other culturalist conferences where flashes of female anger have jolted audiences, only to be swallowed up by the dynamics of Maya consensus making.[12]

The Spanish Conquest and Maya Betrayal

The Spanish invasion was destined to become a major pursuit of the study group since it defined colonial power structures and provoked resistance that has continued over the last five hundred years. The group disputed the classic Western portrayal of awed reactions at the first Maya encounter with the Spaniards (as described in passage 148). The Brinton translation reads, "but it was a fearful thing when they entered; their faces were strange, and the chiefs *took them for gods*." Recinos and Goetz offer a similar version: "In truth they inspired fear when they arrived. Their faces were strange. The Lords *took them for gods*" (1953: 121).[13] Instead, the study group argued that the sixteenth-century Kaqchikel chronicles described Europeans as unnatural and menacing: "*It was really terrifying* when they came, they were not known, the leaders assumed *they were unnatural beings*."[14] Thus in Maya revisionist translations, terror, not awe, foreshadows armed clashes and the Spanish military victory over the indigenous states.[15]

Stories of Pedro de Alvarado's defeat of the Maya leader Tecún Umán have been given legendary status in national schools and state-sponsored histories.[16] According to official accounts, Tecún Umán's heroic though tragic death is the culmination of the conquest. Finding himself in hand-to-hand combat with the Spanish leader, Tecún Umán is said to have taken the unfamiliar horse and conqueror as one. Unknowingly, he plunged his weapon into the horse, leaving the final counterblow to the foreign conqueror. Maya simply do not believe this story, which they feel has been created to assert Maya stupidity and ignorance: their ancient leaders were unable to distinguish man from beast! Such stories, like the long-reputed association of the Spaniards with gods, are seen as legitimizing the inevitable domination of Maya by the European other. Maya see little to admire in this tale of so-called heroic death. From small-town schools to national meetings, this story instantly triggers Maya resentment.

More recently, Maya in Guatemala have begun to search for alternative images of Maya heroism. One Kaqchikel option appears in the *Annals.* The leader Kaji' Imox survived the initial invasion and is now seen as having engaged in a campaign of unconventional warfare against Spaniards for years afterward. Eventually he was killed. But his flexibility in adjusting to Spanish preeminence in the open field of battle, when Maya war maneuvers proved unsuccessful against a technologically superior force, is felt to be emblematic of the tactical ingenuity necessary to resist colonial domination (see, for example, passages 154 and 156). Given the failure of Guatemala's armed insurgency, however, it would be a mistake to read this fascination narrowly. Rather, one can see this tactical ingenuity reflected in the development of hundreds of loosely connected research centers, language committees, and informal education projects throughout the highlands.

The image of Kaji' Imox is compelling to Kaqchikels, who look for exemplars of resistance to counterbalance another painful theme in their history, betrayal. At issue is their state's early alliance with the Spaniards against their historical rivals, the K'iche's. Kaqchikels carry the stigma of being "traitors" at the invasion, and epithets still fly in moments of interpersonal hostility. Waykan explained: "I've heard people say, 'Well, if the K'iche's and the Kaqchikels were enemies, and the Kaqchikels betrayed the K'iche's . . .' They try to use this as a weapon against others to assert, 'You are not our equals.' It's now sometimes used to reject a Kaqchikel or K'iche' proposal." This is not a minor issue, given the size and importance of these groups. K'iche's number over 1 million, making them the largest subgroup in Guatemala. Kaqchikels, the third largest and most active in culturalist leadership, number slightly over 400,000 (Oxlajuuj Keej 1993: 13, 16).

The study group, however, did not want to rewrite history to cover up this enmity if in fact it was the substance of the chronicle. Rather, as Waykan observed, they sought a wider context: "We need a deeper understanding of what happened. It's not enough to say, '*You are fighting each other; you were* enemies.' In so doing we only feed this enmity."

How did the early Kaqchikels see their alliance with the Spaniards? Does an understanding of historical patterns of intergroup warfare make their momentary alliance with the Spaniards more intelligible? In fact, the work group discovered more resistance and more Spanish manipulation of the Maya than has been apparent in the standard Spanish translations.

In the study group, as the linguists came to the narration of the conquest, they paused and for a moment imagined an alternative story in which the Spanish invaders had not enlisted eager Kaqchikels in the attack of their regional rivals. But among all the other errors and ambiguities, the text would not yield this wished-for interpretation (see passages 148–149). After using Kaqchikel forces to vanquish the K'iche' armies, the Spaniards turned their attention to looting their recent allies. The painfulness of Kaqchikel complicity and betrayal, though clearly manipulated in the sense that the Spaniards took advantage of existing divisions to dominate all Maya groups in the end (see, for example, passages 152, 154, and 156), stands as a reminder that Maya unity is something new and vulnerable.

Genealogical Echoes in the Present

Finally, the Maya linguists turned with great interest to the later genealogical section of the *Annals*, the section most translators have not even bothered to transcribe or translate. For the study group, the Pakal B'alam genealogy demonstrated crucial physical and cultural continuity from the mythic origins of the Kaqchikel Maya to the historical moment in the sixteenth century when the oral version of the *Annals* was written down. The continuity of generation begetting generation is double-voiced in a particularly revealing way. The first male ancestor, Pakal B'alam, gives rise to a generation of sons: Pakal Tojin, Pakal Ajmaq, and Pakal Kej. In turn they beget another male generation: Pakal Jun Ajpu, Pakal Ajin, and Pakal Kej. Finally, in the narrator's generation, when the *Annals* were set down in Latin script, Maya names suddenly take a Hispanicized form: Francisco Kechelaj, Diego Méndez, and finally the historian himself, Diego López (see passage "o" in Villacorta).

In essence, the text depicts the mirror image of what the linguists are currently doing in their lives. As is the convention for Maya culturalists, each has readopted a Maya name, drawn from sacred texts or from day-names in the Maya calendar, to displace at least situationally their given names in Spanish. So, during the workshop Pakal B'alam appeared twice: as a famous ancestor and progenitor in the text and as a twentieth-century linguist checking the Kaqchikel transcription of the *Annals* on his laptop computer. Following Benjamin, this flash of recognition is fundamental to historical consciousness, urging the oppressed not to "forget both its hatred and its spirit of sacrifice, for both are nourished by the image of enslaved ancestors rather than liberated grandchildren" (1968: 260). Kaqchikel intellectuals would agree with Benjamin and add that the intimacy of remembering in these small face-to-face groups builds personal commitment to cultural resurgence. Finding oneself in the Kab'lajuj Tijax history or the Pakal B'alam genealogy reaffirms the significance of renaming for revitalization and nationalist identity.[17]

It has become clear, however, that if Maya do not publish research on the chronicles, others will. The translation of indigenous culture is big business along several fronts: schools are under pressure to include more materials on Maya culture; the tourist market includes many who have passionate interests in Indian culture; and human rights struggles, Rigoberta Menchú, and United Nations conferences have spurred international concern. Not to mention foreign anthropologists.

In fact, Oxlajuuj Keej Maya' Ajtz'iib', the language institute that sent some of its members to the history reading group, decided to include a short excerpt from the *Annals* in its new book on Maya linguistics, *Maya' Chii': Los idiomas mayas de Guatemala* (1993). The book was written to be used by activists, students taking adult education courses, and teachers in Maya schools. Interestingly, the group did not use passages from the history work group; rather, it chose a passage about diaspora for its transcendent message. The book's brief introduction frames the selection for Maya readers in the following terms:

This fragment of the *Annals* is a prophecy directed to the groups of pilgrims on their march in search of their own land. This exhortation speaks of the difficulties there will be on the journey, and of their possible future glory. It is transmitted from generation to generation and is one of the literary legacies of the Maya culture.

At once they took their bows, shields,
lances, plumes, paintings,
with bumblebees and wasps,
the mud, the flood, the swamp, the fog.
When we were given advice:
"Great will be your burden,
you will not sleep,
you will not be defeated,
you will not be trampled.
O my children!
You will be strong,
you will be powerful,
you will have strength.

Take your bows, arrows, and shields.
If you pay tribute,
jade, metal, plumes, songs,
for this you will also
possess them and have them,
the jade, the metal, and the plumes,
painted and engraved objects.
All the seven communities have given tribute
even up to the distant hills.
You will have and you will demolish everything.
Lay out your bows and shields,
one will be the first, the other the last,
you thirteen warriors,
you thirteen princes,
you thirteen elders,
assemble your bows and shields
that I gave you.
Then go to lay out
the tribute, your bows and shields.
There is a war there
in the west,
in a place named Suywa,
there you will go to test
the bows and shields I gave you,
Go my children!"
It was said to us
when we came from Tulan,
when the warriors came from the seven communities.
When we came from Tulan
in reality it was terrible
when we encountered the bumblebees,
the wasps, the swamps, the fog, the mud, the flood.
(Oxlajuuj Keej 1993: 105–107)

Culturalists are reviving the heroic imagery of Maya warriors in an attempt to deal with the passivity they see as one of the scars of Ladino racism and its language of inferiority for indigenous populations. Images of self-determination and adversity are weapons for a population that has been defined by conquest rather than by their own historical agency. Most important, this narrative resonates with the experience of displacement suffered by many Maya refugees during the violence and with the struggles youths face with extreme pressures to assimilate. Today's quest echoes the first Tulan migrations and the continuing process of creation in Maya cosmology. The *Annals* are being mined for both personalized and more global imageries, depending on the context and audience.

Ethnohistorical Readings of the Chronicles

The *Annals of the Kaqchikels* amply document, in an elite-centered way, the complex political history of preconquest states, the violence of first contact with the Spaniards, and the aftermath of colonialism. Carmack argues that these writings illustrate the colonial persistence of ancient Maya strategies to legitimize elite control of state policy and sacred knowledge. In fact, chronicles and genealogies were often presented in Spanish colonial courts in support of the rights of Maya elites to political office, tribute, rents, natural resources, and arms (1973: 18–21).

Interestingly enough, the power of hereditary elites was not controversial for the Maya activists in the 1992 history work group. Like most of the national leadership, they are from modest rural backgrounds but have found the path to geographical and economic mobility, at least for the moment, through education and their work in linguistics. Moments of identification across centuries, descent groups, and political divisions are not being used by this branch of the movement to consolidate elite status in the ancient style of monopolies over literacy and knowledge.[18] Rather, these intellectuals are trying to democratize access to knowledge through an activist ethic of community service. Their goal is to promote universal literacy, in contrast to the ancient practices of the culture they celebrate. They also want to see resistance and cultural continuity displace the tragic death of Maya culture in the person of Tecún Umán.

In contrast to earlier scholars who felt the Xajila genealogies were not important enough to translate, family affairs are once again the affairs of a nation. Maya identity politics seeks to tie the intimate and familiar to nationhood in ways that earlier historians and translators would not have imagined. Continuity in descent, culture, and language is being constructed as a challenge to histories of conquest and assimilation.

There were ironies and striking instances of unfinished business in the group's reading of the *Annals*. Sixteenth-century narrators were regarded as primary sources on autochthonous culture yet used Hispanicized names for themselves. Genealogies fell silent on the place of women in androcentric accountings of state building and continuity. Class issues remained unexplored at that juncture. Yet the history group challenged linear renderings of change. They made a place for a return of the suppressed, exemplified in this instance by linguists who used their

Maya names for the occasion, four women warriors on the field of battle, and new elites who seek to share their knowledge and the tools of literacy with impoverished Maya in the countryside.

Conclusion: Anthropologically Contextualizing the Movement

In closing, I want to turn to the choices and political dilemmas we face in contextualizing this movement in current social scientific literatures. First, we can see Maya culturalism as an instance of revitalization, a metaphor I use along with resurgence. Following Wallace's classic ethnography (1972), revitalization is not simply a process of reasserting older cultural forms. Rather, it is a self-conscious cultural resynthesis in the face of extraordinary pressure and conflict, when older models no longer orient people in an increasingly unstable reality. For Wallace, the issue was the politics of a resynthesis, the authors of which have been compelled to reach across cultural divides to imagine a radical transformation of indigenous culture. Competing formulations, visionary inspiration, charismatic leaders, and cultural hybrids are part of the process of revitalization before the politics of institutionalization takes over.

A second literature would include current formulations of ethnic nationalism, imagined communities, and oppositional politics. Following Horowitz (1985), this literature is highly ambivalent about the project of ethnic intensification. Ethnic nationalism is often condemned for destructive essentialism, polarized politics, and state disintegration. In political science and anthropology, there is cynicism about movement leadership, a sense that powerful individuals will take advantage of the moment for their own personal gain, even if it comes to promoting widespread violence.[19] Little room is left for Maya multiculturalism in this formulation.

A third literature examines new social movements, as described by Escobar and Alvarez (1992). In the Latin American case, this research has focused on the recent surge of grass-roots activism working, often militantly, within democratic systems for change through the women's, ecology, labor, Afro–Latin American, human rights, gay rights, and indigenous movements.[20] These movements have global ties and transnational languages yet quite localized and culturally specific goals. Here the Maya movement would be considered a rights-based movement and would be further contextualized in terms of a transnational indigenous agenda that has grown in importance throughout Latin America. As in Clifford's analysis (1988), the issue is how a culture transforms itself to articulate with powerful institutional structures offering access to wider resources.

That the *movimiento maya* fails to rest comfortably in any one of these social scientific literatures helps us characterize the limitations of each. The revitalization model fascinates with its combination of psychology and politics, yet Wallace's formulation (1956) always had an odd functionalism. His ethnography was so much richer historically than his abstract model. Yet even there, his psychoanalytic argument stood in the way of a fuller exploration of historical self-consciousness and agency.

The ethnic nationalist model turns out to be rocky terrain for anthropology because in practice this label quickly reduces multifaceted movements to territorial nationalism, state-endangering opposition, and the corrupt politics of a newly consolidating elite. Young (1976, 1993) initially felt that nationalist movements would not be an issue for Latin American indigenous populations who found themselves fragmented, assimilated into the peasantry, and "deprived of the cultural resources for a collective response to their subordinate status" (1976: 457, 1993). How wrong he was. Yet Guatemala is not the former Soviet Union, the Baltic States, or Rwanda. Maya intellectuals see "nationalist" as a threatening label for their situation because it allows governments to point to international examples of state fragmentation to justify repression in the name of national security at home.

Nor do Maya culturalists find that "ethnic" or "minority" appropriately describes their struggle. In their view, the discourse of "minority rights" emanates from the United States, where it disempowers social movements, promotes assimilation to the mainstream, and limits activists' ability to reconfigure national culture. They reject this language as marginalizing. Moreover, they are aware that this language has been used in Guatemala and the United States to argue that Maya cultural elites who work in nonagricultural occupations outside their home communities are no longer really Maya but rather a "third ethnicity" between indigenous and Ladino. Thus, they become inauthentic representatives of their own people.

Finally, anthropology seems both intrigued and worried by the new social movements literature. Anthropologists are excited about pursuing this local yet transcultural formulation of change. Yet there is a legitimate fear that key issues of cultural meaning will disappear in the transcultural (but strikingly Western-sounding) grammar of movements. It is not uncommon for scholars of new social movements to treat their existence and goals as self-evident. As a result, the focus is on the formal ideologies and established collectivities that people join. Much less attention is directed to the internal dynamics of these movements: to the particular ways participants create and consume culture through their activism, to the ways social relations (not just individual choice) mediate involvements, or to the ironies of identity politics in movements that foreground one of many identities relevant to activists. Perhaps, in its own particular hybrid form, the pan-Maya movement in Guatemala will offer important lessons about nonviolent options to transform political marginalization in multiethnic states that seek a democratic future. The culturalists' recent turn to educational reform has attracted widespread attention in local, national, and international arenas. Though internationally small in scope, indigenous rights movements provide revealing challenges to existing models of development. As this essay has attempted to show, the pan-Maya movement also has much to teach us about the politics of reading culture.

Notes

My appreciative thanks to the following colleagues for their explanations of Maya linguistics to an anthropologist and for generous feedback on early drafts of this essay: Judith Maxwell, Pakal B'alam, Waykan, Kab'lajuj Tijax, Nik'te', Lolmay, and Nora England. In addition to working with the *Annals* study group, I enjoyed many hours in Guatemala with Oxlajuuj Keej Maya' Ajtz'iib' members in informal discussions, other workshops, and conferences where they responded to *kaxlan* readings of chronicles such as the *Popol Wuj*. Ted Fischer, McKenna Brown, Irma Otzoy, Enrique Sam Colop, Charles Hale, and Quetzil Castañeda shared their thoughts and questions for contextualizing the analysis ethnographically and conceptually. Feedback from Steve Rubenstein, Alan Feldman, and Bill Fischer at the 1995 SSRC–Wenner Gren conference on uncertainty and Wende Marshall and Eugenia Kaw in our political anthropology seminar, and from Virginia Garrard Burnett, who read the manuscript for the University of Texas Press, has been very helpful. As always, I alone assume responsibility for the final argument of this essay.

My wider research project deals with language revitalization and standardization, Maya history and analyses of racism, and current efforts to create Maya schools and educational materials. I am interested in how local agendas for change converge and diverge with national activism (see Warren 1992, 1993, 1994, 1995).

1. Todorov (1994) and Sahlins (1981, 1985) are fascinated with the Other as radically different in modes of apprehending and representing the world and politically disadvantaged by these categorical, dichotomizing differences. Obeyesekere (1992) takes on this issue to show the myth-making nature of European society and the self-interested political nature of Hawaiian politics. The balance is tricky. On the one hand, as long as difference is essentialized and seen as hegemonic, the risk is reverse Orientalism instead of an analytically leveled playing field. Alternatively, when difference is collapsed, the risk is a universalized political rationality. Each of these authors seeks a dynamic model, but Prakash (1992) would argue that none has solved the post-Orientalist riddle.

2. Freed from the pressures of their normal work week by Linda Schele's Maya symposium in Austin, Texas, the study group of Kaqchikel-speaking linguists was eager to turn to the chronicle along with Judith Maxwell, professor of linguistics at Tulane, and Helen Rivas, who provided logistical support. Nora

England and I sat in on the sessions, and Nik'te' and Saqijix from Oxlajuuj Keej, who were working on the *Rabinal Achi*, frequently dropped by to check on the group's progress. This was a vacation for all of us, so the tone of the study group was celebratory and informal, with a great deal of spontaneous discussion and cross-language word play. The leadership of the endeavor was collaborative and clearly Maya, with Judith Maxwell as a peer.

3. Here, of course, one sees why Scott's (1990) structuralism, with its emphasis on otherness, sometimes misses the mark. The "hidden transcript" here is as much about internal divisions and worries as it is about the oppressor.

4. Along these lines, Galeano writes: "The sacred myths [of the *Popol Wuj*] announce a time of fighting and punishment for those who are arrogant and greedy. They remind the Indians of Guatemala that they are people and have a history, one much longer than the society which uses and despises them, and so they are born again each day" (1986: 29–30, my translation).

5. Specifically, the group worked on the origins section, which juxtaposes the coming of Q'aq'awitz and Saqtekaw from Tulan to establish the founding Kaqchikel lineages and the creation by Tz'aqol B'itol of the first humans (passages 1–5 in Brinton, Recinos, and Villacorta), the migration of the early Kaqchikels and their wars with neighboring groups (passages 15–16 and 37–38), the Iximche' revolt and the participation of women warriors (passages 99–103), the Spanish invasion (passages 144–149), and the demand for tribute and subsequent wars of conquest involving the Kaqchikels, Tz'utujils, and K'iche's (passages 152–156). On page 188, Brinton comments, "I append the [English] translation of the remainder of what I believe to be the original work . . . ; but as its contents are of little general interest, I omit the [Kaqchikel] text." At that point the group switched to the Villacorta version in Kaqchikel for the Pakal B'alam genealogy (passage "o"), which was, in fact, of great interest.

6. See Tedlock (1983: 261–271) for a fascinating argument that these recountings in postinvasion chronicles represent resistance to Christian narratives of singularity.

7. I include illustrative excerpts based on the work of the 1992 study group in Spanish and Kaqchikel to give readers a sense of the text. Passages are numbered following Brinton, Recinos, and Villacorta. I am departing from the group's strategy for Spanish translation by using the Kaqchikel verse structure, which marks the genre of formal speech and prayer.

8. This is based on the group's retranscription and translations of Brinton's version. One of the ironies of the anthropological process, of course, is that I must provide another level of translation (and thus perpetuate the very problem this group was attempting to remedy) in order to give English readers a sense of the Oxlajuuj Keej texts. My special thanks to Judith Maxwell for reviewing this English version.

In other cases, the issue is easier. Brinton (1885) and Recinos and Goetz (1953) produced English translations, which I draw on when appropriate. Spanish and English translations lose the elaborate language for Maya leadership. In English I have avoided "chief," a term common in other English translations, as well as the intolerant language of "pagans" and "idols," although elsewhere this language becomes the focus of analysis. One unavoidable gap has to do with the levels of meaning in Maya formal discourse. There is no way to represent the simultaneity of meanings and associations in straight narrative, another reason why the discussion of exegesis and translation is conjoined.

9. Obsidian stone.

10. Tz'aqol is, according to Tedlock, associated with "mason, builder, construction" and B'itol with "former, shaper, modeler" (1983: 267).

11. The leader of the Tuquche' forces.

12. At the Primer Congreso de la Educación Maya in August 1994, there were heated exchanges before Maya conventions for consensus smoothed over differences.

13. This is their English translation of Recinos (1950: #148): "en verdad infundían miedo cuando llegaron. Sus caras eran extrañas. Los Señores _los tomaron por dioses_" and Villacorta (1934: #148): "fué cosa terrible cuando entraron; sus rostros eran extraños y los jefes _los tomaron por dioses_."

14. The 1992 Oxlajuuj Keej translation reads: "Realmente _era aterrorizante cuando llegaron_, no eran conocidos. Los caciques supusieron que _eran seres no naturales_."

15. Tedlock's readings of the _Popol Wuj_ and _Annals_ reaffirm this interpretation. He finds provocative evidence of Spanish torture to exact confession in these indigenous accounts (1993).

16. The Guatemalan army (Ejército de Guatemala 1963) sponsored a fascinating scholarly evaluation of the Tecún Umán myth. A panel of highly respected Ladino scholars painstakingly evaluated colonial documents and in the process showed their variations and subjectivities as well as problems in translation. In this sense, the project revealed procedures similar to those advocated by this Maya study group. However, the concluding paragraphs of the book disavow any indeterminacy. The study claims to have definitively proven, through a weighing of indirect evidence, Tecún Umán's battle with Alvarado and the significance of his death. Thus, the national hero is reaffirmed as an established truth in the proceedings of the seminar published by the Guatemalan army press. This study deserves a fuller treatment and contextualization in terms of the state's construction of an encompassing nationalism during an early period of unrest.

17. Alternatively, many Maya adopt calendric names from the 260-day annual count for men and from the 20-day month count for women.

18. The issue of their position as experts who broker and authenticate Maya knowledge is pursued in my analyses of Maya educational texts (see Warren n.d.).

19. See, for example, the new Ferguson (n.d.) collection.

20. See, for example, Hanchard (1994).

6.
The Discourse of Concealment and 1992

Enrique Sam Colop
(Maya Education Foundation)

Colonial Discourse of the Twentieth Century

In the sixteenth century the initial impact of European expansionism was concealed by the euphemisms "pacification" and "liberation"; in the twentieth century the preferred terms are "cultural contact" and "encounter of two worlds," implying the union of two societies for mutual understanding and respect. This discourse shuns honest reflection and tries to justify the colonization that continues today: current economic, political, cultural, and social structures that place the worst burden on native peoples are effectively derived from initial European colonialism. At an ideological level, colonialism is manifested through a discourse that idealizes the sixteenth-century invader and justifies his aggression, a discourse that rationalizes the extinction of Maya culture and languages and justifies the imposition of Hispanic culture and the Spanish language. This is a racist discourse, a discourse of negation of the other.

About what happened five hundred Gregorian years ago, the recipient of the 1990 Nobel Prize for literature, Octavio Paz, writes that the original peoples of Mesoamerica were vulnerable before the Spaniards due to a "technical and cultural inferiority" and that they could not imagine the Spaniards due to their lack of intellectual and historical categories in which to place them. Thus, the Spaniards, says Paz, were considered "gods and supernatural beings" (Paz 1987).

Spanish cultural superiority is interpreted by some as "manifesting itself in a greater capacity for flexible and rational thought, and a pragmatic allocation of energy and material resources," and yet in the case of Yucatán "it is difficult to see much of either in the Spanish campaigns" (Clendinnen 1988: 32). Other authors, such as Severo Martínez Peláez (1970), argue for a Hispanic "superiority" associated with technological development. As an example of this "superiority," Martínez Peláez cites Alvarado's remarks to Cortés about the Indians' ignorance that "the horses were ineffectual on steep and rough terrain" and that the Indians "easily fell in the traps that the horsemen set for them" (1970: 28). Nevertheless, contrary to the view of Martínez Peláez, the *Annals of the Kaqchikels* states: "Xb'an je k'otoj, xb'an k'a jul kej simaj xekamisab'ex. . . . Je k'a k'i kastilan winaq xekan, kere k'a kej xkam pa jul kej. [The Kaqchikels . . . dug holes and pits for the horses and scattered sharp stakes so that they should be killed. . . . Many Spaniards perished and the horses died in the traps for the horses]" (Recinos and Goetz 1953: 125). This version is collaborated by Pedro de Alvarado himself: "They made many holes and pits with stakes covered with earth and grass into which many horses and Spaniards fell and died" (Recinos 1950: 129–130). Such arguments of "cultural superiority" are, at best, partial interpretations. Military strategies, bacteriological warfare, and violations of codes of war do not determine cultural "superiority" or "inferiority."[1] If technological development equaled "cultural superiority," then the United States, since it is technologically more developed, would be more culturally developed than Latin America.

The opinion that the Maya regarded the Spaniards as "gods" is, as Victor Montejo has documented, a Spanish invention repeated to this day (Montejo 1991). The books of Chilam B'alam, for example, do not speak of the Spaniards as "gods" but rather as agents of misery, and the *Annals of the Kaqchikels* bluntly states: "K'ere k'a tok xul Kastilan winaq ri ojer, ix nuk'ajol. Kitzij tixib'in ok xeul, mani etaam wi kiwach, je kab'owil xekina' ajawa'. [Thus it was that the Spaniards arrived here long ago, my children. Truly they inspired fear when they arrived, we did not know their faces, the lords took them for icons]" (Recinos and Goetz 1953: 121; Warren, chap.5).

The term in question is *kab'owil* or *kab'awil*, which Brinton (1969), Recinos and Goetz (1953), and others translate as "god" or "gods." *Kab'awil* in fact means "icon" (good or bad, depending on the point of view, like the Statue of Liberty, the cross, the swastika, or the Virgin of Guadalupe). In the *Calepino Kaqchikel* (Varela n.d.), *kab'awil* is translated as "statue," "idol," "hoax," and "image." Francisco Hernández Arana, one of the authors of the *Annals of the Kaqchikels*, associated the Spaniards with "statues" and "idols" that instilled fear because of their unknown faces and their human callousness; he had earlier described the tragic consequences of the Spaniards' arrival among the K'iche': the torture and sacrifice of their leaders and the destruction of their city. The books of Chilam B'alam of Chumayel and Tizimín say that the soldiers of the "true god" (the Spaniards) are inhuman; and elsewhere, Jesus Christ was associated with one of the "dreaded Lords of death" (Bruce 1983: 275). Thus, what was divine for the Christians was not necessarily so for the Maya.

Cardoza y Aragón states that "actually, there exist two cultures in Guatemala, that of the indigenous and that of the West" (1990: 16). He describes neither "a tranquil coexistence" nor a cultural dilemma, because "the hegemonic culture has almost torn apart the great Indian culture, and the 'ruins of the Indian culture' are what are being revamped by Indian revolutionaries and the dominant culture, which obligates the creation of a culture that, because of all the historical and geographic reasons, will slowly become Mestizo" (1990: 16). Cardoza y Aragón then asks, "Is this ethnocentrism? Is this a racist tone?"

It has been suggested that the roots of Guatemalan *mestizaje* spring from the *Popol Wuj* because this sacred Mayan text was copied and translated by a Spanish priest. Even a university vice chancellor wrote that the *Popol Wuj* is not a Maya work but a mestizo one: "The author or authors were already Mestizos. They already knew Spanish, although not well" (Juárez-Paz 1992: 69). The original *Popol Wuj* was a hieroglyphic book. It was transcribed in K'iche' with Latin characters in the late sixteenth century by K'iche's who recounted the difficult circumstances under which the transcription was made.[2] This manuscript remained hidden for the next century and a half, until Francisco Ximénez was permitted to copy and translate it into Spanish. Since then the first K'iche' alphabetic version has disappeared (see Carmack 1973, who suggests that the original text still exists).

Theories of authorship of the *Popol Wuj* have changed over the centuries, following a telling sequence: for Friar Ximénez, the author was Satan; for René Acuña, he was a Spanish priest; for others, the text was mestizo because Ximénez transcribed it; and finally, some believe the K'iche' authors were not Maya but mestizos since they transcribed it into Spanish. In this attempted usurpation of symbols, it is curious to note that those who draw on the *Popol Wuj* to ground their *mestizaje* do not propose the same with the *Xajoj Tun*, an indigenous text that was also copied and translated by a priest—a French priest. Cardoza y Aragón says: "We have deprived [the Indians] of even their past, exploiting it as our past, and on ending my sentence I discover that I am speaking as a mestizo" (1990: 14). The *Popol Wuj* is, to use a metaphor of Dante Liano (1984), "a birth certificate" of the Maya, not of the mestizos.

The Guatemalan press speaks of a mestizo homeland and of an "inevitable Hispanic integration" through the confluence of Indian and Hispanic blood. The press appears to sympathize with both the celebrators and the detractors of the quincentenary celebration, calling for mutual cultural and linguistic respect as well as a "national unity" based on Spanish. Some journalists, in a spasm of racism, say that their *mestizaje* is a reason for pride and that "genetic destiny" advocates the move toward the Hispanic. Thus wrote a columnist: "*Mestizaje* is indispensable for certain backward peoples of decadent races; they have to be considered from the point of view of anthropology, culture, and other rubrics of progress and the betterment of man and, therefore, of the races. This brings us to eugenics" (Wyss 1992a: 9, 1992b). Rafael Burgos Figueroa, a columnist who claims to know the "true history," writes that five hundred years ago the Spaniards were "ferociously attacked by poisonous snakes, mosquitos, impenetrable jungle, and savage tribes that enjoyed the practice of human sacrifice" (1991a: 9); that by the time of contact Maya culture had already been "taken away by extraterrestrials" (1991b: 11); and that no proof of cannibalism remains because "the gluttons left no scraps or waste behind to prove it" (1991c: 25). Carlos Manuel Pellecer, who asserts that he is a protector of the Indians, writes that the Maya are on the "margin of life, of creative and generous action" (1991a: 12); that they are "furious, vindictive exterminators" (1991b: 12); and that their culture is "elemental" and "there is no evidence that it could advance the interest of tourism" (1991c: 12). Pellecer also equates Maya demands for the recognition of their rights with the death of the Ladino state and the recognition of Maya common law with "returning to the practice of human sacrifice, servitude, slavery, and of course, to the use of splints to shape the head" (1991d: 12, 1991e).

Nevertheless, the Guatemalan press also publishes opinions such as the following: "While the massacres that the Spaniards committed upon arriving to our land are considered a pardonable neglect, ethnic animosity is not recognized as one of the principal causes of an undeclared thirty-year war in which the participation of indigenous groups is minimized because they are deprecated to the point that they became rebels" (Mejia 1992: 12); or the following: "It has been a long time since the Spaniards were protagonists of our history. The protagonists are, in contrast, the Ladinos who have the Indian and Guatemala in a situation that has to be recognized as feudal" (Liano 1992: 61). Finally, the following editorial questions Ladinos who refer to the Maya as their property:

> I have wondered and asked, when some idiot refers to indigenous
> Guatemalans as "our" little Indians, if it is true that they have
> inherited "a herd of Indians" among the multiple properties that
> their parents or grandparents have left them. At every opportunity,
> I am asked to clarify this innocent question . . . and I do: How
> many little Indians did your parents leave you? Have you inherited
> them already or are you going to inherit them? How jealous I am!
> You lucky son of a gun! I did not inherit even one. . . . In you one
> can see the spirit of a frustrated slave-owner. (Carrillo 1992: 31)

Misinformation and racist opinions are also presented in universities and schools. The university text *La patria del criollo* speaks of Indian culture, in particular native languages, as "less developed" (Martínez Peláez 1970: 600), explaining that "the language of a society reflects the degree of development of which it is a product. A more advanced technology always supposes a more developed language, in vocabulary and expressive possibilities. Indigenous languages, as spoken today, are known to be plagued by proper words that have no translation" (Martínez Peláez 1970: 768).[3]

Martínez Peláez abuses the Sapir-Whorf hypothesis: lexicons do not define languages. Languages borrow and phoneticize terms constantly (Spanish speakers say or write, for example, *naif* [knife], *picop* [pick-up], *apartied* [apartheid], *disket* [diskette], *mol* [mall], *wisky* [whiskey], and *nais* [nice]). With respect to "expressive possibilities," Spanish discourse lacks the complementary dialectic of Maya discourse; in morphological terms, Spanish lacks the inclusive/exclusive pronouns that some Mayan languages have; in syntactic terms, Spanish apparently does not have intransitive clauses with a degraded object (antipassives) as do Mayan languages, French, Choctaw, and others. Does this mean that Spanish is less developed? No, it is simply a different language. Martínez Peláez proposes learning Spanish as a means of decolonizing the Maya, but, if his theory is correct, it would be better still to learn Japanese or German since these languages are "more developed" than Spanish.

Martínez Peláez adopts the theory of ladinization advanced by North American and Mexican anthropologists in the middle of this century. He states: "It is well understood that an Indian dressed in jeans and wearing boots is no longer Indian. And even less so if he speaks other modern languages besides Spanish. And less still if the *cofradía* has been changed for the labor union, and the sweat bath for antibiotics" (Martínez Peláez 1970: 611). In this same spirit, the aforementioned university vice chancellor, echoing a prevalent line of thought, writes that Rigoberta Menchú Tum is no longer an "authentic" Maya, she is mestiza (Juárez-Paz 1992).

Estudios sociales, a text for secondary students, under the title "Encounter of Two Cultures" states that while Anglo-Saxons proposed the elimination or reduction of the slavery of "aborigines," the Spaniards and Portuguese "said that the most suitable thing was to levelize the Indian to Spanish and Portuguese culture, but to achieve this it was indispensable to unify them juridically" (Castañeda 1962: 173). The text continues by affirming (and contradicting itself) that the unification held fast when "the natives organized their communities in the form to which they were accustomed" (Castañeda 1962: 173). Regarding the religious aspect of European expansion, the text assures the student that "a new religion full of love and peace" came to substitute "the sanguine rites that the natives practiced to please their multiple gods" (Castañeda 1962: 141–142). The students, however, are not informed that this new religion, forged in an epoch of torture, burned men alive and hung them while friars prayed around them. This textbook repeatedly refers to Maya culture with depreciatory terms such as "folklore," "popular culture," "artisans," and "superstitions."[4] Likewise, in the prologue to *Crónicas indígenas de Guatemala*, Francis Polo Sifontes, a member of the Guatemalan Academy of Geography and History, refers to Maya literature as a "peculiar literature" that has been translated into all the "civilized languages" of the world (in Recinos 1984).

In primary school texts, we are misinformed that Tz'utujil is a dialect of Kaqchikel, that Awakateko is a dialect of Mam, that Q'eqchi' is a dialect of Poqomam (Ruiz Recinos 1972). Another text, *Guatemala historia gráfica* (Gordillo Barrios 1987), teaches students that the pre-Columbian Maya "worshiped nature . . . [and] some animals such as the coyote, the raccoon, and the tapir"; that there was a god the Maya "could hardly define but considered the most powerful of all" (86); that Kaqchikel means "fire thieves" (99); that the Indians considered the Spanish "gods because of their color"; and that during the first years of the colony the Indians received the priests with "special attention given as a result in grand part because of the little culture that they already had" (167).

Conclusion

1 B'aqtun, 5 K'atuns, and 7 Tuns (500 solar years) after the beginning of European expansion on this continent, colonialism continues in force. It is part of the dominant ideology: "We are the conquistadors. They were our parents and grandparents that came to these beaches and gave us our names and the language we speak," acknowledges Mario Vargas Llosa (1990). "We continue colonizing the Indian," says Cardoza y Aragón (1990), adding, "In Guatemala Pedro de Alvarado is long-lasting" (1989).

In this colonialism, the Other is interpreted, imagined, and represented, and his future is prescribed. With few exceptions, the contemporary Maya and all things Maya are associated with the "past" and "backwardness," and so it is decided that they must renounce their culture and languages and integrate themselves into the "national culture" and speak the official language. The fixation that the Indians should resemble the Ladinos (culturally and linguistically) is so great that the former are interpreted as an inverse image of the latter. It is affirmed that if the Ladino is racist or discriminatory in action, the Maya is the same in reaction. In this configuration it is thought that as Spain expelled the Muslims after eight hundred years of occupation, the Maya are going to expel the Ladinos today. Thus, for some, the very fact that the Maya try to exercise their human rights is equivalent to hating Spain and the Spanish language and signifies a return to "primitive states."

In this dominant ideology, pluralism and peaceful coexistence seem to commit outrage against the evolution of the state, but a "national unity" cannot be constructed while denying an existent plurality. To do so is to construct a future while walking toward the past. The Maya, in contrast, do not base their future on the past; they add their future to their history and to the history of humanity. After 12 October 1992 came 13 October, which in the Maya Long Count is 12 B'aqtuns, 18 K'atuns, 19 Tuns, 9 Winäqs, 6 Q'ij (1 Kame, 9 Yax in the Calendar Round).

Notes

Parts of this article have been published in Sam Colop (1991). This article was translated from the Spanish by Edward F. Fischer and R. McKenna Brown.

1. For greater detail, see Clendinnen (1988), especially pages 32–37.

2. In teaching the Latin alphabet, the friars had an evangelizing aim, but the Maya writers discerned an instrumental function. Tedlock (1985) says that as Christian symbols served in the massacre of ancient deities, the Latin alphabet served to massacre the ancient texts.

3. David Vela says that the Mayan languages had remained stagnant until the middle of the sixteenth century and were relatively "very poor for expressing current contexts and values" (1990: 3).

4. This belittling of that which is of the Other is masterfully captured by Galeano in "Los Nadies":

Que no son, aunque sean.
Que no hablan idiomas, sino dialectos.
Que no profesan religiones, sino supersticiones.
Que no hacer arte, sino artesanía.
Que no practican cultura, sino folklore.
[They do not exist, even if they exist.
They do not speak languages, but rather dialects.
They do not profess religions, but rather superstitions.
They do not make art, but rather crafts.
They do not practice culture, but rather folklore.] (1991: 59)

7.
Old Writing and New Messages: The Role of Hieroglyphic Literacy in Maya Cultural Activism

Circe Sturm (University of California, Davis)

The Maya of Guatemala are beginning to reappropriate the hieroglyphic writing of their ancestors despite considerable linguistic and economic obstacles. Their greatest challenges are the incomplete decipherment of hieroglyphic writing and the scarcity of educational materials available in Guatemala. Prior to the Spanish invasion, many Maya were literate in their indigenous writing system, but in modern Guatemala, Maya must struggle against socioeconomic odds to become alphabetically literate. Only when the prerequisite of alphabetic literacy is achieved can Maya begin to relearn their hieroglyphic writing system.

Although many theorists have failed to recognize the social and political significance of literacy, the Guatemalan example clearly demonstrates the need to ground writing system theories in specific social and political contexts. Writing is always charged with sociopolitical valences and can even be subject to attack, as when the written legacy of the Maya was systematically destroyed during the Spanish invasion. The modern use of Maya hieroglyphic writing is an expression of self-determination and political resistance against non-Indian hegemony. By examining how writing in a resuscitated script relates to larger cultural and political contexts, this essay will attempt to sharpen our understanding of contemporary Maya issues and increase our awareness of the biases inherent in academic endeavors.

This essay begins by discussing various manifestations of Maya cultural activism and the political strategies of the self-identified *pueblo Maya*, particularly with regard to how inconsistencies in their self-presentation insulate Maya cultural activists from political repression. Then, relating hieroglyphic writing to the larger sociocultural spectrum, I demonstrate how it functions as an expression of political resistance and discuss the problems inherent in its application in a modern context. Finally, I conclude by detailing some of the ethical issues that have arisen between Maya and foreign scholars concerning hieroglyphic writing.

Is Maya Cultural Activism Revitalization or Nationalism?

The pan-Maya movement in Guatemala has been described as Maya ethnonationalism: the "conscious effort to construct a pan-Maya identity and collectively formulate Maya political demands" (Hale and Smith 1991: 6). According to Smith, Maya nationalism focuses on "cultural symbols of Maya identity—languages, community forms, clothing, and religious practices—as expressions of non-violent self-determination" (1991: 30). Nonetheless, some Maya resist the label of nationalism and emphasize that revaluing Maya culture will result in tolerance and cultural pluralism both within individual Maya communities and between the Ladino and Maya communities at large. This particular form of Maya resistance is being defined by various social actors, including Maya intellectuals and community leaders, as well as non-Maya scholars from Guatemala, Canada, Europe, Japan, and the United States.

In a recent interview with one Maya intellectual, it became apparent why the debate over appropriate terminology continues. I asked the director of Cholsamaj (a Maya publishing house), Leopoldo Tzian, which term he preferred, Maya nationalism or Maya revitalization; he responded:

> Basically, you could refer to this as a process of cultural revitalization. Of course, you could also identify us as a national movement, since we refer to ourselves as a *pueblo* [nation, people]. The phrase "Maya nationalism" that you have expressed to me is what we understand as the national fight or the national movement; in this sense, we are the Maya Nation. We understand nationality as being equivalent to *pueblo*, thus we refer to ourselves as the Maya *pueblo*. (Emphasis mine)[1]

Although this statement is nationalistic in its tone, Tzian a few moments later said, "If we are going to talk about a traditional approach, obviously this one is not nationalistic." He clarified the apparent contradiction:

> This is not a nationalism that unleashes an armed conflict like what happened in Europe; neither is it a nationalism that in the end becomes the same, that is to say that goes from being an oppressed people to being an oppressing people within a "nation-state." On the other hand, yes, [the Maya movement] is a nationalism that pursues equality between nations through a redefinition of Guatemala as a multinational state comprised of the Maya people,

the Ladino people, the Xinka people (which is almost extinct), and
the Garífuna people; it is a nationalism that wages an active
struggle of cultural revitalization that is involved with the social,
the economic, and the political, but passive from the point of view
of being neither warlike nor aggressive.

Tzian's statements are cautious, and any mention of nationalism is
qualified. They reflect the difficulties that both Maya and non-Indian
scholars have in finding a political category for the pan-Maya movement.
   Part of the problem results from the fact that the pan-Maya movement comprises two distinct fronts. One front is overtly political and has
traditionally been labeled popular; it encompasses trade unions, students, and others who identify with one another because of their shared
experiences with repression and class inequities. Also, the popular front
is largely Marxist and bases its actions on theories of class. The other
front focuses less directly on politics and class issues and more explicitly
on ethnic and cultural commonalities (Bastos and Camus 1993).[2]
   I refer to the culturally based expression of the pan-Maya movement
as Maya revitalization, which I consider a broader and more inclusive
term than "nationalism" and one that transcends traditional political
categorizations. The term "revitalization" also avoids the confronta-
tional tone associated with popular resistance, which Maya cultural
activists avoid in practice in order to circumvent the same repression
that has plagued their more outspoken peers. By focusing on linguistic
and cultural rights, they are perceived as less threatening to the status
quo and to the Ladino-run Guatemalan government.

Hieroglyphic Writing as an Expression of Maya Revitalization

Evidence of Classic Maya hieroglyphic writing is found at a number of
sites in an area covering the Yucatán peninsula of lower Mexico,
Guatemala, and the western extreme of Honduras. It is believed that the
Classic Maya writing system originated between 200 B.C. and A.D. 50
(Schele 1991: 1). The Classic period (A.D. 250–900) is defined by the
erection of monumental architecture and stone stelae, on which
hieroglyphs were carved to record political and religious events such as
dates of royal accessions, deeds of war, and ritual bloodlettings.
   At the beginning of the Postclassic period (A.D. 900), monumental
stelae virtually disappeared. Nevertheless, glyphs continued to be written in bark-paper screenfold books called codices. For the most part, the
surviving codices are almanacs that record historical, calendrical, astronomical, and ceremonial information. There is evidence of Classic
period codices on ceramic pots and in carved iconography, but these
codices have not survived to the present. Thus, the remaining codices are

but a small fragment of the original corpus; it is likely that the codices recorded many other types of information, analogous to Mixtec and Aztec practices. The production of hieroglyphic texts was halted by the Spanish invasion, when the Spaniards burned all but a few codices and virtually destroyed the literary history of the Maya—and knowledge of the writing system along with it.

Although the calendrical sections of the hieroglyphic corpus were largely deciphered by the 1890s, only in the past thirty years has any significant progress been made in the decipherment of other parts of the script (Coe 1992: 107–108, 231–258).[3] Three decades ago, the most important epigraphers, Sylvanus Morley, J. Eric Thompson, and Thomas Barthel, believed that the script was purely logographic (with each sign representing a word), an assumption that slowed their progress. A breakthrough occurred in the early 1950s, when Russian scholar Yuri Knorosov discovered that the script was a combined syllabic-logographic system with polyvalent signs: most frequently, a hieroglyphic sign stood for a consonant-vowel syllable (syllabic), but occasionally, the same sign could also stand for a particular word (logographic). His revolutionary discovery served as the foundation for all later decipherments. Once the connection was made that many glyphic symbols operated phonetically, decipherment proceeded in leaps and bounds, though much work, including decipherment of the syllabary, is still in progress.[4]

Since the glyphs were associated with politics and power in the pre-Columbian past, it is not surprising that in their modern context they have recaptured similar associations. Modern Maya who use the glyphs are reclaiming their past, with the hope of encouraging greater autonomy in the Maya's future. The past they reappropriate helps to build a larger pan-Maya identity, based on a common pre-Columbian history. For example, the glyphs, associated with lowland language groups in precolonial times, are at present written by highland language speakers.[5] This blurring of historical and geographic detail becomes a practical and powerful tool with which to subvert non-Indian hegemony and construct a sense of pan-Maya community.

In Guatemala, Maya revitalization is closely linked to education and literacy. The Maya leaders of the revitalization movement, almost all of them literate, include students and intellectuals, community-based professionals, and members of local nongovernmental organizations and cooperatives (Smith 1991: 30). Fischer (1996) adds an important dimension, arguing that the Maya leaders of the revitalization movement are largely urban-centered. Significantly, highland Maya who have access to educational materials on the hieroglyphs and to institutions of higher education, which in Guatemala are located predominantly in the capital city, are most actively adopting the glyphs as a form of political resistance.

Although the glyphs are occasionally used by Maya in private communications (i.e., letter writing and signatures), they generally appear in public settings as a part of print media.[6] The complexity of the production of print media makes it difficult to determine who is employing the script and to what end. There is often no single "author" for the implementation of hieroglyphic writing because the communicative acts of a group, and not a single individual, are involved. For example, the artist who incorporates glyphs in the design of a book cover is sometimes detached from the organization or individual who chooses to print the materials. Since literacy levels in Spanish and/or a Mayan language frequently correspond to levels of active involvement in print media, these users of the glyphs may be considered members of an emerging elite. Peasant farmers are not a primary source of modern glyph proliferation, since alphabetic literacy and especially any level of hieroglyphic literacy are still luxuries in Guatemala, a result of an economic and political system that limits educational opportunities.

The public and printed nature of hieroglyphic writing is an important part of Maya revitalization and may, as Benedict Anderson has suggested in a different context, be laying the base for Maya ethnonationalism in two distinct ways:

> First, and foremost, [printed materials] create unified fields of exchange and communication . . . in the process [the readers] gradually become aware of hundreds of thousands, even millions, of people in their particular language-field, and at the same time that only those people so belong. These fellow readers, to whom they were connected through print, form . . . the embryo of the nationally imagined community. (Anderson 1983: 44)

Although literacy is limited to Maya intellectual elites, the hieroglyphic "field of communication" involves the majority of Maya and crosses class boundaries. All Maya, including both peasant farmers and urban-based intellectual elites, "read" the glyphs symbolically, which occurs regardless of an individual's ability to decipher a literal message. They recognize the glyphs as "Maya" and, thus, participate in Anderson's "field of communication."

Hieroglyphic writing is one way in which the leaders of the revitalization movement "imagine" themselves as part of the masses, thereby lessening the distance between themselves and their villages. This statement is not meant to imply that Maya intellectual elites have lost touch with their roots in their home communities. Frequently, the hard work of their families, who remain in the village, provides the only opportunity for Maya to become educated. However, an education often requires physical separation from the village and may provide a basis for class, ideological, and/or economic distinctions between the Maya elite and their peers in the home community who are less fortunate. Revitalization specifically seeks to bridge these distances; it builds pan-Maya identity by resisting traditional class distinctions and focusing instead on a shared culture and the shared experience of oppression.

Old Writing, New Messages

Modern highland Maya are effectively using the script as a form of political resistance, overcoming traditional and historical limitations, and creating new and sometimes systematic modes of representation. According to Kaufman's (1976b) glottochronology of Mayan languages, Proto-Mayan split into the Wastekan, Yukatekan, Western, and Eastern families. Historical/comparative linguistics has proved that for the Classic period the language the glyphs originally recorded was related to the Yukatekan and Western lowland languages. Although there are few existing examples of hieroglyphic writing in the highlands (i.e., Kaminal Juyu') and no known Classic period texts, some scholars believe that highland hieroglyphic writing was more extensive than the archaeological evidence suggests. Tedlock (1985, 1992) asserts that the *Popol Wuj*, a postcolonial highland text, was originally written in hieroglyphs. Various ethnographic and ethnohistoric sources report books among the highland K'iche' as late as the early eighteenth century (Ximénez 1967), and there is lexical evidence in K'ichean languages for the words "paper" and "write" (Campbell 1977).

A practical consideration in the script's modern application to highland languages is that the Maya hieroglyphic writing system is both logographic and phonetic. Because of the script's flexibility, modern Maya must choose the manner of representation from various alternatives. Thus, any problems encountered in adapting the script to highland languages vary according to the choices made by Maya about the nature of the individual signs or graphemes.

Occasionally, modern Maya use the script phonetically based on a syllabary that is not completely deciphered. Since the Mayan languages are phonetically similar, the existing syllabary can represent the majority of Eastern Mayan languages with only a few specific additions for each. In particular, the "lowland" syllabary lacked the signs to represent the uvular stops /q/ and /q'/ and the liquid consonant /r/ that are present in highland languages. Thus, in the summer of 1991, members of Oxlajuuj Keej Maya' Ajtz'iib', a group of Maya linguists, developed a set of signs that when attached to or placed within the standard syllabic sign specify a highland pronunciation. An example of the adaptation of the syllabary to the highland languages is found in figure 1, where the writer modifies the syllabic symbols for /ya/ and /k'a/ by attaching a small

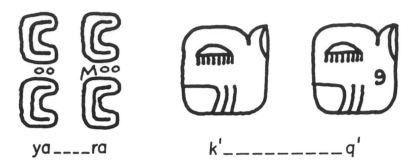

Figure 1. After COMG (1991).

spiral loop; they are then pronounced as highland /ra/ and /q'a/, sounds to which they are historically related.

Originally, Oxlajuuj Keej developed a different sign to represent each phonetic shift. This set of signs was published in various prescriptive grammars of Mayan languages by the Proyecto Lingüístico Francisco Marroquín (PLFM). Oxlajuuj Keej has since decided that one standardized symbol is sufficient. Thus, the *caracól* (a snail or spiral loop) now represents all phonetic shifts between the "lowland" hieroglyphic syllabary and modern highland languages. This spirited innovation of Oxlajuuj Keej permits highland language speakers to use the ancient writing system to represent their own languages, and its standardization and simplification make it accessible to a larger Maya community.

Even though highland Maya can now use the syllabary to write their own languages, the most frequent modern use of hieroglyphs remains logographic. In the same interview with Tzian, I asked him whether logographic or syllabic use was more common. He replied: "Considering that the proposed syllabary is a recent interpretation, . . . if the logograph exists, we use the logograph and if the logograph doesn't exist, then we use the syllabic sign." Modern logographic applications are lifted directly from historical examples that are common to all Mayan languages (i.e., dates, the Maya zero, days for the Cholq'ij calendar), while syllabic use is relied upon more for modern Maya words and neologisms (i.e., the names of institutions such as Oxlajuuj Keej, Cholsamaj, and Rajpopi' ri Mayab' Amaq). In fact, the most common modern use of hieroglyphic writing is the bar and dot number logographs as page numbers in various political, linguistic, and cultural texts.

As a policy, Cholsamaj requires that every text it publishes bear the Maya bar and dot numbers on its pages. Tzian explains Cholsamaj's intentions: "Why do we learn Roman and Arabic numerals but not Maya numerals? This is a recovery of Maya knowledge. We, the Maya people, are so tired of the colonial discourse. One form of positive resistance is to begin to learn what is our true history." In an interesting adaptation of the hieroglyphic system, Cholsamaj uses the day-sign cartouche to frame the bar and dot numerals. In this way, it clearly distinguishes the bar and dot numbers from the surrounding text and draws attention to the numbers for educational purposes.

The bar and dot system is an appropriate choice for Maya cultural activists, since it was originally pan-Maya, not limited to specific geographic areas, and its essential form has not changed through time. The use of dots is representational, where each dot represents the value "one"; the viewer attributes this value independent of culturally based knowledge. On the other hand, the use of bars is not representational, since the value associated with the bar— "five"—is not represented by the bar pictographically and must be culturally transmitted. The Maya bar and dot numeration system combines the two forms to create a logographic system.

Logographic representation may prove to be an important concept in indigenous language policy and self-determination, since logographic use of hieroglyphs can facilitate the standardization of representing various Mayan languages in a modern context. Logographic main signs were traditionally used to represent language-specific words and to refer to particular concepts. Thus, the concept of "deer" might be represented by the same logograph in different languages but interpreted as a specific word meaning "deer" according to the particular language of the reader. On the other hand, "deer" might also be written phonetically with a syllabary. In that case, the phonetic rendering of "deer" would be language specific.

Symbolic and Literal Functions of Hieroglyphic Writing

Modern Maya hieroglyphic writing can be categorized as literal, symbolic, or both. Whereas the literal use is semantically specific, the symbolic use of Maya glyphs does not convey a concrete meaning. Rather, the meaning is only suggested, and its interpretation is relative to the sociocultural background and political orientation of the individual reader. If the glyphs are used in a historically accurate manner and the reader is illiterate in the writing system, then the glyphic writing functions symbolically, because the reader does not have the necessary knowledge to interpret the specific meaning of the glyphs. Likewise, the script can be creatively adapted as a symbol, in which case literacy is not the decisive factor for communication since the application is unique and not part of the writing system proper.

Maya hieroglyphic writing functions both literally and symbolically when its use is either historically accurate or creatively refigured and that use is accompanied by an explanation or translation of individual elements written in alphabetic text. In this manner, the addition of text lessens the subjective and interpretive role of the reader, and the meaning becomes fixed. In all functional categories, the assumed literacy or nonliteracy of the reading audience and the intended specificity of meaning are primary factors influencing the function of the script. Modern Maya use glyphs differently, and their choice is determined by what they want to say and their assumptions about the viewer's "reading" abilities.

In figure 2, the Academia de las Lenguas Mayas de Guatemala (ALMG) uses refigured stylistic elements of glyphic writing as a logo to represent its organization. This example is not simply symbolic since it incorporates both alphabetic script that specifically states the name of the organization and the logographic bar and dot numbers. Although the use of the bar and dot numbers is historically accurate and, thus, semantically specific, the primary meaning conveyed by the image is symbolic.

The use of a stylized Calendar Round on the front of a Majawil Q'ij pamphlet is also mainly symbolic (figure 3). However, here glyphic elements are applied in a manner that is more textual. Again, bar and dot numerals are utilized, but beside them occur the specific logographs for each Maya day-name. Since the majority of Maya would not recognize the logographs, the day-names are also written in alphabetic text. The glyphs combined with text teach the reader the meaning of the logographic representations; thereby, the limitations of hieroglyphic illiteracy are overcome with alphabetic literacy.

The next example also has a didactic function. In figure 4, the adopted name of a Maya author is written on the title page of his book in Maya hieroglyphs and the alphabet. Like the Majawil Q'ij Calendar Round in the second example, the glyphs are meant to be read logographically, but the reader's level of literacy in the logographic system is not assumed;

Figure 2. ALMG logo.

Figure 3. From the logo of Majawil Q'ij.

Pakal B'alam

Figure 4. After B'alam (n.d.).

the alphabetic text ensures that the correct meaning is conveyed and, at the same time, teaches the reader elements of the logographic system. This example is similar to the ALMG's use of glyphs in its logo, though here glyphs form the personal symbol of an individual rather than of an organization.

In figure 5, the problem of hieroglyphic illiteracy is approached differently. The image is accompanied by an explanation that teaches the reader to recognize a particular glyph block as a whole. The organization, the Coordinadora Cakchiquel de Desarrollo Integral (COCADI), uses a glyph collocation on the front of its book, *Cultura maya y políticas de desarrollo*. The glyph block is historically accurate and contains both logographic and phonetic elements, but no alphabetic text co-occurs alongside the glyph collocation. However, COCADI does include an explanatory alphabetic text located on the copyright page: "Maya writing utilized in Piedras Negras, Petén; it means the 'taking of power.' On the cover we use it in order to illustrate that cultural

Figure 5. After Raxche' (1992).

pluralism means reclaiming 'the power of decision' over the development of one's own culture by each of the peoples that constitute
Guatemala" (Raxche' 1992). This states the historic site where the glyph
block was originally used, the basic meaning of the collocation as a
whole, and the specific meaning COCADI intends the collocation to
convey in its particular application. The COCADI example attempts to
bridge a gap between the symbolic and textual conveyance of meaning
with an alphabetic explanation. The success of that attempt is limited
by the distance of the explanation from the glyph collocation and relies
on the initiative of the individual reader.

The COCADI example is particularly important, because it epitomizes the relationships between meaning, text, and context that are
central to hieroglyphic use as an expression of Maya revitalization. In
figure 5, the *ahau* (lord) head is located atop the open hand; this
collocation was used in the precontact period to represent kingly
accession. The accompanying alphabetic text translates the hieroglyphic
message as "the taking of power." Interestingly, this same collocation
appears on the title page of several recent Cholsamaj publications (figure
6). However, the meaning is no longer translated; instead, it appears on
a hand-drawn stela. The hieroglyphic text begins with a Long Count that
specifies the date of publication of the book or pamphlet and ends with
"the taking of power" as its verb. In other words, the actual publication
of the book signifies a metaphorical reclamation of power for the Maya.

In figure 7, each word in the name of a Maya organization is
represented by primarily phonetic elements that form a glyph collocation. Here a specific textual meaning is conveyed by using the hieroglyphic syllabary with alphabetic text. As discussed previously, the

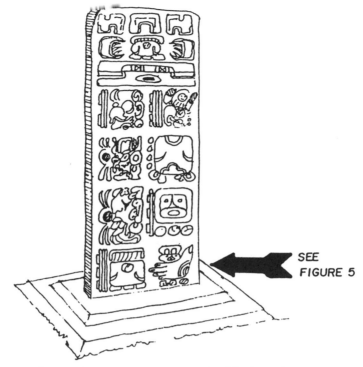

Figure 6. After Oxlajuuj Keej Maya' Ajtz'iib' (1993).

Figure 7. After Oxlajuuj Keej Maya' Ajtz'iib' (1993).

capacity of the hieroglyphic syllabary to represent words across modern Mayan languages and convey meaning to a larger Maya audience was historically limited. The image shown in this figure demonstrates how those limitations are overcome by modern Maya.

The name of the Maya organization Oxlajuuj Keej Mayaab' Ajtz'iib' (now known as Oxlajuuj Keej Maya' Ajtz'iib') in figure 7 roughly translates into English as "Thirteen Deer Maya Writers." Oxlajuuj Keej is the date in the Maya Calendar Round on which the organization formally began. However, *keej* is not the original lowland Maya day-name of the Calendar Round represented by the hieroglyphics. The original lowland day-names are not meaningful to the modern highland Maya. Consequently, the words are replaced with the equivalent from K'iche, a modern Eastern Mayan and highland language.[7] Both *oxlajuuj* and *keej* are represented by the hieroglyphs logographically and not phonetically: *oxlajuuj* is represented by the head-variant glyph for thirteen, and *keej* is represented by the *manik* or *chi* hand glyph.

Although logographs are used to represent the initial words, the phonetic hieroglyphic syllabary is used to represent the last two words of the organization's name. In a phonetic reading of the glyphs, each glyph has a syllabic consonant-vowel value, but the vowel of the last syllable can be ignored. Therefore, *mayaab'* is written with three glyphs from the syllabary—*ma, ya,* and *ba*—even though there are only two syllables in the word. The same is true for the word *ajtz'iib'*, which is written with the glyphs for *a, tz'i,* and *bi.*

Maya Intellectual Rights

Given the above examples, one might conclude that history is repeating itself. But while the modern adaptation of the lowland script by highland Maya to represent their own languages may have a historical precedent, modern Maya find themselves in the difficult position of having to reacquire hieroglyphic literacy and re-create the method of adaptation. Maya are also frustrated by the limited availability of educational materials on hieroglyphic writing. This latter point is related to a broader and more important topic: Maya intellectual rights to those materials and to participation in the discourse concerning the decipherment of the script.

In an ironic twist of history, Maya intellectuals who wish to attain hieroglyphic literacy find themselves dependent on the knowledge and expertise of foreigners, specifically the epigraphers who specialize in the decipherment of Maya hieroglyphic writing as both professionals and hobbyists.

Almost six hundred participants attend the largest annual hiero-glyphic workshop, the Maya Meetings at the University of Texas in Austin. Of these participants, only several hundred can actually read the glyphs. In fact, the field of epigraphy may be further limited if one only includes those individuals who work on decipherment. These twenty or so leading epigraphers work in a handful of universities located in the United States, Europe, Canada, Mexico, Japan, and Guatemala. Hiero-glyphic literacy is a limited phenomenon, difficult to attain, not only for highland Maya in Guatemala but for the majority of people in the world. Many Maya cultural activists demand that these individuals share a responsibility to "give back" to the people they study in whatever form possible.

Given this obstacle, how is it that some Maya gain sufficient hieroglyphic literacy to use the glyphs in a modern context? While many Maya are familiar with bar and dot numbers and day-name glyphs in the sacred calendar, more detailed information on the hieroglyphs comes from two specific sources. First, Heinrich Berlin published an introduction to the Maya hieroglyphs and various related articles in Spanish in 1958, 1959, and 1977. Although there are other publications in Spanish on Maya hieroglyphic writing, particularly in Mexico, Berlin is one of the few written sources widely available in Guatemala. Second, a few epigraphers began offering hieroglyphic workshops to Maya in 1987. These include Linda Schele (University of Texas, Austin), Nikolai Grube (Universität Bonn), and Federico Fahsen (Guatemala).

Schele, committed to improving the intellectual dialogue with the Maya, has given hieroglyphic workshops to groups of Maya since 1987 (see Schele and Grube, chap.8), each of which has attracted between twenty-five and forty participants, with some repeating the experience in different years. The majority of the participants come from a literate, highly educated sector of the Maya population, but, since 1992, Maya who come from more varied economic and educational backgrounds have participated.

These workshops are totally voluntary for the professional epigraphers, who pay their own expenses and often a portion of the expenses of the participants. But the efforts of these few individuals cannot counteract all the historical pressures that place modern Maya in a position where they are dependent on outside knowledge. For Maya to attain hieroglyphic literacy, they require a larger number of qualified teachers, economic support from foreign individuals and agencies, and translations of existing written materials. Although a Spanish translation of Schele's hieroglyphic workbook is used in the workshops, this and Berlin's articles and introduction are essentially the only sources written in Spanish readily available to Maya in Guatemala, and, of course, no academic discourse is available in Mayan language translations.

Given the limited resources, it is not surprising that trained Maya epigraphers are almost nonexistent. Many Maya resent that they are unable to participate in a debate that in certain ways defines their own cultural heritage.[8] The Maya use of and interest in hieroglyphic writing have purposes that are different from those of Western academics; while these purposes are not necessarily mutually exclusive, they differ in important ways. The role of epigraphy needs to be redefined in a proactive manner that encourages the full participation of the Maya in its discourse.

According to one Maya scholar, the violent behavior attributed to the ancient Maya by epigraphers and archaeologists is juxtaposed against the Guatemalan army's violent repression of living Maya. Present-day massacres are then minimized because international attention is directed by the media to the bloody ancient Maya and diverted away from harsh realities of the present (Montejo 1991: 5). Thus, some Maya believe that epigraphic interpretations and other academic assertions have definite and often negative political consequences in their lives; epigraphers, archaeologists, and other social scientists must become more sensitized to the sociopolitical impact of their investigations.

Shifting Authority and "Speaking Nearby"

Epigraphers, even while intending to avoid an authoritarian role, in reality give voice to silent stone and books, speaking for and about the Maya past and present, when, responsibly, they can only "speak near" the glyphs (Trinh 1982). Adopting such epistemological modesty would help restore the balance of authority between Maya and foreigner. It is indisputable that Western epigraphers teach and Maya listen and that epigraphers view themselves as authorities on the glyphs. Montejo asserts that the "scientific" practice of modern Mayanists "goes without challenges, because of the language of power (English) in which scholarly accounts have been written, and because of the persistent belief that the scientific community has the 'authority' to tell us what is or is not 'legitimately' Maya" (Montejo 1991: 1).

Western epigraphers have developed a sophisticated system for glyph decipherment. By their own standards, they are indeed the experts, and it is noble for them to share their knowledge, since much of it is valuable and useful. But imagine the state of epigraphy today if it were dominated by Maya working autonomously. How different might our understanding of the Maya past be? Until economic equality is reached between Maya and Westerners, a subtle recreation of colonial patterns emerges despite the best intentions. Perhaps the politics of Maya studies are dictated by the larger economic and historical relationship between Maya and "others."

The question then arises as to what practical actions we can take to ethically and responsibly assist in rectifying the injustices of a colonial past. I suggest that at least on an individual level we begin by translating our own works into Spanish. In addition, part of the fees for First World academics who attend hieroglyphic workshops could support the translation of existing academic works. Fund-raising efforts could be con-

ducted at these meetings, the focus being to financially support developing institutions administered by Maya in Guatemala. With economic
resources generated from abroad, Maya could better make their own
decisions about how to proceed with broadening hieroglyphic literacy.
Since we are the economic beneficiaries of the past, it is mostly in this
arena that our support can help balance the colonial equation.

Some scholars warn against mixing academics and politics, implying
that the combination of the two will result in the distortion of the
"objective" truth as it exists "out there." But as Montejo warns, "Anthropologists have insisted on their 'authorities' by promoting the
versions of the truth and interpretations that have prevailed. After all, a
continuous monologue has persisted and will persist if anthropologists
do not accommodate themselves to the politics of the communities they
study" (Montejo 1991: 7).

It is our intellectual responsibility to approach the study of hieroglyphic writing in the most productive and least biased manner possible.
An awareness of the internal biases within the field of epigraphy and an
increased sensitivity to present-day sociopolitical issues will benefit
academic understanding. Furthermore, in the Maya quest to be heard in
the multivocal discourse of academia as well as in the international
political arena, it is essential that the Maya revitalize their ethnic
identity in the most politically effective and autonomously developed
form possible.

Notes

This essay has benefited substantially from comments made by Nora England, Martha Macri, Linda Schele, and Randolph Lewis on earlier versions.
However, it expresses my opinions, and I alone am responsible for its contents.

1. All translations are mine.

2. Tzian distinguished Maya organizations based on whether or not they
were overtly public, carrying out demonstrations and marches that specifically
confront the existence of civil self-defense patrols (PACs) and their resulting
forced military recruitment and that support the specific struggle, which he
labels "union" and "popular" (class based). For these organizations, Tzian
believes that in the majority of the cases, the fight for Maya rights is opaqued by
defending "collective struggle." On the other hand, Tzian distinguished as a
group those organizations that focus on the revitalization of the Maya via "socio-
productive activities, such as education in the communities, but not contrary to
these other struggles." The specific terms that Tzian used to separate the
different groups were those whose work is "union-based" and "popular" and
those that promote a revitalization of the *pueblo Maya*. He considered Cholsamaj
part of the latter.

3. Michael Coe (1992), in *Breaking the Maya Code*, provides a useful and
concise history of the decipherment of Maya hieroglyphic writing.

4. The syllabary comprises the total list of syllabic values for hieroglyphic

signs. A syllabic reading is created when a hieroglyphic sign is assigned a consonant-vowel syllabic value.

5. Modern Maya who use the glyphs are geographically located in the western highlands, but the languages they speak are classified as Eastern Mayan. Confusion may result, since lowland languages, located in the east, are classified as part of the Western Mayan language family.

6. In a previous essay I refer to the use of hieroglyphs in print-media by approximately sixteen different Maya organizations and individuals (see Sturm 1992). However, further research suggests that these numbers are unrepresentative. The actual number of presses and organizations employing glyphs is much smaller; Cholsamaj and Nawal Wuj are run by the same people, who are responsible for the majority of glyph proliferations. Nevertheless, the number of documents with glyphs is steadily increasing.

7. In figure 7, the same logograph is interpreted as *manik* in Western Mayan languages and *keej* in Eastern Mayan languages, both meaning "deer."

8. Several visiting Maya scholars attended the 1992 and 1993 Maya Meetings in Austin. In an unpublished paper presented at the 1992 conference, Maya scholars criticized those foreign epigraphers and academics who benefit from studying the Maya past yet remain unwilling to share their knowledge of hieroglyphic writing with living Maya people.

8.
The Workshop for Maya
on Hieroglyphic Writing

Linda Schele (University of Texas, Austin)
Nikolai Grube (Universität Bonn)

In the summer of 1987, the Centro de Investigaciones Regionales de Mesoamérica (CIRMA) in Antigua, Guatemala, sponsored the Ninth Maya Linguistics Workshop, a meeting of linguists from Maya communities and the United States. After the meeting, CIRMA arranged a trip for the workshop participants (both Maya and foreign) to Copán, Honduras. Knowing that Linda Schele was working at Copán that summer, Judith Maxwell suggested that Schele guide the group through the site. The workshop group arrived on a Friday. The guided tour of Copán took place the following Saturday and Sunday and included a visit to the tunnels under the famous Hieroglyphic Stairs, readings of the monuments in the Great Plaza, and explanations of the significance of the buildings and their sculpture.

During lunch on the last day, Martín Chacach, then director of the Proyecto Lingüístico Francisco Marroquín (PLFM), invited Schele to Antigua that same summer to teach a group of Maya about the ancient writing system. Schele agreed to go. Also present were Kathryn Josserand and Nicholas Hopkins, who had worked with Schele in previous workshops, so Schele invited them to join the endeavor—and the first Maya workshop on hieroglyphic writing was born.

A digression into the history of the hieroglyphic workshops is in order here. In 1977 Nancy Troike, then a research associate of the Institute of Latin American Studies at the University of Texas at Austin, invited Schele to give a workshop on the decipherment of the Maya writing system as it was then unfolding. That was the first in a series of seventeen annual workshops given at the University of Texas. These meetings have grown to include as many as six hundred participants in the various events.

The development of Spanish-language materials for the workshops was a gradual process. Schele gave two workshops at the Universidad Nacional Autónoma de México in 1978 and 1979, the latter being the first given in Spanish. In 1986 and 1987 Schele also gave workshops in

Spanish at the Universidad Nacional de Honduras in Tegucigalpa, for which she prepared a full set of transparencies. The first half of her English-language hieroglyphic workbook was translated into Spanish at that time by Jorge Treviesa, a Honduran who had recently completed his master's degree at the University of Illinois. The second half of the workbook was later translated at CIRMA by Nora England and Lola Spillari so that a full set of Spanish-language materials would be ready for the 1987 Antigua workshop.

That first workshop in 1987 lasted three days. At Martín Chacach's request participation was limited to Maya, a practice that continues today. The approximately forty participants represented twelve Mayan language groups. Linda Schele, Kathryn Josserand, and Nicholas Hopkins taught, and Nora England helped with logistics. The workshop was jointly sponsored by the PLFM and CIRMA and was held in CIRMA's archaeological laboratory, as have all of the subsequent Antigua workshops.

The first workshop was designed to teach the Maya participants some of the history of the writing system, how to spell using syllable signs and logographs, the syntax of the system, a set of common verbs and titles, and, on the last day, how to do a structural analysis of the Tablet of 96 Glyphs from Palenque. Though this last work was not finished, a team of Q'eqchi' speakers led by Eduardo Pacay read their translation of the first half of the tablet and thus became the first modern Maya to read an ancient text in their own language.

In 1989, again at the request of Martín Chacach, the PLFM, and CIRMA, Schele returned to Antigua to give a four-day workshop on the same material. In this workshop, the translation of the Tablet of 96 Glyphs was completed and read in twelve Mayan languages, English, and Spanish. Starting in 1986, Schele had been collaborating in research at Copán with Nikolai Grube, now of the Universität Bonn. In 1990, while they were working in Copán, she invited him to join her in giving the third workshop. He accepted, thus establishing the team that has given all subsequent workshops.

In approaching the third workshop's theme (the making of history), Grube and Schele divided the thirty-five participants into two groups. Each of them then led a group through the decipherment of the texts relating the history of Yaxun-B'alam (Bird-Jaguar) of Yaxchilan. Each group took half of the texts, so that in three days the teams had deciphered the entire corpus.

In the remaining two days, teams from both groups were assigned tasks of interpretation. One team worked on the preaccession history of Yaxun-B'alam; one on the postaccession history; one on the layout of the site and the juxtaposition of text, imagery, and architecture; and one on an overview to coordinate the other teams' work. Schele and Grube, assisted by Nora England, answered questions, made suggestions, and proposed strategies, but the goal was for the Maya themselves to develop the historical interpretation. The afternoon of the final day was reserved for a presentation of the results of each group's work and for a general discussion and debate of the results. After the workshop, Schele and England took a group of twelve participants to the site of Tikal for a week of study. They focused on the process of historical interpretation within the site itself, deciphering texts on the original monuments and discussing architectural programming amid the original architecture.

In the summer of 1991 Grube and Schele returned to Antigua, though a formal workshop could not be held. Instead, Schele and Grube traveled with members of Oxlajuuj Keej Maya' Ajtz'iib' (OKMA), a Maya research group coordinated by Nora England, to the archaeological sites of Iximche' and Mixco Viejo. At Iximche' they participated in the opening ceremonies of a Kaqchikel artisans cooperative and went with a group of Kaqchikel Maya through the site, where they discussed and interpreted the architectural program of the city. The following Sunday, Schele, Grube, and six members of OKMA traveled to Mixco Viejo, again examining the architecture and spatial organization of a Postclassic Maya city.

That same summer, members of OKMA decided to adapt the ancient hieroglyphic writing system of the lowland Maya to their highland Mayan languages, which possess consonants that do not exist in the original system. In particular, adaptations were needed to represent syllables containing /q/, /q'/, and /r/ and all retroflexive consonants in languages such as Mam. They developed a series of signs that are attached to or placed inside the ancient syllable signs to specify their pronunciations as highland sounds. For example, a loop is attached to a *yi* sign to convert it to *ri* (for illustrations, see Sturm, chap. 7 in this volume). These signs, along with an explanation of how the ancient writing system worked, have been included by members of OKMA in prescriptive grammars (e.g., Ajpub' 1993; Lolmay 1993). Thus, a few signs invented by speakers of highland Mayan languages have made it possible for them to write their own languages using the ancient writing system.

The development of this system of additional signs heralded the use of the writing for a whole series of functions. Cholsamaj, a Maya publishing house, began using glyphs in its logos and publications. Glyphs began to appear in diplomas, announcements of weddings, births, and other such events, official invitations for meetings and conferences, newspaper headings, a memorial to Adrián Chavéz in Quetzaltenango, business cards, and yearly calendars for appointments, as well as other kinds of published materials. Unlike the use of glyphs merely as decorations, these texts not only contain messages written in modern highland languages, they also transmit critical information about identity, origin, and political status and awareness.

The participants of the first three workshops were largely educated, highly literate Guatemala Maya. They came from various linguistic programs, especially the Academia de las Lenguas Mayas de Guatemala (ALMG), the Programa Nacional de Educación Bilingüe (PRONEBI), OKMA, the PLFM, and the Universidad Rafael Landívar. Community leaders from various towns also participated.

In 1992 this situation began to change thanks to the help of anthropologist Duncan Earle. He took Schele to meet the family of the man who had taught him the skills of a K'iche' *aj q'ij* (day-keeper or shaman) in the early 1970s. Schele invited Manuel Pacheco, the forty-five-year-old son of the *aj q'ij*, to the Antigua workshop in July, and he became the first Maya shaman to participate in the workshops. Although Pacheco had little formal education, he had been a diviner since age thirteen, giving him a profound knowledge of traditional K'iche' religion. His contribution was invaluable, and the depth of his knowledge profoundly affected the younger Maya. Manuel Pacheco demonstrated that no formal education is required to understand, participate in, contribute to, and benefit from the workshops. The ancient texts hold information relevant to the entire Maya community, not just those our academy classifies as the elite.

For the 1992 workshop, CIRMA and OKMA requested that an additional two days be added to prepare those who had not attended earlier workshops. Federico Fahsen, a Guatemalan epigrapher, joined Schele and Grube as a teacher. The introductory sessions were held on a Thursday and Friday, and the main workshop was held during the following week. The theme was Maya creation as recorded in ancient texts and books, and the workshop was particularly notable for the discussions on culture, as well as for the mechanical decipherment of texts. Content was drawn from the imagery and inscriptions on Classic period stelae, tablets, and pottery, from the Paris Codex, from the *Popol Wuj*, from modern astronomy and ethnographies, and, last but not least, from the knowledge of the participants.

For the participants this workshop appears to have been the most meaningful of all that we have given. The Classic period story of creation relates directly to modern Maya religious, social, ritual, and agricultural practices. Observations of their reactions and conversations with participants the following year suggest that this body of information most strongly forges links between contemporary experience and the ancient, pre-Columbian past.

At the end of the workshop, a group of participants wished to make another trip, this time to Palenque in Mexico to see the original tablets that record much of the imagery of creation. Schele, England, and Grube prepared letters explaining the purpose of the trip, and CIRMA provided a guarantee of financial responsibility. Nevertheless, the Mexican consulate in Guatemala City denied visas to the Maya. As a result, the research trip was taken to Copán, Honduras, where the Maya descendants of the builders of that city were welcomed. A writer and photographer from the German magazine *Geo* participated in the final days of the workshop and in the subsequent trip with the permission of the Maya participants (see Rojas and Löwer 1993).

At the request of various Maya participants in the ongoing workshop series, Federico Fahsen gave an eight-month-long course in 1992–93 on hieroglyphic writing at the ALMG that ended when the group lost access to the overhead projector it had been using. As with the main workshops, this course was limited to Maya participants. Its effect has been extremely important because people were able to reinforce the skills they learned in the workshops and for the first time had a long-term experience with many different texts. Participants now have the confidence, skill, and knowledge to begin giving their own courses in their towns and villages. Fahsen has been asked to give another course and several workshops in different towns, such as Palín and Cobán. Several study groups have begun, especially in Chimaltenango and Tecpán. The teaching and dissemination of the writing system are moving into Maya hands.

In 1993 Schele and Grube returned to Antigua for the fifth workshop sponsored by OKMA and CIRMA. The theme was the Dresden Codex (a pre-Columbian Maya book with astronomical and divinational texts) and how its structure relates to the highland tradition of divination still extant. In this workshop, participants included four *aj q'ija'* (Manuel Pacheco and a friend from Joyabaj, as well as a day-keeper from Rabinal and one from the Mam area); five bilingual (Spanish/Mayan) teachers from Santa Catarina Ixtahuacán; and a Mopán speaker from San Luís Petén, who was a considerable help in translating since Mopán is a lowland language closely related to the Yukatek of the Dresden Codex.

Participants received copies of the Villacorta version of the codex (Villacorta 1934), which they glued together into the accordion format of the original book. The presentations and analysis concentrated on understanding the interplay of calendar, text, imagery, and prognostications. Most of the almanacs were analyzed, and the astronomical data were studied. Special emphasis was given to how these almanacs might have been used and how they related to historical and modern activities of highland Maya day-keepers.

Several important new developments occurred in 1993. Grace Bascope, a graduate student at Southern Methodist University, had made contact in Valladolid with an organization of bilingual Yukatek teachers, Mayáon, dedicated to the preservation of Yukatek Mayan language and culture. Through her and David Freidel, Bartolomé Alonzo Caamal, the president of Mayáon, invited Schele and Grube to give a workshop to his organization. They accepted and flew to Mérida to give the workshop, in which all fourteen participants spoke Yukatek. The contents were essentially the same as in the first two Antigua workshops: the first days concentrated on the spelling, syntax, and contents of the writing system, while the last three sessions involved the analysis of the Tablet of 96 Glyphs. The final result was the full transcription of the Tablet of 96 Glyphs into Classic Chol, modern Spanish, and modern Yukatek.

The workshop was tremendously successful in demonstrating to the participants that the glyphs can be read and that there is a vital register of Maya cultural tradition preserved in them. The final event, as with the Guatemalan workshops, was a visit to a pre-Columbian site, this time Chichén Itzá. One participant, whose family name is Kokom, said that he had come to Chichén Itzá three times before but had never seen the imagery or contemplated what it meant. On this trip he saw his family name written in the glyphs for the first time.

Mayáon requested that another workshop be given in 1994. We anticipate that a regular series will develop from this original contact. In future workshops we hope that Maya from the Yukatek and Guatemalan groups will meet and exchange their experience and expertise.

In 1993 Lolmay (Pedro Oscar García Mátzar) asked for a workshop in San Andrés Semetabaj, a town overlooking Lake Atitlán. Sponsored by Nimak Jay (the council of Kaqchikel Maya elders), the workshop was given on August 8 and 9 by Linda Schele and Federico Fahsen. Kay Warren, an anthropologist who has worked in San Andrés since 1970, also participated. The Kaqchikel participants included town and religious leaders, bilingual teachers, nuns, and people from the outlying hamlets. As requested by Lolmay, the theme was Maya creation. As with earlier workshops, the new information was enthusiastically received, although there was some discomfort because of religious and generational conflicts within the community resulting from the Maya revitalization movement.

The workshop was extremely effective and signals a new development in the Guatemalan series. It is apparent that many Maya who have participated in the workshops now know enough to begin teaching other Maya. We anticipate that future workshops will be collaborative, with Maya epigraphers giving the introduction and preparing their communities for more specialized topics presented by foreign colleagues. Eventually, it will be the Maya who are presenting the new discoveries they have made.

By 1993 the presentation of Maya epigraphy had become more public in Guatemala. Pakal B'alam (José Obispo Rodríguez Guaján) of Tecpán began giving a fifteen-minute radio program every Sunday morning that focuses on Kaqchikel culture and gives the Long Count of the day and other information about hieroglyphic writing. Also, Radio K'iche' in Santa Cruz Quiché regularly includes information on the calendar and the writing system in its programming.

We do not feel that we have the right or the knowledge to speak for the Maya, either individually or collectively. Nor can we chide or prescribe for the larger academic world in which we work. We can only talk about our personal motivations, expectations, and observations of the process in which we are engaged.

We have a set of rules that we apply to our dealings with the Maya and these workshops. First, we must be invited. We do not feel that we can arrive in a Maya community as "missionaries of the past." We cannot teach epigraphy and Maya cultural history to people who do not already have a profound interest in the subject. Invitations are a sign to us of the existing and growing interest in the field of study we pursue.

Second, the workshops must be collaborative. The first workshop came about serendipitously, but the succeeding ones were collaborations between Grube, Schele, and Fahsen and various Maya organizations. In the future we hope and expect that much of the material will be presented by Maya to Maya. The participation of Maya teachers in the workshops already contributes to the diffusion of this growing body of knowledge, with hieroglyphic writing and the history and cosmology as preserved in the ancient texts becoming part of teaching materials used in primary and secondary schools. For example, a Maya press prints notebooks for schoolchildren with the bar and dot number system on the back. We are aware that in the future collaboration between Maya and non-Maya historians and epigraphers will take place on a more equal footing, much like the present relationship between Maya and foreign linguists.

Third, the workshops are open only to Maya, as originally requested by Martín Chacach. This practice has continued because it provides the most effective forum. The participants share experience and language in a way that cannot include members of the dominant culture of the region. In our experience, when members of the dominant culture are present, they tend to monopolize discussion and restrict the bonding that occurs in an all-Maya group. Perhaps the future will see a time when workshops given by Maya as well as foreigners can be attended by anyone interested, but for now we will follow Maya guidance in this matter.

Fourth, we do not prescribe to the Maya what they should do with the writing system as a modern instrument of politics and culture, nor what their attitude should be toward the history and cosmology preserved in the ancient texts. When Maya ask us questions about the ancient texts, we are obliged to answer as truthfully as we can. In questions of religious belief and cultural definitions that now preoccupy the Maya community, we feel that we must speak on a personal level and not as authorities. We have been told by Maya leaders that we are part of the debate that fuels the Maya revitalization movement, but we feel that we should minimize our roles whenever possible and aid the Maya to become scientific authorities in our fields.

We see the Maya community on the brink of entering into a dialogue with the history and cosmology preserved in the ancient texts and artifacts. We recognize that Maya epigraphers and historians of the future will challenge our interpretations and forge their own. We acknowledge that there are Maya now who do not agree with our interpretations and prefer their own. We also see that the Maya are in a process of making new myths of identity that use the hieroglyphic record in ways that do not agree with our perspective. We see all of this as part of the process by which history is made, and then remade, by different generations, by different constituencies, and by different individuals. We recognize that the Maya community is complex and varied. The Maya, like all people, have a right to decide how to use hieroglyphic writing and the information it contains for themselves.

This essay began partially in reaction to an American scholar's characterization of the relationship between epigraphers and the Maya as a colonial one. To use the word *colonial* evokes questions of subtle and profound import. We come from the United States, Germany, and the elite strata of Guatemalan society. By some definitions, anything that we do must be colonial, in intent if not practice. At the same time, we perceive pressures from colleagues and the Maya community to give back something to the descendants of the people we study. Resolving the conflict between these two views cannot be done to the satisfaction of all involved.

Yet we feel obliged to act. Our personal solution is to respond to the call for sharing our specialized knowledge, while hoping we can avoid being colonialist in our performance. We have found that colleagues like Nora England and Judith Maxwell, who have long experience with the Maya community, are good examples because they have participated in a process of sensitization. In the long run, however, the Maya themselves are our teachers. They instruct us when we use a term loaded with meanings we do not perceive. They tell us the terms that they prefer be used about their languages and culture. Moreover, the workshops themselves are not one-sided. We teach the Maya what we have learned from archaeology, epigraphy, and ethnohistory, but they inform us about meanings, interpretations, and associations that people from our world could never come to know without their help. Our work is a true collaboration from which we benefit greatly.

Finally, we come to the question of academic responsibility to the people we study. Our experience has been one that was not anticipated, sought, or planned. When Martín Chacach first asked Schele to give a workshop to Maya, a door of opportunity opened. We stepped through as an experiment, and the results have flourished beyond our imagination, but if the invitation had not been presented we believe that we would have followed the traditional detached stance of Western science. Serendipity put us on a different path.

When we stepped through the door of opportunity, we found experienced linguists awaiting to advise us on how to establish collaboration. In 1970 Nora England, Terrence Kaufman, and others began just such a collaboration with Maya that continues fruitfully today. We learned from them, and in partnership with our Maya colleagues we have been engaged in the endeavor of returning something to the modern community of Maya peoples.

In our experience, other disciplines, like archaeology, have not concerned themselves with returning knowledge and experience to the Maya community. We believe the world has changed in the last decade and that in the future academics of the developed world must consider the needs and goals of the people whom they study. The cultural scientists who should be in the forefront of this kind of interaction, in fact, are often the most unaware. We counsel our colleagues to try it. They will learn far more than they teach, and the returns are beyond value.

We have characterized that first workshop as a serendipitous happening, but this is only our perception. In 1987 the Maya communities of Guatemala were just emerging from a nightmare of violence and embarking upon a path of revitalization that has been and still is generating major changes in their communities at all levels. We have observed these changes and participated in activities associated with them all over Guatemala. We cannot speak for the Maya in all their constituencies concerning their goals, hopes, and tactics, but we do know that hieroglyphic writing and the history and cosmology preserved in the ancient texts are playing an increasingly important role in the process that is unfolding. It is also clear to us that the Maya are using everything they can find about the ancient world of their forebears.

Our appearance on the scene was fortuitous to us but not to them. The Maya would be engaged in the process of using the ancient writing with or without us. And that is something important for us all to contemplate. If we share our knowledge and expertise with the Maya, they will become collaborators in the endeavor of science and discovery. If we do not, they will construct their understanding of the ancient world from translations of books forty, fifty, or a hundred or more years old. It is in our best interest and theirs to take them into account in all the research and writing that concern the world in which they live.

9.
Maya Clothing and Identity

Irma Otzoy (Maya Education Foundation)

Since the sixteenth-century Spanish invasion, Maya people have endured particular types of economic, social, and political subjugation. So, in addition to realizing internal cultural changes, Maya have developed new strategies of ensuring the very survival of their culture to confront the different faces of colonization.[1] In this chapter I analyze the use of Maya clothing as *one* cultural element that embodies the processes of historical struggle, cultural creativity, and political resistance of the Maya people. Except where specifically noted, this study focuses on the Maya of Guatemala.

Studies of Maya Clothing and Textiles

A brief review of the literature shows that Maya forms of dress have been the focus of a great number of studies, generally realized by erudite foreigners or non-Maya Guatemalans. This research covers a variety of perspectives, from technology and economics to hermeneutics. A number of studies give geographic overviews of the feminine and masculine articles of clothing and other local textiles associated with towns in Chiapas (Mexico) and Guatemala (see Morris and Foxx 1987; Osborne 1965; Wood and Osborne 1966; Pettersen 1976; Rowe 1981; Asturias de Barrios 1985), while a smaller number focus on just one piece of clothing and its geographic and gender associations (see Schevill 1985). Ehlers (1990) has reported on the economic and technical aspects of cloth production, and Carlsen and Wenger (1991) have presented a historical analysis of the different types of thread dyes used in textiles.

A few researchers merit special attention for venturing further in the interpretation of Maya textiles, tying weaving technology to Maya cosmology (see Prechtel and Carlsen 1988). Carlsen (n.d.) identifies ways in which Maya religious and communal identity are implied in weavings. Similarly, Tedlock and Tedlock (1985) have analyzed the dialectical relationship between language and technology as expressed in the Maya art of weaving. Hendrickson (1986, 1995), who studied Maya dress and its social function in Tecpán in the midst of the political tension of the 1980s, thoroughly compares Maya female dress to the clothing of Ladino women and presents an analysis of the respective roles of each type of clothing in the social construction of Maya and Ladino identities in a municipal context. Finally, a recent study of Maya weavings conducted by Julia Kellman (1991), focusing on three women from the Kaqchikel area, analyzes the artistic, economic, and cultural issues implied in the acts of weaving and wearing a *huipil* (a traditional blouse worn by Maya women). Her approach is significant because of its emphasis on the artist (weaver) over her art (weaving).

Colonialist Perspectives of Maya Dress

As an external cultural sign, Maya dress often acts to distinguish Maya from the rest of the Guatemalan population. Maya dress includes garments woven or embroidered by hand that are distinguished by their type of manufacture, design, form, motifs, and styles, which vary not only from one region to another but also according to the taste and creativity of the weaver and those who view them. The pieces that cover the upper and lower parts of the body, and the belts of both men and women, constitute the most visible portions of Maya dress, and these show marked regional variation.[2] Maya clothing is produced by artisans and, at least historically, woven on backstrap looms by women. Nevertheless, factors such as the availability of foot looms and the scarcity of time and money have modified this precedent. For many Maya it is now more economically practical to wear Maya clothes woven by men on foot looms.

In a society such as Guatemala, whose history is impregnated with European colonialism, it is not surprising to find records of all types of restrictions and impositions placed on the aboriginal society by the colonizers. Some studies even suggest that the Spaniards may have imposed a policy of standardizing the native population's clothing in order to facilitate controlling Maya communities and evangelization (see Anawalt 1990). While there is no solid evidence for this, there are Spanish decrees such as the royal warrant issued on 25 October 1563, which reads: "that no person, man or woman, be allowed to wear any textile that was brocaded . . . nor one that had gold or silver in its weaving . . . even if these threads were false imitation . . . as also it was prohibited that silver or gold should be used for the cloths that were used on horses and mules" (quoted in Osborne 1965: 23). While this quote demonstrates that there were restrictions on the dress of the indigenous people (as well as certain immigrant classes), modern Maya styles suggest that the royal order was largely ignored. Gold and silver have always been scarce in the Maya area, but brocade and embroidery are common in contemporary Maya dress, and many Maya weavings contain silver-plated and gilded synthetic threads. This ability to conserve their weaving allows the Maya to dress in a style that pleases their artistic, moral, and spiritual senses while also being culturally distinct.

Some recent Ladino views of Maya dress have been put forth to discourage the Maya from weaving and wearing their unique clothing. Interpreting Maya dress as a colonial creation and therefore a symbol of oppression, these non-Maya claim that to weave and wear Maya dress only perpetuates the "legacy of Spanish colonialism" (see Martínez Peláez 1970: 605–610; Méndez de la Vega 1989: 51). Such a perspective portrays the Maya as defenseless victims of colonization who, being culturally incapable of creation, had to adopt Spanish weaving technology, motifs, and styles.

Even if the technique of foot-loom weaving arrived with the Spanish (Osborne 1965), the backstrap loom, used to make the most elaborate textiles, is of pre-Columbian origin, as evidenced by pre-Columbian Maya representations of the deity Ixchel (Cordry and Cordry 1968: 46). Spanish narratives from the colonial period also report that Maya textiles existed before their arrival. Consider, for example, the description given by Francisco Ximénez of finely woven clothing and of the dresses of prominent women used in what is today Chiapas: "These huipils were white with red and yellow roses, a very beautiful costume" (quoted in Osborne 1965: 22). Likewise, Fuentes y Guzmán describes the clothing of prominent Maya men, who "wore colored cotton garments with many designs incorporated in the material, blue and red on a white background being most prevalent. The material was very fine and closely woven" (quoted in Osborne 1965: 20). Pictographic and hieroglyphic pre-Columbian texts, sixteenth-century documents such as the *Popol Wuj*, and fragments of pre-Columbian textiles found in various archaeological sites provide evidence for the creativity, complexity, and indigenous origin of Maya textiles. Therefore, the Ladino perspective that Maya textiles are a colonial creation is unfounded and ethnocentric.

Furthermore, one must be cautious when defining particular motifs as originating with Spanish or non-Maya sources. For example, the "bicephalous bird," a design found in a large number of diverse Maya textiles, is frequently interpreted as the Hapsburg eagle of Carlos V of Spain. Of course, the eagle of the Hapsburgs does not have a "truly" Spanish origin itself since it was the emblem of the dukedom of Austria. In addition, the bicephalous eagle (as well as other motifs of double-headed animals) was a common motif in the art of the Hittite Empire (circa 1200 B.C.), and it has appeared throughout history and prehistory in the artistic traditions of Anatolia, sub-Caucasus Europe, and the Danube Valley (personal communication with Peter C. Reynolds, 1992). The bicephalous bird motif is also found in pre-Columbian art throughout the Americas (Enciso 1953; Spinden 1975; Schevill 1985). Even if the Maya did borrow the bicephalous bird design from the Spanish rather than from neighboring Mesoamerican peoples, this in no way implies that the symbolism of the motif is indeed Spanish. It is probable that the motif was adopted by the Maya precisely because it fit in with an already existing system of Maya metaphors and that it is continually reinterpreted in a manner consistent with Maya philosophy and experiences. At present, the bicephalous bird acts as a symbol of Maya ancestors and at the same time as a symbol of physical and cultural survival after the contact with the Spanish. Thus, the specific historical origin of an element does not determine whether or not that element is Maya. To the contrary, the incorporation of new symbols into the Maya meaning system permits textiles to serve as a dynamic expression of the Maya experience.

A more common Ladino attitude toward Maya dress than the intellectual position of "colonial creation" has been to stigmatize it as "primitive," "backward," or "antiquated." This has occurred despite the fact that Maya dress has been used (some would say abused) by non-Maya Guatemalans in various ways (Hendrickson 1986). For example, businesses of the petite bourgeoisie use Maya textiles to construct high-fashion pieces exhibited in chic boutiques and sold to tourists in select areas of Guatemala City and the rest of the world. While there are textiles made and sold by Maya in the streets, stores, or small booths in tourist areas of Guatemala, these differ from the former in terms of the social class of the target market and the related fact that the clothing sold in the boutiques has the potential to be valued by Ladinos if it becomes stylish in the United States or Europe.

Non-Maya also sometimes wear clothing that the Maya themselves wear. Today, both inside and outside Guatemala, one sees non-Maya Guatemalans who wear Maya-style clothes, apparently in the context of daily life, a phenomenon unheard of in our parents' youth.[3] Foreigners (several anthropologists, for example) have been buying and wearing Maya clothing for some time, and the change in Ladino attitudes toward Maya clothing can be interpreted as a reflection of the haste with which non-Maya Guatemalans imitate North American and European trends. One Maya *campesino* observed: "It wasn't until North Americans began to use our *morrales* [a woven bag used by Maya] that the Ladinos began to give a little respect to our things." One extreme example of such imitation is the Ladino I once encountered in Guatemala City dressed completely in Maya clothes, with bleached-blond hair and an affected foreign accent. This person's Maya garb was based on an entirely foreign image, an image that he himself had created.

Ancient Vestiges of Maya Dress

While the majority of studies of Maya textiles have concentrated on twentieth-century Maya dress, a few have focused on the pre-Columbian era. In spite of the limitations presented by the latter type of study, some scholars have been able to describe pre-Columbian Maya styles of dress and compare them with contemporary styles (Morley, Brainerd, and Sharer 1983; Morris and Fox 1987). Such analyses are mostly based on indirect archaeological data found on stelae, murals, and ceramics. Nonetheless, the few textile fragments found in the Maya area have greatly increased our knowledge of this Maya art.

Some of the most spectacular discoveries of ancient textiles have occurred at Cieneguilla, Chichén Itzá, and Río Azul.[4] Of the Cieneguilla finds, Johnson writes that "the most unusual and important aspect of these ancient textiles is the method by which they were patterned. Two rare techniques, not previously recorded for Middle America, are represented in these comparatively few specimens: hand painting and resist-dyeing (batik)" (Johnson 1954: 140).

In the Sacred Cenote of Chichén Itzá (which dates to the late Classic period), more than six hundred textile fragments have been discovered. Joy Mahler, who studied the textiles (which were largely made from cotton thread), states:

> These textiles . . . present . . . a variety of weaving techniques and some indication of geometric designs. . . . Although the bulk of the material consists of plain weaves, either with single warps and wefts or single warps and paired wefts, the total range includes brocades or embroideries, pile cloth, gauze, warp-float patterns, . . . openwork, and twills. . . . This enumeration of techniques suggests an approximation to the complex weaving of [the Quechuas and Aymaras of] Peru. (Quoted in Tozzer 1957: 198)

At Río Azul textiles that date to the early Classic period were found (Carlsen 1985, 1986). The textiles were discovered in adjacent tombs—numbers 19 and 23—covering two skeletons of ancient Maya elites. One of the textiles in Tomb 19 was a woven bundle with thick fibers. The other, a shroud, was finely woven with drawn work of cotton and possible brocade. Comparing this latter textile with other data, Carlsen states: "Because of the mineralized condition, dye analysis was unsuccessful, however, it is not an unreasonable assumption that this open-weave garment may have been woven in a white-on-white or 'shadow weave,' such as portrayed by Maya nobles on the murals at Bonampak" (Carlsen 1986: 147). Carlsen also correlates these ancient Maya textiles with modern weavings: "There are descendants of the ancient Maya that still weave textiles in styles suggesting that of the Tomb 19 'shroud.' In the Guatemalan highlands these towns would include Coban, San Juan Chamelco, Senahu, Quetzaltenango, Altotenango, and Santa Lucia Utatlan. . . . There are also [native peoples] from the Mexican highlands that weave in similar styles" (Carlsen 1986: 140). In fact, Carlsen's description of the ancient Maya textiles of Tomb 19 largely applies to modern Q'eqchi' weavings, which show a variety of subtle white-on-white designs in woven *huipiles* (*po't*).

The combined techniques utilized in the construction of these ancient textiles, along with the contents of their woven texts, indicate gradual changes in Maya dress and in the forms created by the Maya in innovation and diversification of their dress until the present. Thus, not only has the analysis of pre-Columbian textile fragments contributed to the understanding of change and continuity in Maya art, it has also established a sociocultural connection between the ancient and modern Maya.

Weaver and Wearer of Maya Dress: Politics and Aesthetics

The articles of clothing called *pa's*, or belt (worn by Maya women and some men), and the *xti q'u'*, or *xerca* (an apron used by some men), are developed from what may be called a loincloth. The *tupui, tocoyal*, and *xaq'ot* (a type of hairband worn by some women) evolved from a headdress used by the ancient Maya as seen in stelae and murals. These articles, together with the *po't* (*huipil*), are highly indicative of Maya heritage. I will focus here on the *po't* because of its artistic beauty and its technical complexity, and, above all, because it is the Maya article of clothing most full of meaning. As Hendrickson expresses, the *huipil* is the "most symbolically dense article" of clothing (Hendrickson 1986: 175). I have chosen an article of women's clothing since almost all Maya women use Maya clothing, while a much smaller percentage of Maya men do so. This fact is frequently explained by Maya men as an unfortunate result of the social, economic, and cultural pressures exerted by Ladino society. During the colonial period, Maya men felt the need to involve themselves in the economic and administrative matters of the country, but such involvement did not come without a price. In 1836, for example, a government order stated that "no Indian may hold the office of *regidor, alcalde, síndico*, nor any other parish position, without wearing shoes or boots, a shirt with a collar, long trousers, a jacket or coat, and a hat that is not made from straw or palm leaf" (Carrillo Ramírez 1971: 49). These restrictions forced some Maya men to reduce the use of or totally abandon their aboriginal dress (although sometimes they would wear a Maya scarf underneath the non-Maya clothes). Nevertheless, under similar social circumstances, and taking part in diverse activities, many educated and professional Maya women retain their Maya dress even today. Hendrickson explains that this divergent social response is tied to a different appreciation of men's and women's Maya garb by the Western masters of Guatemalan society: the dress of Maya women "conforms to . . . 'Western' standards of femininity," but the dress of Maya men "does not contain elements which emphasize masculinity," according to the same Western standards (Hendrickson 1986: 102).

Both Maya men (Hendrickson 1986: 144) and women (Otzoy 1988: 107–108, 115, 119) explain this situation by saying that Maya women are more valiant than men. This response suggests that Maya women feel the strongest sense of cultural responsibility to transmit their values to future generations. In any case, Maya men and women alike recognize that Maya women (and particularly Maya women with formal education) have the courage to openly defy a society that discriminates against them. This feminine courage recalls when Q'aq'awitz (a Kaqchikel grandfather-ancestor) faced Q'axq'anul, saying, "Ja ri achi['j] ru [K']ux, ma[ki] tu xib[']i[j] rij" [He has the heart of a hero, that fears not]; his victory was also the victory of the whole nation (Brinton 1969: 96; Recinos 1950: 73). In wearing Maya clothing, Maya women demonstrate their identity and impart a lesson of active cultural resistance. Maya dress also provides the world with a text to be read.

Howard Nemerov (1980: 11) writes that "both painter and poet write in languages"; weavers also write in languages. The language of Maya dress has a woven multivocality that can be divided into at least two levels: the iconographic and the iconological. Iconographic language refers to the form and content expressed in images (as, for example, figures, designs, and motifs in the weave). The iconographic language is interrelated with the iconological language, and both include sociocultural motifs that underlie the making and utilization of an image (Mitchell 1980: 4). Iconographically, Maya dress "speaks" about the creativity of the art and the history of the people, their present existence, and the continuity of the future through motifs and designs. Iconologically, the weavings include a "visible language" (aesthetic selections) and a "language of silence" (with political significance) of both Maya actors— the weaver and the wearer—within a given sociocultural context.

The motifs, designs, and figures in Maya weavings have, as Tedlock and Tedlock (1985) argue, a mixture of iconic, indexical (or indicative), and symbolic aspects. The iconic is most often an image (such as an animal, plant, or other object); the indexical may indicate the social bonds of a person (to a village, community, or nation); and the symbolic maintains established conventions in its creation (for example, a decorative motif or theme associated with a specific community). Iconographically, the language of Maya dress may be examined in a local, regional, or extraregional context. Maya weavings are constantly changing and are diverse even within a single community (see Hendrickson 1986; Asturias de Barrios 1985), though they contain special attributes that make them distinctive to a specific geographic or linguistic region.

There are three types of *huipiles* associated with the town of Comalapa (Chixot): the *rijpo't*, the *aj San Martín po't*, and the *käqpo't* ("red *huipil*"). The choice to use a particular style depends on various factors such as age, social position, occupation, custom, the occasion, and personal and/or familial preferences. Due to its character, which includes all-occasion as well as special-occasion uses, as well as its wide acceptance among young Maya women, I will examine the text of the *käqpo't* of Comalapa. The *käqpo't* of Comalapa is constructed of two panels (*ka'i' nik'aj*) of fabric whose major text (register) is written (woven) from bottom to top and is read (when worn) from top to bottom as follows:

Writing
1. *rutikib'al*   its/his/her sown ground, at hip level
2. *ruk'ajin*   its/his/her half, at belt level
3. *runik'ajal'*   its/his/her center, at chest level
4. *rutele'n*   its/his/her carrier, at shoulder level
Reading
1. *rutele'n*   its/his/her carrier, at shoulder level
2. *runik'ajal'*   its/his/her center, at chest level
3. *ruk'ajin*   its/his/her half, at belt level
4. *rutikib'al*   its/his/her sown ground, at hip level

Thus, the Maya weaver writes a text within the warp and weft of the weaving, and a Maya can read the text of a textile from top to bottom when the article is worn. The *rutele'n* as well as the *runik'ajal'* are very visible and constitute the most important parts of the text of the *käqpo't*. The *rutele'n* section is always red, woven with a red thread called *rukreya* which is highly valued among the Kaqchikels and Tz'utujils (see Asturias de Barrios 1985; Carlsen and Wenger 1991). The distinctive *rutele'n* symbolizes the close association of the Kaqchikels of Comalapa with the *käqpo't*. The *runik'ajal* design can be selected from a gamut of old and new motifs, according to the personal tastes of the weaver and wearer. According to Asturias de Barrios (1985), there exists approximately 125 old figures (*ojer ruxe'*) and a larger number of new figures (*k'ak'a ruxe'*). The older designs include geometric and zoomorphic motifs. For example, there exist diverse variants of the "diamond" motif, which have been described as symbols of prestige, respect, and importance.[5] The motif of the diamond is very similar to the design found in the Maya noble dress represented in Lintel 24 at Yaxchilán. Among the zoomorphic figures there are variants of eagles, doves, rabbits, jaguars, monkeys, and serpents. New motifs include alphabetic writing and machines, innovative artistic elements that express the expansion of Maya culture. Tedlock and Tedlock refer to this fact as the "interculture" of Maya culture: Maya culture "places a positive value on dialogues with other cultures" (1985: 142). Therefore, the art of K'iche' weaving, the same scholars explain, "is an art of possibilities" that selects and creates in a dynamic and conscious manner (Tedlock and Tedlock 1985: 142).

At the regional level, weavings share designs and motifs that distinguish a Maya linguistic group. For example, Berlo and Senuk, in comparing and determining the motifs associated with Maya-Ixil textiles, state that "some of the same geometric and animal motifs found in the textiles of Chajul and Nebaj occur in Cotzal, yet they are used in a different manner and in a strikingly different color scheme" (1982: 7). At a larger level, the language codified in Maya weavings "speaks" of the Maya as a people, of their roots, of their lives, and of their causes. In dealing with the language of Maya weavings it is pertinent to cite the words of Clifford Geertz: "to study an art form is to explore a sensibility, that such a sensibility is essentially a collective formation, and the foundations of such formation are as wide as social existence and as deep" (1985: 99). Consequently, the study of Maya textile art requires inquiry and examination of the sensibility of the Maya (their motives, sentiments, emotions, satisfactions, regrets, and pains), attributes that are intimately tied to weaving and wearing Maya clothes. To begin, I will examine some commentaries by two Maya women living in exile who are themselves weavers. Rigoberta Menchú states:

> I saw a paper about a village of weavers by an anthropologist . . . He did a study that depicts the weavers as if they were a great wonder. "How pretty this is . . . how nice that is," forgetting the daily reality, the suffering of our people. This is a lack of consciousness, a lack of will. To depict it as wonderful—this is what the army and the Guatemalan government do. (Quoted in Branfman 1987: 54)

Likewise, a North American scholar summarizes Elana Ixk'ot's comments about weavings:

Elena Ixk'ot remarked during her visit to the University of Iowa on the western preoccupation with Maya weaving without any accompanying interest or knowledge of the life of the community or in the woman whose work it is. She pointed out that understanding and appreciation must take place within the context of community or all meaning is lost. (Quoted in Kellman 1991: 20)

The above comments make it clear that the Maya art of weaving must be seen in a larger context—the aesthetics and politics of Maya daily life. As Rigoberta Menchú succinctly states, "It is the same to speak of the *tejidos* [weavings] as it is to speak of the earth. Those things have equal value because the *tejido* is the expression of it all" (quoted in Branfman 1987: 53). For the Maya, the earth is as essential for their subsistence as weaving is for their culture. Both land and weavings form the medullary bases of their existence. It is not surprising then that the land and weaving of the Maya have been the target of reprisals. Historically, the Maya have fought for their land and their weavings and have always been determined to maintain them.

Aesthetics and politics are inextricably bound to the weaving and wearing of Maya clothing. The notion of politics refers here to the more subtle promulgations (spoken or not) of Maya sociocultural resistance. In a larger sense, Maya politics includes land, identity (and all that it implies—culture, history, and descent), as well as the right to self-determination. Thus the historical, artistic, and cultural aspects of weaving and wearing Maya clothing are an expression of Maya resistance. This Maya sociocultural resistance includes the conscious feeling of belonging to a people and implies an interaction of moral, ideological, material, and spiritual necessities of daily life. Consider, for example, the resurgence of the old *xilon*-style *huipil* worn by young Maya women in the Kaqchikel area during the 1980s. While some Kaqchikels explain that the popularity of the *xilon huipil* was due to its beauty, others attribute its use to a sense of respect toward their Maya heritage. Hendrickson writes that the *xilon* example represents "a female expression of Indian pride at a time when other, more overt expressions resulted in the proponent's death" (1986: 228). In this context, the fact that Maya wear and weave their distinctive dress may be interpreted in the terms used by Schutz in his explanation of world-life: "a pragmatic motif governing our natural attitudes toward the world and daily life. The world, in this sense, is something that we have to modify with our actions, or that modifies our actions" (Schutz 1970: 73).

Just as the recognition of the Maya as a people with human rights is a prerequisite for justice, wearing and weaving Maya dress is an artistic observance of, and a demand for, sociocultural liberty. Sociocultural liberty includes respect for and understanding of the changes and continuity expressed in Maya weavings and the recognition that both the changes and continuities result from acts of self-determination.

In the sixteenth-century documents the *Popol Wuj*, the *Título de los señores de Totonicapán*, and the *Annals of the Kaqchikels* one finds passages that make reference to Maya dress (e.g., Recinos 1950: 221, 65, fig. 1). The mythological origin of the designs and symbolism of clothing is expressed in the *Popol Wuj* when B'alam Kitze', B'alam Aq'ab', Majukutaj, and Iki B'alam were instructed by Tojil, Awilix, and Jakawitz:

> Inscribe [the cloaks] with the signs of our being. They're for the tribes. . . . Give them to the maidens [Xtah and Xpuch] . . . [so they will take them to their lords] . . . give them the cloaks to try on, the maidens were told . . . [the lords] were shown the figured cloaks . . . : one with a jaguar, one with an eagle, and one with yellow jackets and wasps drawn on the inside, on a smooth surface. And they loved the way the cloaks looked. They costumed themselves. The jaguar . . . was the first figure to be tried on by a lord . . . another lord costumed himself with the second figured cloak, with the drawing of an eagle . . . it just felt good to him . . . [the third lord] costumed himself with the one that had yellow jackets and wasps painted inside. And then he started getting stung by the yellow jackets and wasps. He couldn't endure it, he couldn't stand the stings of the insects . . . It was the third drawing that defeated them. (Tedlock 1985: 191–192)

In K'iche', as in all contemporary Mayan languages,[6] the verb root *tz'ib'* ("to write," alphabetically or hieroglyphically) encompasses other forms of "writing" such as painting and drawing. In the passage from the *Popol Wuj* cited above, to draw is to write, a writing that was woven in fabric in the capes of the three K'iche' lords, "the lords who founded the three principal [K'iche'] lineages" (Tedlock and Tedlock 1985: 124). The sign of the lords was placed *chuwach*, or in the face of each cape (literally), but was also visible *chupan*, or in the interior of the capes, which Tedlock and Tedlock reasonably explain as double-faced brocade, a technique found in many modern weavings (see Asturias de Barrios 1985).

The change and continuity in the designs and motifs of weavings express cultural creativity while symbolizing continuing Maya political resistance. In the *Popol Wuj* one finds that symbols of jaguars and eagles, in contrast to those of yellow jackets and wasps, pleased the lords and were conserved by them. In contemporary Maya weavings the motifs of the jaguar and eagle are abundant, while those of the yellow jacket and bumblebee are not, a fact that reveals much about the sublime power of the *Popol Wuj* in contemporary Maya thought. Perhaps then, for the Maya, weavings are not museum artifacts or exotic collectibles but rather manifestations of continuing experiences. Hence the constant creativity.

There are "stable" and "modifiable" elements in Maya weavings. Stable elements are those motifs and structures that remain more or less constant and represent continuity, including the white-on-white weaving art of the Maya-Q'eqchi' people; the frog motif of the Maya of Chiapas, Mexico; and the "diamond" motif in the weavings of the Maya-Poqomam (as in Palín) and the Maya-Kaqchikel (as in Tecpán, San Juan Sacatepéquez, and Comalapa).

During the onset of Spanish colonization, the capital of the non-Maya population was constructed in the Kaqchikel territory, near the Poqomam region. As a result a large number of Spanish colonial enterprises were instigated in this area. The Spanish campaign of evangelizing, felt most consistently and directly in the Kaqchikel territory, was devastating to indigenous religious beliefs and practices.[7] Nonetheless, the Kaqchikel people resisted. Consider, for example, what the *Annals of the Kaqchikels* record for the year 1526:

> In the course of this year we breathed a little, as did also the kings
> Cahi Ymox and Belehe Qat. They had lost all hope before the
> Spaniards, and they maintained themselves at Holombalam, O my
> children! One year and twenty days had passed since the places had
> been made desolate by Tunatiuh, when the Spaniards arrived at
> Chiixot. On the day 1 Caok [27 March 1527] our slaughter by the
> Spaniards began. They fought with the nation and persisted in war.
> Death ravaged us again, but the whole country continued to refuse
> tribute. (Brinton 1969: 185; cf. Recinos 1950: 131)

Maya resistance has always existed. Even under Christian domination, the Maya found the capacity to express and safeguard their culture. The Poqomams and Kaqchikels have carefully conserved their religious beliefs through other cultural practices such as weaving. Consider, for example, the case of the *rupan laq* (or *rupan plato*) of Comalapa:

> [R]upan [laq], whose literal translation is "its/his/her interior,
> plate," is a deep, ceramic, majolica ware dish that has a peculiar
> design, a tiger for example, in the bottom. . . . There exists a variety
> of figures called *rupan [laq]*. All of them resemble rhombuses or
> rhomboids and represent the ceremonial dish of the same name.
> [One of them] is a rhombus that contains four small rhombuses

inside; [another] is a rhombus that has a series of rays around it.
(Asturias de Barrios 1985: 32)

Comalapan weavers explained to Asturias de Barrios that the figures in
the form of rhombuses (or "diamonds") called *rupan laq* refer to a "very
precious [ritual object] associated with the *cofradías*." Asturias de
Barrios then shows that "[these] figures have much prestige. They are
frequently brocaded on special *huipiles* and *sobre-huipiles* [*rij po't* or
over-*huipiles*]" (1985: 32). This example illustrates how Maya weavers
transform real objects of a ritual character or other special significance
into woven motifs. In creating forms for preserving, producing, and
reproducing that which has value to them, the weavers are thus design-
ing for survival.

Material constraints and geopolitical factors have also acted to change
Maya dress. For example, Maya no longer use jaguar skins or (non-
domesticated) bird feathers in the construction of their clothing because
these are now scarce, if not totally depleted, resources; and even if these
resources were available, other factors (such as technological restraints
and environmental conservation efforts) would limit their use. In a
similar way, Maya have developed a type of "common identity" as an
answer to the geopolitical restrictions imposed on the use of Maya
clothing. In the recent past, Maya tended to wear clothing associated
with their place of origin. Today, a growing number of Maya do not
follow this standard, wearing pieces or even complete outfits from
another Maya area. Some non-Maya have criticized these new Maya
combinations of dress, believing that they confuse local and international tourists. Once a Ladino woman from Guatemala City said to me,
"Today the Indians wear their clothing all mixed up. They wear pieces
from different places. What they are doing is confusing the tourists"
(Otzoy 1988: 136). Notwithstanding this woman's preoccupation with
tourism, I do not consider that anything Maya should be totally alien to
the Maya.

Since the beginning of Spanish colonization, the majority of Maya
have lived in highland rural communities. Urban areas and the most
fertile lands have been appropriated by non-Maya people. For centuries,
the relative isolation of Maya communities functioned, to a certain
point, as a social barrier that aided the survival of Maya culture. Maya
wore, and still wear, their distinctive dress as a symbol of their identity
and as a tie to a local or linguistic community. Today a growing number
of Maya live in cities. In urban areas, in contrast to rural communities,
Maya have to coexist and interact more with non-Maya. In this situation, Maya encounter new challenges and create new strategies for
sociocultural continuity. In the past, some Maya resorted to wearing

non-Maya clothing to avoid social, racial, and cultural discrimination in the cities. Today, Maya students and professionals directly challenge such discrimination by wearing Maya dress and maintaining other external cultural elements in the cities. These Maya are creating new forms of cultural survival and are joining together in various Maya cultural and educational organizations. The basic goal of these organizations is to meet, share knowledge, and enhance Maya solidarity in the cities. In this context, Maya dress plays an important role as a symbol of cultural survival and solidarity. In the *Agenda con el calendario maya*, published by the Guatemala City–based Maya publishing house Nawal Wuj, brief notes on Maya dress are included. One reads, for example, that "to wear [Maya dress] is to accept the invitation written by our ancestors: 'Our children, do not abandon us'"; that "to wear Maya dress is to tell ourselves and others: I am Maya, we are Maya, we continue and will continue to be Maya"; and that "to teach the boys and girls to weave is to make them literate in the art of expressing themselves with colors, threads, and Maya forms and designs" (Cholba'l Samaj 1991).

Although among Maya with a "formal" education women have been the most consistent in the wearing of Maya clothing, it has not always been easy for them to do so. A female Maya university student told me: "I do not know why, but it is our clothes that they [Ladinos] do not like. [Maya dress] is like something that bothers them; it is like a taboo."

Of late, some formally educated Maya men have been bothered by this situation. In this respect a Maya professional stated to me that it is necessary for Maya men to find more external symbols of their Maya identity. According to him, this is necessary "for the public reaffirmation of one's identity. Private affirmation (personal, and for and with one's people) is not sufficient; reaffirmation toward other people is necessary." If Maya men were first to establish (forced or voluntarily) an interethnic interaction in Guatemala, Maya women were the ones that assured the maintenance of one of the principal Maya cultural emblems. Now these Maya women and men form a base that is interacting, resisting, and flourishing as a people. Maya dress is a symbol of "being" Maya; *retal qak'ojeik*, says the *Popol Wuj*.

Notes

A version of this article has been previously published in Spanish as "Identidad y trajes mayas" (Otzoy 1992). This chapter was translated from Spanish by Edward F. Fischer and R. McKenna Brown.

1. The faces of colonialism are described as classic, internal, and neocolonial in the scheme of Altbach and Kelly (1984: 1–5).

2. For a detailed inventory of pre-Columbian dress, see Anawalt (1990); for the twentieth century, see Osborne (1965).

3. By "in the context of daily life," I am referring to the opposite of the use of Maya dress during a special event, contest, or any type of Ladino event. I refer here to the use of certain items of Maya dress and not the use of a complete Maya outfit, although beginning relatively recently the latter is seen among the non-Maya population, who, as some Maya joke, are becoming "Mayanized" or "Indianized," a phenomenon that deserves a separate analysis.

4. With respect to the textiles found at Chichén Itzá, see Tozzer (1957: xi); for Cieneguilla, see Johnson (1954), O'Neale (1942), and Wauchope (1942); for Río Azul finds, see Carlsen (1985, 1986).

5. These include the "rose" or "bundle" discussed by Osborne (1965) and the *rupan laq* mentioned by Asturias de Barrios (1985).

6. This does not hold true for one Mayan language, Huastec (see C. Brown 1991).

7. In the *Annals of the Kaqchikels*, for example, one finds that at the beginning of the 1540s Fray Juan de Torres was already evangelizing the Kaqchikels and working on a translation of the "Christian Doctrine in the Guatemalan Language [Kaqchikel]" (see Recinos 1950: 139).

10.
Women, Weaving, and Education in Maya Revitalization

Carol Hendrickson (Marlboro College)

When I first worked in Tecpán, Guatemala, people were not talking about Maya revitalization. I was there in 1980–81, just as the violence of the most recent round of civil strife began to escalate in the central highlands. While the urban center of Tecpán remained relatively quiet throughout my stay, that was not the case with some of the surrounding rural areas and a number of neighboring municipalities.[1] I was interested in local people's thoughts on and involvement in what was euphemistically referred to as *la situación* and so asked Tecpanecos (the residents of Tecpán) to whom I felt closest if members of the community were involved in guerrilla activities. I remember one answer in particular: a friend responded by saying that Tecpanecos (and here the term was being used to refer to indigenous Tecpanecos) were more involved in education. At that time, I did not exactly take the reply to be a non sequitur, but it was unexpected—what could be considered a safe response but also one that answered my difficult question with a thoughtful insight.

Now, more than a decade later, that response seems to capture brilliantly what was going on then in quiet ways and what is going on now, in the 1990s, in increasingly public ways. For, in fact, the battle for indigenous rights and an active presence in Guatemalan society is being fought with notable success by Maya who are pursuing their educations far beyond the levels attained by their parents, commanding the power of professional positions (as teachers, social workers, health promoters, agricultural specialists, linguists, and researchers), becoming increasingly savvy in the internal workings of the national government, and reaping the economic, educational, political, and social benefits of expanded ties to Maya from other communities and transnational groups sympathetic to Maya projects. Surrounding these activities and making them even more public and meaningful is an active articulation of desires and goals as well as a growing recognition of alternative routes to fulfilling these. In thinking about the Guatemalan case, I am reminded of the observations made by Jean and John Comaroff that

> the assault on local societies and cultures is the subject of neither "consciousness" nor "unconsciousness" on the part of the victim, but of recognition—recognition that occurs with varying degrees of inchoateness and clarity. Out of that recognition, and the creative tensions to which it may lead, there typically arise forms of *experimental practice* that are at once techniques of empowerment and the signs of collective representation. (1991: 31)

While the Comaroffs are writing about a time early on in the colonizing process, before relationships between the colonizer and colonized have any real history and a social consciousness is formed, I believe that similar mental and social processes occur under shifting historical circumstances. Of course I would not claim, for example, that the horror and violence of the 1980s in Guatemala somehow erased memories and allowed for a clean start in power relationships. However, it does seem that an abhorrence of violence and the perceived failure of the insurgency and counterinsurgency tactics in the highlands have led many people to reject certain routes of resistance and action and to vigorously seek new conceptualizations of social problems and new means to their ends. It is from such current "experimental practice" in the highlands that different activities and organizations focusing on Maya history and identity have developed and come to be recognized in a collective sense. These activities have been labeled cultural salvage, Maya revitalization, Maya nationalism, and the Maya cultural rights movement (or just *el movimiento*, "the movement"), terms that denote not a neatly bounded set but rather an open-ended class of organizations and activities characterized generally by a focus on Maya issues, a conscious articulation of a cultural purpose, an interest in the Maya past for use at the present, and participation by Maya from throughout Guatemala.[2]

Because my own research in Guatemala (Hendrickson 1995) has focused on *traje*, or Maya dress, and the ways in which its production and use reflect and help create the social identity of those who make and wear it, I am interested in the roles of weaving and *traje* in revitalization activities. In addition, because Maya women as a group are ideologically associated with *traje* and, in actuality, wear *traje* much more than Maya men, I focus on women and weaving. The data suggest that while recent efforts by Maya activists have moved important cultural issues into a realm of acceptable political discourse at a national level (that is, into a space without the stigma of the militarized politics of the last decade), *traje* cannot really be considered one of these. I will examine why, in general, *traje* and weaving lack an active role in the cultural arena and ask how this affects the roles of Maya women both in the context of revitalization activities and in the larger society. In particular I see the role of education as fundamental in *el movimiento*, a fact of particular consequences for the roles of weavers and weaving.

Before examining the Guatemalan situation further, I want to consider another case of changing cultural consciousness, that of the Kayapo of the Brazilian Amazon. Terence Turner (1991), an anthropologist who has worked with the Kayapo since 1962, writes about his first experiences in Brazil and what he sees now as the Kayapo's earlier "lack of a viable political response to their subordination to, and dependency upon, the representatives of Western society" as well as "a lack of consciousness of the political significance of their own culture in the new context of inter-ethnic coexistence" (ibid.: 293). Some twenty-five years later, he writes about the transformations in his own thinking as well as that of the Kayapo. Where he earlier saw a people who did not seem to understand in a conscious sense any sort of social theory of their own cultural being, he now sees a people who are "consummate ethnic politicians" (ibid.: 311) with a well-articulated sense of cultural consciousness. This articulation of Kayapo politico-cultural identity gets translated into concrete public actions and demands made to the government and other Brazilian agencies on issues concerning mining, dam construction, border disputes, and the like. The means by which these messages get carried beyond the Kayapo themselves include videotapes produced by the Kayapo, the national and international media, and the work of outsider social scientists, aid agency representatives, and media stars (Sting, for example) who are sympathetic to their issues. The Kayapo people who enjoy prestige and hold positions of leadership appear to be chiefs (that is, older males with status positions within the traditional social structure) and younger males who have been educated away from home and who can act as skilled and experienced mediators between the Kayapo and the Portuguese-speaking world of Brazilians. Women are not silent and inactive, but men seem to have the key positions, articulating cultural concepts and mediating between the indigenous and nonindigenous worlds.

How, then, does this relate to the Maya situation in Guatemala? I would argue that the Maya of Guatemala have traveled a route parallel to that described by Turner for the Kayapo. As I mentioned earlier, a quiet but powerful transformation has taken place in recent years. While indigenous Guatemalans in the past spoke Mayan languages, conducted Maya rituals, wore Maya *traje*, and revered Maya ancestors, this was not done in a self-conscious manner. There was little attempt or perceived need to articulate a sense of the cultural system to non-Maya or to other

Maya outside of the immediate group. While the "closed, corporate communities" of Maya society were not so hermetically sealed as early ethnographies might have it, there seems, nonetheless, to have been a centripetal force that focused community awareness within the municipality. As a result, there was relatively little interaction between different (especially distant) Maya communities, and the routes that did exist (for example, the market system) were generally limited to narrow concerns like economic exchange. Indigenous interactions with non-Maya were likewise limited, especially when these ranged beyond the day-to-day concerns of town life. Gossip, petty transgressions, and other weapons of the weak were (and are) used against those with more power (Scott 1976). On rarer occasions, uprisings occurred against the dominant group. These actions, however, have not had an impact on the structure of power relations in Guatemala, and Maya have continued to live in a minority status and have suffered because of it.

This brings me to the activities and individuals that, by the early 1990s, were seen as part of *el movimiento*. Because the other chapters in this volume deal with many of these, I include only a few details to give context to my points. In particular I want to stress the importance of language as both a topical focus and a medium of expression in so much revitalization work; the primacy of language is best seen in the prominence of the Academia de las Lenguas Mayas de Guatemala (ALMG) and the Programa Nacional de Educación Bilingüe (PRONEBI) within the movement. However, language is not the only activity falling under the revitalization label. For example, the ALMG also promotes the revitalization of *costumbre*, or traditional indigenous practices, in terms of religious customs, sociopolitical organization, and the use of Maya dress (Nelson 1991: 6). Other organizations, such as the Coordinadora Cakchiquel de Desarrollo Integral (COCADI), have been organized to promote rural development on a number of fronts such as agriculture, construction, and arts and crafts production, including weaving and the production of *traje* pieces for sale.

Who are the Maya in the leadership roles of these organizations? The vast majority are well educated by Guatemalan standards, having completed at least a high school–level degree. A large number continue at university level or participate in special classes (e.g., ones provided by foreign academics, especially linguists). They are generally young: many were teenagers during the violence of the early 1980s. They are both male and female—predominantly male, but females are not mere tokens in this elite group. They come from throughout the highlands, although certain municipalities (Tecpán among them) have a disproportionate number of active participants. And they generally know each other because of ties through school, work, and/or panhighland cultural activities. They are proud to be Maya, and because education (as opposed to armed opposition) is a generally agreed-upon good in Guatemalan society, they can use their training and professional positions to promote publicly issues of Maya interest having to do with, for example, language, education, ritual, health care, weaving, and *traje*.[3]

These Maya highly value language skills, being articulate in the spoken and written forms of Spanish and a Mayan language. The importance of strong oral language skills emerges in public situations. There is an art to public speaking in Guatemala that does not depend solely on education, although, for younger adults, it is now thought to go along with schooling.[4] Words well spoken convey information from written and oral sources and help to define the situation under discussion. Words are also central to the revitalization movement for articulating a Maya consciousness, promoting Maya activities and symbols of collective representation, and spreading these ideas among Maya and non-Maya alike.

Along with speaking, writing has become an increasingly important means by which Maya articulate an indigenous consciousness and gain an authoritative voice within wider spheres of influence. University training, of course, has been important in fostering the production of written materials. Writing groups have formed; there are Maya publishers; and a whole array of Mayan language publications, including children's books and news bulletins, are available (Richards 1994). All of this has been an important way that Maya have been able to take back their own lives, to turn their own "real lives into writing" (in the words of Foucault 1979: 192) so that writing might serve their own purposes and their own sociopolitical efforts rather than the purposes and efforts of others.

The study of linguistics has thus taken on great importance. In studying linguistics Maya students develop a technical knowledge of language that is highly scientific and hence arguably "neutral" or lacking cultural biases. By mastering the language of the discipline they enter into communication with a worldwide network of scholars with whom they can become coequals. Further, in a country that has had surprisingly few niches for the study of indigenous culture within the established university systems, the study of native languages has turned out to be an important center of indigenous revitalization efforts; and education in linguistics—both inside the university system and out—is an important training ground for leaders in the Maya revitalization effort.

Given the importance of language, spoken, written, and studied, where does this leave such silent subjects as weaving and *traje*? They are included among the concerns of various Maya organizations centrally involved in regional and national Maya revitalization efforts, though never ʔ one of their primary concerns (especially not within the better-funded or more prominent groups). One "problem" with weaving, conceived of as the primary means of producing *traje*, is that the activity itself is not validated in a school or university setting. A person might be able to study about weaving for a degree (though even here the opportunities are few and the study stigmatized),[5] but he or she cannot weave and have that contribute in any significant way to a diploma. In fact, women in Tecpán regularly claim that, as girls, they made the choice not to weave when they decided to pursue school and fill their hours with homework. Some of these highly educated women within the revitalization movement have expressed an interest in learning backstrap weaving, in essence to make up for a lost cultural experience; however, in my experience, these expressions of interest generally remain at the level of desire with the women, at best finding time to embroider blouses and thus contribute their own labor to the production of an acceptable form of *traje*. Finally, backstrap weavers make very little money for the enormous amount of time they put into making *huipiles* (Maya blouses) and other handwoven articles of indigenous dress (well under a dollar for an eight-hour day in all the cases that I have studied). Class considerations, therefore, come into play, with weavers (especially weavers who are not also textile entrepreneurs) making the equivalent of a subminimum wage. Thinking only in terms of this income (and not additional money from a spouse), this wage puts strict limits on weavers' opportunities in the sphere of revitalization, where a certain amount of wealth is needed to travel, sponsor rituals, and pursue higher education.

Weaving and *traje* as subjects of study also suffer in the translation to the academic world. Different authors have noted (e.g., Weiner 1992: 12) that cloth and clothing have not so much been ignored in the social scientific literature as given little prestige. Seen as "women's work" and a "craft" akin to "basket weaving" (with all the negative connotations that the latter phrase carries), the study of cloth and clothing and the visual information that they convey has been marginalized and seen as less serious than the study of such social scientific "objects" as, say, markets, family structures, and community organizations.[6] The fact that weaving and *traje* embody themes having to do with politics, economics, and social structure is not always obvious, and there is a feeling that a person interested in the study of dress in general and *traje* in particular needs to campaign to make the subject a legitimate one at the same time that he or she strives to make the content of a study understandable. This characterization holds true for the study of weaving and clothing in a North American university setting, and the system of biases and prejudices translates more or less directly into Guatemalan higher education. In Guatemala the stigma also relates to the fact that the presentation and discussion of *traje* are often confined to "folkloric" events, which give no sense of the potential of indigenous dress as a politico-cultural artifact (see Hanchard 1993).

Furthermore, the study of weaving and *traje* remains by and large a women's subject. While Mayan languages, religion, and archaeological sites are legitimate topics for both sexes to study, I am unaware of any Maya males (and few non-Maya males) who have chosen to investigate the subject of *traje* production and use. In addition, the institutions that most directly and generously support weaving and research having to do with weaving and *traje* in Guatemala are the Instituto Guatemalteco de Turismo (INGUAT) and the Museo Ixchel de Traje Indígena. Both are controlled by non-Maya, focused to greater or lesser extent on tourists (and, in the case of the Ixchel Museum, national and international scholars, though relatively few Maya), and centered in Guatemala City. I have never heard these organizations mentioned as being part of the revitalization effort, and, in fact, their activities can be seen to support a model of *traje* that is largely apolitical and educational efforts that are generally aimed at a non-Maya audience.[7]

Finally, an irony of the situation is that while individuals involved with revitalization efforts generally express a desire to retain the use of *traje* on a daily basis, the vast majority of Maya males (including virtually all in leadership positions) do not wear *traje*. Women in the same positions do, and, in fact, they wear particularly beautiful pieces that emphasize their cultural worth and what Kay Warren (1993: 46) describes as their role as "metonymic representations of community."

Women's *traje* is admired and used by non-Maya in a number of situations from the most casual to the most elegant and refined. It beautifully complements a whole range of symbolic dimensions in Western female fashion at the same time that it can be seen as quintessentially Maya wear. Thus Maya women in *traje* wear clothing that is capable of balancing two fashion aesthetics while remaining uncompromised in its ethnic orientation. This balance is useful in the world of revitalization activities, which so often are played out within a regional or national arena and under the scrutiny of a wide variety of individuals. Men in *traje* do not have the luxury of clothes that easily fit a dual aesthetic. In general, men's *traje* does not signal complementary information within Maya and non-Maya realms. Speaking from a biethnic perspective, the values manifested by the colorful, handwoven shirts and the calf-length pants of some male *traje*, for example, do not match those of, say, blue jeans and T-shirts or suits and ties. Men in *traje* are therefore seen as "less" masculine, serious, and competent, and whatever else they do in a biethnic world is compromised by these symbolic dimensions associated with their dress.

In pointing out different ways that weaving and *traje* fall outside the activities of *el movimiento* as I have broadly characterized them, I do not mean to ignore the very real ways that they do play a role. Maya men are using different forms of clothing (for example, Maya cloth sewn into bomber jackets) that signal participation in revitalization activities, and individual weavers and some local groups are studying old *traje* pieces in order to incorporate elements of the past into weavings of the future. Nonetheless, as I have tried to show, there are some very basic difficulties in locating a place for weaving, *traje*, and women (in their roles as weavers) within the revitalization movement. A key to understanding why this is so has to do with education, to which Maya activists owe so much for their achievements but which, also, does not perfectly accommodate work with all dimensions of the culture. The incorporation of weavers, weaving, and *traje* into revitalization work thus remains a challenge to the ongoing "experimental practice" of those who are attempting to bring to consciousness Maya issues and Maya identity in Guatemala and in the international sphere.

Notes

1. Tecpán witnessed a number of violent attacks later in 1981: in May the local priest was murdered by men said to have been military hirees, and in November "unknowns" blew up the municipal hall, killing the mayor.

2. I should add that there are people living in Maya communities in Guatemala who, while aware of the different activities that I and others include under the "revitalization" label, would not recognize the labels per se or know what they refer to. Many other people are not even aware of the activities, with or without the labels. Others who are aware of the activities are extremely critical of the participants and their goals and motivations (even though, I should add, the critics sometimes engage in activities that, on the surface, may seem similar to ones that draw their ire, only in their own cases the actions are conceptualized very differently).

3. By saying this I do not mean to imply that now anything is possible for Maya who are educated, articulate, and willing to take a public stand. Subjects like human rights and land distribution, for example, are still extremely politically charged, and a person takes definite risks speaking out on these issues.

4. Older ritual specialists developed their oral skills within local Maya communities, and now some younger Maya are apprenticing with these individuals in order to develop a knowledge of ritual language. This flow seems to be part of a larger dialectic between local, more experience-based learning and pan-Maya, institutional-based learning and adds another dimension to observations by Warren (1992: 211) of what she sees as a turning away from "experience-based memories" with the increased use of "ethnic nationalist explanations in building a wider ethnic revitalization."

5. The current efforts in bilingual education may be changing the attitude toward the use of Mayan languages in schools, but, as far as I know, nothing is

being done to modify the stigma of weaving as a valid educational activity. The stigma attached to a "craft" like weaving, of course, is not unique to the Guatemalan educational system.

6. Highland weaving considered as an "art" would not easily fit into an academic mold either. It is not a system of genius innovators and signature pieces. Weavers do have marks and styles that distinguish their work from others, and in general *traje* is produced and worn without a focus on the creator. This more "egalitarian" orientation is reflected in such factors as price: the price of a piece is virtually always determined by a set of "objective" criteria (including materials, fineness of weave, and type of design motifs) that have nothing to do with who produced the piece.

7. Funds from INGUAT are given to weavers' groups in support of projects such as cooperatives that aim at broadening their access to tourist markets.

11.
The Mayan Language Loyalty Movement in Guatemala

R. McKenna Brown (Virginia Commonwealth University)

This chapter examines a particular aspect of the growing revitalization, nationalist, or pan-Maya movement in Guatemala that relates to the Mayan languages. Borrowing from Fishman (1988) the term "language loyalty movement," I refer to those efforts that seek to deter and reverse the loss of the languages and to gain for them a broader, more formal, legitimized institutional role in Guatemalan national life.

First, I will tie these phenomena in with what we know or feel about Maya studies today, specifically, the importance of self-determination and the concept of the successful Indian as negotiator of multiple cultural systems. Second, I will describe several characteristics of the language loyalty movement and place them in the broader context of work on such movements by Fishman. Finally, I will discuss the need for a prescriptive model for domestic language use and the related implications for language maintenance.

Throughout, I suggest that the present context of Maya studies and the movement itself represent transitions on a very large scale and interact with the shifting roles between Western scholars and Maya as studiers and studied, shifts that are significant at many levels. Ten years ago Maya studies was dominated by Westerners whose research agendas, methods, and publications mainly served, with a good deal of impunity, English-speaking Western academia. The Maya participated mostly as objects of study or as informants, donating information about their languages and cultures upon request. Today the Maya are taking an increasingly active role in Maya studies, using Western scholarship as a means to regain control over their linguistic and cultural destinies and demanding that foreign scholars who work in Maya communities help them in this struggle.

As a sociolinguist studying language maintenance and shift during this period, I discovered that it was not enough to simply report decreasing use of Mayan languages. Ethically, I was compelled to share the tools of my field with the Maya and to assist them when possible in finding ways of maintaining and promoting the use of their languages.

Western scholars who play the role of advocate for the peoples they study and who allow that advocacy to shape their research have traditionally been suspect among their peers, and the changes in Maya studies today have not lacked for controversy. The current dynamics in Maya studies offer us a chance to rethink our notions of scholarship as apolitical and our relationship and responsibilities to the peoples among whom we work.

Bilingualism versus Language Shift, or What It Has to Do with Science

In 1992 *Lingua Franca* published an article by Arthur Allen on the controversy among Maya scholars, particularly epigraphers, regarding efforts to give back to the Maya what is learned about them. Archaeologist William Sanders was quoted as saying, "I couldn't care less whether the modern Maya preserve their ancient cultural traditions [because] it doesn't have anything to do with science" (in Allen 1992: 53). Though Sanders referred specifically to epigraphy, this argument might well extend to other fields, including linguistics and cultural anthropology, and invites comparison with language maintenance.[1]

I argue that whether the modern Maya preserve and, more important, gain control over their ancient cultural traditions, among which language is a prime example, is one of the most pressing issues facing Maya studies today. That the issue even surfaces as a topic worth debate reflects profound changes in the social sciences from a time when the exclusion of Maya from scholastic inquiry on their cultures was perceived as, well, unremarkable. We are witnessing a recalibration in the traditional relationship between the studied and the studier that affects virtually every aspect of scientific inquiry, from research agenda to methods to dispersal of findings. Whether or not every researcher will accommodate his or her practice to a new order is not the point. The mere fact that the disinclined researcher must confront the option and refuse it reflects an important change in science.

Scholars of Mayan languages must be aware of the broader context in which they work (see England 1992a). The issue of a new status for minority languages is part of a global transition in postcolonial dynamics. The minority status of the languages we study is not accidental but rather the result of Western impact on local communities. As the influence of European powers and their languages recedes, the return to local autonomy is often accompanied by agitation for increased status for local languages. Fishman mentions that "the phenomenal increase in languages of education and government since the end of World War II is a result of such recoveries from external and internal colonization . . . such revival and rebirth movements [attempt] to overcome and undo the punitive dislocations to which their constituencies were exposed" (1988: 112).

Discussion of Mayan language maintenance today must take into account another of Fishman's observations: that the causes of bilingualism are not the same as the causes of language shift. Bilingualism (the acquisition of a language of wider currency in addition to the mother tongue) is often a pragmatic response to political and socioeconomic forces. Language shift, on the other hand, usually is brought about by significant proportions of parents speaking their second language to their offspring, a choice motivated by affective factors. (Of course, the former is a necessary precondition for the latter.) Hence this topic finds us smack in the intersection between the macro and the micro, where both the effective manipulation of state policy and the mobilization of emotions will determine the preservation of this ancient cultural tradition.

Both Maya and non-Maya alike often conceive of Spanish acquisition as somehow un-Maya and perceive the monolingual (in a Mayan language) as somehow "purer" than the bilingual in Spanish and Maya. However, since the Spanish invasion, the survival of Maya culture has often depended on the successful mastery of Spanish cultural elements, including language, as an addition to, but not a replacement for, Maya culture (see Lovell 1991). For example, in his study of four Kaqchikel towns, Annis (1987) portrays the successful Indian as negotiator between two worlds. Success in the cash economy often accompanies and contributes to success in the subsistence (or *milpa*) economy. Annis found that evangelical Protestantism, which he and others interpret as a rejection of the values of the *milpa* system, appealed most to the fringes of Maya communities, especially to the land poor.

Undeniably, acquisition of the Spanish language and other accoutrements of the Western world not only enhances the Maya ability to stay Maya but also provides the arms, as it were, to do battle against many types of hegemony. An excellent example is Rigoberta Menchú (1985), who recounts that she learned Spanish, the language of her oppressors, in order to communicate with Maya of other language groups and ultimately to argue the case for her people within a global forum. Thus, Spanish language acquisition is not incongruous with the Maya identity. Bilingualism can be seen as a linguistic manifestation of the ability to straddle the divide between two worlds. In many areas, particularly at the municipal level, higher education, entrepreneurship, and other successful exploitations of the Western system are widely valued by the Maya today.

However, there is no denying that the Mayan languages are not only sharing more space with Spanish but losing ground to it. An alarming proportion of younger Maya are not learning their parents' mother tongue or are learning it incompletely. An example comes from my own research on Kaqchikel Mayan language vitality in four Kaqchikel communities (R. Brown 1991) in which over five hundred household surveys were conducted in the municipalities of Santa Catarina Barahona and San Antonio Aguas Calientes and its two dependent hamlets, San Andrés Cevallos and Santiago Zamora. Respondents were asked to evaluate the Kaqchikel fluency of the children in the household. When fluency levels are divided by the age of the mother (fig. 1), the oldest group of mothers has the largest proportion of offspring with high Kaqchikel fluency and the smallest proportion of offspring with no Kaqchikel fluency. Inversely, the youngest group of mothers has the smallest proportion of offspring with high Kaqchikel fluency and the largest proportion of offspring with no Kaqchikel fluency. The younger the mother, the less fluent in Kaqchikel her children are likely to be.

A comparison of the reported Kaqchikel fluency levels of offspring by age confirms this hypothesis (table 1). The younger the child, the lower the Kaqchikel fluency level is likely to be. These data suggest that over

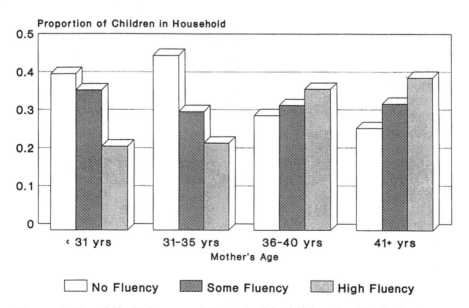

Figure 1. Kaqchikel Fluency of Household Children by Mother's Age.

Table 1. Average Age of Offspring by Fluency Level

Fluency Level	Kaqchikel Fluency			Spanish Fluency		
	Age 1st Child	Age 2nd Child	Age 3rd Child	Age 1st Child	Age 2nd Child	Age 3rd Child
1	15.8	13.1	11.3	18.5*	10.0*	11.0*
2	19.3	18.8	15.1	23.2	19.3	18.8
3	24.3	22.4	21.9	20.8	20.3	19.0

1=none   2=limited   3=fluent
* fewer than 3 cases

time children are acquiring less fluency in the Kaqchikel language. Though studies of language shift in Maya communities are few, those that exist report similar trends (Annis 1987; Garzón 1985, 1991; Richards 1985). That the languages are being spoken less and that Spanish is gaining territory in situations in which Kaqchikel was previously spoken is widely recognized and a source of great concern to growing numbers of Maya.

The Maya response to language loss is gaining ground at many levels, perhaps most notably the institutional. Already, much has been written about the newly formalized ALMG, various writers' groups, and PRONEBI. The Maya perspective has been eloquently articulated by Cojtí Cuxil (1992, chap. 2 here), Sam Colop (chap. 6), and Otzoy (1992, chap. 9 here). Fischer (1992, 1996) looks at the history of economic development in the highlands to situate the emergence of the movement. Specific linguistic issues, such as purism, standardization, and neologisms, have been dealt with by Chacach (1987), Maxwell (1992), England (1992a, 1992b), and others. At present, I would like to make a few generalizations about the specifically linguistic concerns.

Language Loyalty Movements

The Mayan language movement in Guatemala may be fairly characterized as (1) led and organized by a largely urban, educated minority of Maya; (2) apolitical, at least in the sense of the left-right dichotomy of Guatemalan politics; (3) seeking to mobilize the language-ethnicity link; and (4) seeking to increase prestige of Mayan languages for speakers and nonspeakers through education and the publication of linguistic works. I address each of these characteristics below.

Urban Leadership

The study of language shift must accompany a study of nonlinguistic phenomena such as urbanization and industrialization. In the Guatemalan case population displacement due to the 1976 earthquake and political violence in the 1970s and 1980s, as well as the attraction of higher education and professional employment, led to massive Maya emigration to the capital city. Growing numbers of Maya now lead, at least temporarily, urban lives; and most of the leaders of the current movement are urban dwellers. Many of the critics of the movement, especially of the unified alphabet, argue that the Mayan language activists do not represent the great majority of rural Maya. In particular the Summer Institute of Linguistics, which is linked to an extensive network of evangelical churches throughout the countryside, has protested vigorously that the new alphabet violates the human rights of the Maya masses.

However, it is not unusual for the leaders of a language loyalty movement to be somewhat atypical of their brethren. In fact, it may be the very difference of their experience that enables them to lead such struggles. Fishman notes:

> advocates of languages that are undergoing displacement are often much more exposed to (and identified with) the values and methods of their linguistic competitors than were their less exposed (and less threatened) predecessors. As a result, they are more likely to adopt organized protective and publicity measures from more "advantaged" co-territorial (other-tongue) models to serve language maintenance purposes. (1988: 44)

Critics also claim that many Mayan language activists are not fully fluent speakers themselves and that they do not fully participate in the traditional culture of their rural counterparts; somehow this divergence negates any right to claim representative authority. However, from what we know of other such movements, a more authentic Maya voice is not likely to emerge. As Fishman observes:

> a language undergoing massive displacement may be retained most fully by increasingly atypical and self-consciously mobilized population as displacement progresses. Nevertheless, it is also clear that ideologies normally mobilize only a relatively younger, more active, and perhaps more alienated or dislocated segment of any language population. Language maintenance may depend most on nationalist ideologies in populations whose lives have otherwise

been greatly dislocated, and it may also depend least on such ideologies in those populations that have best preserved their total social context against the winds of change. (1988: 184)

A basic irony obtains that must be recognized: urban dwellers are more inclined to language shift than rural dwellers. Yet language revival movements, language loyalty movements, and organized language maintenance efforts have commonly originated and had their greatest impact in cities.

Further results of my research in the four Kaqchikel communities mentioned found that the group reporting stable intergenerational bilingualism was the youngest and most highly educated. Respondents were asked which language they used most with their parents and with their offspring: Spanish, Kaqchikel Maya, or both. The initial intent of these questions was to identify the *shift generation*, those parents who spoke Kaqchikel Maya with their parents but Spanish with their offspring, thus triggering a language shift to Spanish. They were expected to be the younger and more educated group of parents because of the assumed impact of national education and other growing cultural and economic forces. About 15 percent of the entire sample reported that they used only Kaqchikel with both parents and offspring, and about 10 percent reported using only Spanish with both generations. The shift generation made up about 25 percent of the sample (table 2). Over half the respondents reported using both languages with their offspring, whether they spoke only Kaqchikel with their parents (about 30 percent) or both Kaqchikel and Spanish (about 20 percent). Contrary to expectations, the most highly educated and youngest group of respondents were those reporting use of both languages with parents as well as with offspring (see fig. 2). They represent a pattern of stable bilingualism upon which the survival of their Mayan language may depend. Thus, the general distrust of urban, educated elites as authentic voices must be reconsidered. Contrary to common assumptions, they may constitute a necessary ingredient in successful language revival.

The Apolitical Posture of the Movement

Fischer (1996) and others have noted that the progress and survival of the revitalization movement is owed in large part to the ability of its leaders to carve out a new political space in which to agitate. The revitalizationist agenda carefully avoids explosive topics such as land reform and consistently maintains a discourse of cooperation with the state. This is not new for such movements. Fishman notes the Yiddishist movement in Eastern Europe around the time of the Second World War and the

Table 2. Classification of the Sample Population by Intergenerational Language Use

		Language Used with Parents		
		Kaqchikel	Both	Spanish
Language	Kaqchikel	1	X	X
Used with	Both	4	5	5
Offspring	Spanish	3	2	2

1.	Only Kaqchikel	13.7%	(56)
2.	Only Spanish	8.8%	(36)
3.	Shift Generation	25.5%	(104)
4.	Beginning Bilinguals	32.1%	(131)
5.	Stable Bilinguals	19.9%	(81)

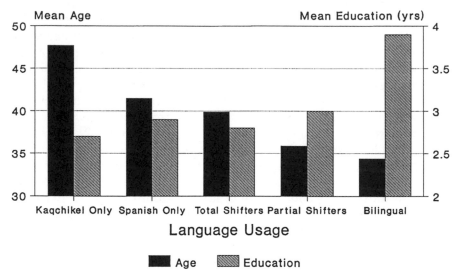

Figure 2. Age and Education by Language Use.

Raetoromans of Switzerland as two examples of language movements that did not have an explicitly political agenda. He writes that these movements turned "to ethnicity and to the presumed language-and-ethnicity link, rather than to either social-class ideologies or religious philosophies alone" to situate their position (1988: 81).

Historically, in Maya social studies issues of economic welfare and political justice have received more attention than intellectual and identity issues. One hears periodic grumbling in Guatemala that the Mayan language movement dodges the "real" issues facing Indians today and diverts important resources toward frivolous concerns. However, linguistic and educational reforms may prove the safest and surest paths to real structural change. Also, historical precedence has demonstrated the safety of avoiding political confrontation, and, within the context of Guatemalan politics, the mere fact of survival may be interpreted as success.

Mobilization of the Ethnicity-Language Link

The notion that a mother tongue embodies the essence or soul of a people is not new. Fishman credits Johann Gottfried Herder (1744–1803) with many seminal ideas on this front, including that "language was also the surest way for individuals to safeguard (or recover) the authenticity they had inherited from their ancestors as well as to hand it on to generations yet unborn" (1988: 14).

Maya activists today seek to raise the Maya's consciousness of their roots. A common theme of *pláticas*, the occasional talks to groups that are one of the prime forums for revitalization issues, is the value of the languages as a link with the glorious past and as a link to authenticity. They seek to mobilize affective factors in the struggle between language maintenance and language shift. The Maya need not be reminded that they are distinct from the national culture; rather, the objective is to heighten awareness of the Mayan languages as both a symbolic and functional marker of identity, to change how people think and feel about their languages. That many Maya routinely use their languages in daily life is not enough. Fishman notes that "whereas everyday, unconscious ethnicity is quietly involved in the myriad of daily actions that go into language maintenance and language shift, heightened and politicized ethnicity movements, including language loyalty movements . . . are involved in conscious and often rowdy publicity-seeking actions on behalf of language maintenance or language shift" (1988: 28).

For Fishman, the concept of *borders* is also important to language continuity. As national languages have national borders to protect them, he writes that "where minority cultures are strong enough to protect their cultural boundaries, they produce the same defenses for their ethnocultural mother tongues. They separate populations into insiders and outsiders and they define the cultural desiderata—including language—which are required for inside membership" (Fishman 1988: 148). Defining such borders becomes more complex in the context of a pan-Maya movement, where there is actually a trend away from localized markers of identity at the municipality level, such as *traje* and community-bound acceptance of language variation in preference to markers of a pan-Maya identity. Younger women now wear *huipiles* from communities other than their own, and efforts to restore men's use of a distinctive Indian dress have produced a newly fashioned jacket with no specific municipal affiliation.

Many of the activities associated with revitalization in such arenas as bilingual education and institutions like the ALMG and COCADI take place in Spanish. And as the *functional* value of Spanish increases in establishing a pan-Maya identity, so grows the *symbolic* value of the Mayan language spoken at home.

Regarding political borders, many Maya now seek to emphasize that the Maya world (*el mundo maya*) that their people inhabit is now spread across three nation-states (Mexico, Belize, and Guatemala). They choose to elevate ethnic and language boundaries over national ones, though greater contact and collaboration with the Maya in Mexico and Belize remains an ideal hindered by political relations among those nations.[2] Maya history, especially as recovered through epigraphy and archaeology, gains additional importance in reconstructing the bonds that unite all Maya through time and space. Municipal, linguistic, and national borders become secondary to the distinction between non-Maya and all Maya together.

The tools of linguistic reconstruction are further employed in the quest to develop standardized codes and invent neologisms to replace Spanish loans. Thus the scenario we have today is one in which the Maya are putting Western science to use in the struggle to find strength in unity. Western science, however, seems ambivalent about its application to explicitly political goals. Norman McQuown (1990), in the introduction to a volume on Maya linguistics, while agreeing with Demetrio Cojtí's (1990a) list of contributions needed from foreign linguists, cautions as well against falling into the same universal traps of confusing science with ideology and identifying descriptive methodology with political orientation.

In an interesting side note, a well-known epigrapher was quoted in Arthur Allen's article as finding the adoption of the name Pakal (from a famous Classic era ruler of Palenque) by a modern Kaqchikel speaker "scary as hell" because "they didn't even speak the same languages" (1992: 57). It seems the epigrapher doubts that the Kaqchikels are capable of grasping the basic principles of language classification and does not trust them to establish their own ethnic bonds.

I argue that as the Maya bring their own agenda to Maya studies and imbue them with their own systems of meaning, science is greatly enriched. Moreover, in this case, the Kaqchikel individual knows his own history well, including the fact that there was more than one Pakal, and one was indeed Kaqchikel.

Prestige

As Fishman (1988) warns, the term "prestige" should be approached with caution because of its ambiguity. Individuals vary greatly in their appraisals of prestige of a language, and one language may have various levels of prestige for the same speaker depending on function. For example, in New York City, many hold the Italian language in great esteem as a language of opera yet disdain its use in everyday life.

In the case of Guatemala there is broad consensus that many of the language-internal phenomena produced by intense contact (for example, loanwords) reduce the prestige of the Mayan languages for both speakers and nonspeakers alike. The notion of *purity* operates here, and many varieties of Mayan languages are disdained because they are perceived as "contaminated" or "diluted" by the infusion of foreign—most commonly Spanish—elements. For example, the Kaqchikel spoken in the four communities previously mentioned reflects the close proximity and interaction with the Spanish urban centers since colonial times. Spanish loanwords include numbers, conjunctions, and common objects such as "table." Kaqchikel speakers from these and other communities, as well as Ladinos, commonly refer to this Kaqchikel as inferior because it is less "pure."

A growing body of literature attests to the value of the Mayan languages in linguistic and extralinguistic terrains (England 1992b; López Raquec 1989). A common theme is that the Mayan languages possess rich structures that allow for subtlety not found in Spanish or other Western languages. Additionally, the publication of various types of grammars enhances the prestige of the Mayan languages (Lolmay 1993; Ajpub' 1993; Saqijïx and Nik'te' 1993).

Domestic Language Use and Related Implications

One of the most urgent needs of revitalization is to reverse the trend toward language shift. Through the mobilization of ethnic identity, parents must be persuaded to speak regularly to their offspring in Maya, and they must be guided in how to help their children meet their future language needs. First, understanding the shifting parents' motivation is necessary. Maya parents recognize that Spanish language acquisition is necessary to prepare a child to deal with schooling, Spanish literacy, and mastering the intricacies of the dominant bureaucratic system. However, adequate opportunities outside the home for Spanish acquisition are lacking.

Most parents do not see public school attendance as a good point to begin learning Spanish. Many parents recall their own traumatic expe-

riences arriving at school with no command of Spanish and the abuse
they suffered from Ladino teachers who did not respect their language or
culture. They do not want their children to repeat this experience.
Despite the improvements and expansion of bilingual education today,
the great majority of classrooms are still not able to adequately serve the
monolingual Maya student; and despite the practice of speaking Spanish
in the home, many Maya parents still recognize the value of Mayan
languages and do not claim to be intentionally precipitating their
demise. Parents may not speak Maya at home for a number of reasons,
including the belief that language is such an essential part of a people,
like skin color, that it need not be consciously taught or learned to be
acquired. Many parents are not aware that language is only acquired
easily during childhood, and so if there is any sense of linguistic urgency
it will probably be aimed toward Spanish.

Parents readily accept the value of intergenerational continuity for
the Mayan languages. What is needed at present is a practical guide to
raising bilingual offspring. Parents need to be assured that bilingualism
is indeed feasible, and they need specific suggestions on how to distribute the two languages within life at home. Specifically, they need
strategies to teach their children Spanish in a Maya-speaking home. At
present, an officially recognized model for domestic language use is still
evolving. Increasingly a topic at meetings and workshops, such a prescriptive model will take time to develop, consensus building being
what it is.

Conclusion

The Mayan language loyalty movement shares many traits with other
movements around the world. The Maya's struggle to preserve their
cultural traditions involves the mobilization of hearts and minds in a
changing global economy and a changing sphere of Maya studies. That
language plays such a pivotal part in this quest speaks to Fishman's view
that "the recurring role of language in such movements is eloquent
testimony to the ability of this sublime symbol system to symbolize the
fondest and most fervent dreams, hopes and wishes of which mankind
is capable" (1988: 203).

The Maya's efforts to regain control over their linguistic and cultural
destiny have reshaped their relations with the Western academic world.
Scholars of Maya studies today are obliged not only to reconsider many
fundamental tenets of their science but also to rethink their personal
involvement in their work. To respond to William Sanders's statement
that the preservation by the Maya of their ancient cultural traditions
hasn't anything to do with science, I would argue that it has very much
to do with it.

Notes

1. In all fairness, it should be noted that the entire article was pervaded by a very cynical tone, and the author seemed to aim to paint everyone involved in as unflattering a light as possible.

2. In the case of Mexico, indigenous policies have been very different, in rhetoric if not in effect. Mexico historically has co-opted the Indian voice, so that Ladino lackeys of the government are the first to shout "arriba el indio" and to represent Maya at conferences, in publications, and at cultural events. The reality of discrimination faced by the Indian is reflected in the current armed conflict in Chiapas. Also, the displacement of Guatemalan refugees into Mexican territory has worsened the situation. In contrast, the neglect of the Guatemalan state in Indian affairs left a vacuum that the Maya have occupied more easily.

In the case of Belize, the cantankerous relations since the British occupation of the last century and the continuous exhortations of the Guatemalan state to regain stolen patrimony have soured relations. Currently, there are increasing numbers of Q'eqchi' Maya migrating to Belize, where the border is more apparent on a map than in the extremely rural jungle setting.

12.
The Role of Language Standardization in Revitalization

Nora C. England (University of Iowa)

The focal point for Maya cultural revitalization in Guatemala is language.[1] Maya are concerned with language maintenance in the face of increasing signs of language shift, they are concerned with expanding the domains of usage of Mayan languages, especially written language, and they are concerned with achieving a balance between language as a marker of local identity and what is viewed as the increasing fragmentation of Mayan languages. Language prescription, or the establishment of standard rules for language usage, particularly written usage, has come to take on an important role in Maya cultural revitalization. This chapter examines that role from both philosophical and practical points of view. A complex set of factors operates in language standardization and prescription, but among them historical authority is beginning to take on overwhelming importance.

That language is the focal point for cultural revitalization has been quite explicitly stated as an assumption: "Of course we must deal with language first, and then with other matters." We might ask why it seems so obvious to Maya that language should be the issue of first concern. Mayan languages are still spoken actively by an overwhelming majority of the Maya population, they are unequivocally "Maya," and they are the principal means through which Maya philosophy and worldview are transmitted, as well as being in and of themselves an important symbol of identity. However, it is becoming increasingly obvious that Mayan languages are endangered, after half a millennium of successful resistance to Spanish encroachment. There are twenty Mayan languages spoken in Guatemala and another nine in Mexico; only one (Chikomuselteko, formerly spoken in Mexico) has disappeared since Spanish contact, but several are in severe danger of disappearance (especially Itzaj, Popti' or Jakalteko, and Poqomam in Guatemala), and all show signs of increasing language shift, especially in the last twenty years. Maya who are concerned with cultural maintenance and revitalization are as aware of the signs of shift as any social scientist: an increasing number of Maya children do not speak a Mayan language.

One of the numerous factors that is contributing to shift is that many parents believe, with justification, that Spanish is useful to their children, and they also believe, with little justification, that a child who grows up in a Maya community will "naturally" acquire the language of that community whether it is used in the household or not. As a consequence, they speak to their children in Spanish to promote the acquisition of the "foreign" language and do nothing to ensure the acquisition of the "native" language. The results are becoming increasingly obvious to all, as more and more children grow up without being able to speak a Mayan language. Leaders in revitalization are struck forcefully by the fact that what they have been able to take for granted as the principal symbol of Maya identity—language—is being markedly eroded. This realization has resulted in a transformation in attitudes toward language, from passive acceptance of Mayan languages as local codes and identity markers to active concern with the promotion of Mayan languages in the home community and in wider spheres of usage.

Another question of some theoretical interest is whether the Maya sense of the importance of language as a direct transmitter of Maya worldview and philosophy is warranted. This seems, in most cases, to be an unquestioned assumption among Maya revitalizationists. Only very occasionally does any Maya claim that Spanish is inevitably the future language of the Maya population and that it does not, in fact, matter what people speak, and then such sentiments are immediately rejected or, worse, dismissed contemptuously as "Ladino thought." Woodbury, in a recent paper, takes on the task of defending the proposition that languages are, in fact, "linked to essential cultural content" (1993). In a very interesting analysis of the Yup'ik demonstrative system as used in narrative, he shows that the demonstrative system itself is substantially different from English, that it encodes certain of its meanings because of its traditional and customary use in a specific geographical and cultural context, that it can be used to achieve broader artistic and communicative goals of verbal performance, and that special (as opposed to ordinary) meanings can be set up in the course of the narrative.

Woodbury concludes that if Yup'ik were to be lost, the demonstrative system would of course also be lost, but even more, a whole set of expressive techniques that presuppose Yup'ik ideas would also disappear. He furthermore suggests that English, if it replaces Yup'ik, will not preserve the Yup'ik category system in another code, or at least is incapable of preserving the covert parts of that system. In the first generation of bilinguals much of the category system theoretically could be preserved in some sort of "nativized English" in which there would be one-to-one correspondences with the Yup'ik demonstratives, but in succeeding generations of monolingual English speakers, the mainstream English demonstrative interpretations would be likely to take over. "There could well be too few clues in the English of the bilinguals who preserved the Yup'ik conceptual scheme for that hidden scheme to be effectively learnable" (Woodbury 1993).

Woodbury's convincing argument suggests that Maya are right to be concerned with language loss or shift precisely because it necessarily entails cultural loss as well, and that the assumption that the Maya worldview is essentially different and more complete when transmitted in a Mayan language rather than Spanish, for example, is correct. Warren's chapter (chap. 5) provides further evidence of this in her discussion of some of the issues of translation that arose with the *Annals of the Kaqchikels* study group. What the Kaqchikel members of the study group found, in addition to relatively simple errors of translation that were due to lack of adequate control of Kaqchikel on the part of the translators, were a number of quite complex errors or misrepresentations that required a deep metaphorical understanding of the surface language of the text in order to understand the basic message. Mayan languages typically rely heavily on metaphor, puns, paired associative terms and concepts, and other literary and figurative devices in both ordinary and formal talk. They furthermore are grammatically quite distinct from Spanish in a number of very important ways. Basic word order, the verb-noun agreement system, the demonstrative systems, areas of special lexical elaboration, the treatment of the category of number, and ways of showing the direction of action are radically different. While Spanish is of course an adequate code for daily expression, it certainly is not the *same* code as a Mayan language and can hardly substitute for it without loss.

In reexamining language as a focus of revitalization, it has become clear that Mayan languages are not only endangered, but they also have steadily suffered an erosion of domains of usage. Once they were written languages, but in the recent past they have been largely unwritten. Once they were used in all domains of communication, but today they are increasingly being used in affective rather than instrumental domains, and even these are being reduced as families switch to Spanish as the principal language.[2] As a consequence, one of the principal concerns in language revitalization has been to increase the domains of usage of Mayan languages.

The domain that has received particular formal attention is the domain of writing. Literacy is an often-used "proof" of cultural superiority, so Maya are quite naturally led to question whether such proofs must, first of all, be unavailable to them and, second, be restricted to Spanish. Writing is also useful for wider communication, and the Maya revitalization movement is interested in mass communication. Furthermore, writing is particularly useful for historical preservation, and in a movement that is so concerned with history, from the points of view of reinterpreting it, putting it to use in the present, and controlling it for its own community, writing is an obvious symbolic and practical tool.

Maya of course had writing—the only true writing system developed independently in the Americas. While Maya hieroglyphic writing was still in use at the time of the Spanish invasion, if perhaps in a restricted manner, it soon fell victim to forced culture change, along with the hundreds or perhaps thousands of books the Spaniards destroyed. A number of Maya learned to read and write using a Spanish-based alphabet in the sixteenth century and produced at that time one of the most important world literatures, including the *Poopool Wuuj*[3] and the *Annals of the Kaqchikels*, among others. The literate tradition developed in the sixteenth century survived in the Yucatán until at least the middle of the nineteenth century, in the various additions to the *Books of Chilam B'alam*, but it seems to have become rapidly attenuated elsewhere, with the only important later document in the highlands being the *Xajooj Tuun*, or *Rab'inal Achi* (written in K'ichee' in the nineteenth century). In the twentieth century there have been individuals who have known how to read and write in Mayan languages, but the knowledge has not been widespread and has not led to any appreciable literary production.

In order to reextend the domain of Mayan languages to the literary and written, it has been necessary to create a number of practical tools and to begin to consider, in detail, what literacy means. Mayan languages have had, since the sixteenth century, a Latin character alphabet, but during the present century slightly different versions of the alphabet have been used by almost every institution or individual who has been interested in writing. Mayan languages have lacked all the other tools of literacy: there are no monolingual dictionaries, thesauri, style manuals, or reference grammars. Where any of these materials exist, they have been largely produced by foreign scholars for a scholarly audience. Dictionaries, therefore, are bilingual, sometimes in English and Mayan, and grammars are usually written in English; style manuals do not exist at all. Therefore, even producing the basic materials that promote and complement literacy is a formidable task.

In addition to the practical tools that facilitate literacy, intellectual tools must be developed to promote it. Writing, in order to be as widely understood as possible, depends on a set of interrelated agreements among writers and readers about what the written symbols mean, about what version of language is appropriate for written texts, and about the specific conventions of writing that are required and acceptable. All of these matters fall into the general category of standardization: choosing a single variety of a language for writing and the symbols and conventions that are to be used to represent it. Mayan languages, since at least the sixteenth century, have lacked an agreed-upon standard for the purpose of writing.[4] Standardization has therefore received considerable attention in the revitalization movement.

In Guatemala, Mayan languages, in addition to lacking a standard written variety, have generally also lacked an agreed-upon "prestige dialect." With the exception of Q'eqchi', where the Cobán dialect is generally recognized as "the best," most Maya are rather localist in language loyalty. What is spoken in the home community is usually regarded as the best and most proper (correct) way of speaking, with the exception of a few communities that are so advanced in language shift that their members readily acknowledge the speech of some other town to be better. Almost all the twenty Mayan languages in Guatemala are highly diverse in terms of dialect differentiation and subdialect local variation, so the choice of a standard dialect becomes an important issue. Even a language like Awakateko, spoken in only one municipality, has two highly differentiated dialects. Languages like K'ichee' and Mam, with over 1.5 million speakers, respectively, have dozens of local varieties and a relatively large number of quite distinct dialects. In the case of Mam, these verge on mutual unintelligibility at the geographical extremes of the language area.

The question, then, is, If there is no readily recognizable and accepted standard spoken code, how should a standard written code be chosen? There are several interrelated questions here. First of all, who should do the choosing? Second, what criteria can be proposed and actually used in making choices? Third, how can the choices be put into effect in actual written materials? Given the complexity of the language situation in Guatemala, the relatively large size of the Maya population and its heterogeneity, and the relative powerlessness of the Maya in state institutions coupled with the inherent danger in political organization, the actual process of standardization is quite complicated.

Who Should Choose?

Maya all agree that Maya should do the choosing. The real beginning of the process of standardization can be dated from the meeting held in June 1987 at the Centro de Investigaciones Regionales de Mesoamérica during which a "unified alphabet" for the Mayan languages was proposed as the first instrumental act of the recently constituted (but not yet officialized) Academia de las Lenguas Mayas de Guatemala (ALMG). Naturally, any public act has its antecedents, and the Primer Seminario sobre Alfabetización de los Idiomas Mayas (1978) and the Segundo Congreso Lingüístico Nacional (1984) were important precursors to the 1987 alphabet meeting (López Raquec 1989). Almost a hundred Maya met in 1987, established criteria for the selection of alphabets for their languages, listened to opinions of non-Maya experts who attended the meeting but were excluded from voting, and voted on the selection of a common alphabet. This alphabet was "legalized" by presidential decree in November of the same year and is now the "official" alphabet for Mayan languages in Guatemala.

A number of observations can be made about this first standardization meeting. First of all, it is obviously critical that Maya conducted the meeting and excluded non-Maya from voting. This immediately signaled that from that time onward, Maya were to be in charge of decisions about Mayan languages. This reflects a central point in the philosophy of the ALMG: "the Academia de las Lenguas Mayas de Guatemala seeks the linguistic self-determination of the speakers of Mayan languages" (López Raquec 1989: 88, translation mine). This had not been the case before 1987. Previous alphabets and other decisions about the use of Mayan languages had been made by non-Maya, principally independent foreign linguists, Summer Institute of Linguistics (Wycliffe Bible Society) translators and fieldworkers, and Guatemalan government officials.

Second, the reason behind the meeting was that Maya were concerned about the "proliferation" of alphabets for their languages and regarded such proliferation as due to the influence, largely foreign, that a number of different individuals and institutions had had on Maya writing.

Third, the participants at the meeting consciously rejected being guided by Spanish orthographic principles when such principles were not particularly well suited to Mayan languages. Specifically, they rejected the *c/qu* spelling for the velar stop ([k]), instead using *k* for the velar stop and *q* for the uvular stop ([q], a sound that does not exist in Spanish). Where Spanish or old Spanish spelling conventions were suited to Mayan languages they were retained, for instance, in the use of *j* for the velar/uvular fricative or *tz* for the alveolar affricate ([¢]). This rejection of unsuitable Spanish spelling conventions was based on a clear but revolutionary principle: the purpose of writing Mayan languages was to be for the inherent value of literacy in Maya and for the promotion of writing as an extension of their domains of usage and not just as a means for teaching literacy in Spanish. It was considered that the previous twentieth-century efforts at literacy in Mayan languages had all been based on using these languages as transitions to literacy in Spanish and that this was an essentially assimilationist attitude that was explicitly rejected at this meeting.

The decision that Maya were to be the ones in charge of "linguistic self-determination" elicited immediate negative reactions, principally from the Summer Institute of Linguistics (SIL). As soon as the unified alphabet was made official through presidential decree, SIL fieldworkers mounted an intensive propaganda campaign to have the alphabet rescinded. Their tactics included promoting letter- and petition-writing campaigns supposedly initiated by rural Maya (since a number of these were signed with thumbprints, it is hard to imagine that the signers had made a principled evaluation of the alphabet), to broadcasting a number of radio advertisements against the alphabets which said, among other things, that now people's Maya last names would be misspelled and mispronounced, and ultimately to making a "human rights" complaint about the alphabet.

There are a number of reasons why the SIL might have opposed the new alphabet. The institute had published a number of Bibles and other religious tracts using somewhat different alphabets; there were a number of evangelist converts who were literate in these somewhat different alphabets. However, the principal reason seems to have been one of control. SIL fieldworkers were outraged that Maya, and not even evangelist Maya, were making the decision. In reality the "new" unified alphabet and the "old" alphabets were not substantially different. Several letters were changed, but the majority of the graphemes remained the same. One of the principal negative effects of the SIL campaign against the new alphabet was that it promoted the basic idea that it is essentially difficult to read in a Mayan language and that any change (even if relatively minor) would make it impossible. This of course is nonsense. The unified alphabet is an excellent alphabet that represents all of the phonological distinctions that need to be represented, and the various old alphabets were quite good as well. Reading, using any of the alphabets, is at least as easy as reading in Spanish and considerably easier than reading in English, for example.

The alphabet of the ALMG is still the official alphabet for Mayan languages, most of the furor over its adoption has diminished, and the ALMG itself is engaged in considering some minor reforms to its initial proposal. It is quite clear, however, that if any reforms are undertaken, these will be judged and approved by Maya and not by outsiders.

Standardization involves much more than alphabet selection. Wherever there is variation in the spoken language, whether due to dialect variation or to variability in the speech of single individuals or within single communities, decisions about the permissibility of the various forms must be made. Are all the forms acceptable "standard usage" or only some of them? If only some of them, which? Are contractions to be permitted, or only full forms? Are words borrowed from Spanish permissible or not? Maya attitudes about the other choices to be made are equally clear. It is the speakers of the languages that are ultimately responsible for decisions regarding their use.

Many of the decisions that must be made are highly technical, which leads to certain problems of decision-making authority among Maya. There is a tension between a popularist approach to decision making and a technical approach. The popularist approach usually is based on numerical dominance and local interests. That is, in deciding between different forms, those used by the most people or those used in "my community" should be chosen. The technical approach, while not free of these evaluations, attempts to base decisions on a linguistic analysis of the language. The analytic questions that emerge are, if there is variation in speech, which of the forms are more complete (that is, preserve more linguistic information), which are older (that is, preserve more of the historical record), which are more transparent (that is, are more readily understood by people who do not use them). There are well-established linguistic techniques for answering at least the first two of these questions, and the third can be put to empirical test.

There is a small but growing group of Maya who are highly trained in technical linguistics. While these individuals are generally well respected, there are simply not enough of them to do all the work that needs to be done, and they are mostly young people with relatively few years of experience. They still lack somewhat the necessary authority to be accepted universally as the appropriate decision makers. This, coupled with impatience with slow results and certain local interests (that is, the "my way is best" school) that may not be represented among the groups of technically trained linguists, leads to a continuing tension between popular and technical approaches. This tension will undoubtedly work itself out in ensuing years as everyone gains more experience.

There are a number of institutions that are directly involved in issues of writing in Mayan languages. They all contribute in a still somewhat uncoordinated fashion to the standardization process. The ALMG is the institution with presumed authority for ultimate decision making, but because of its very recent formation and because it lacks technically trained personnel, it has not yet been able to assume this role effectively except for the establishment of the alphabet. The other state institution involved in standardization is the Programa Nacional de Educación Bilingüe (PRONEBI), and in many ways it provides the biggest challenge to the authority of the ALMG. PRONEBI has been characterized as an essentially assimilationist institution (cf. Cojtí Cuxil 1991: 107ff.), but whether that is the case or not, it has immediately pressing needs for decisions on writing in Mayan languages, and where those decisions are not provided by the ALMG (and sometimes even when they are), PRONEBI writers simply make the decisions themselves. Since the materials that are written by PRONEBI are destined for the schools, they have the potential for making a great impact on Maya literacy. PRONEBI writers themselves are not necessarily in agreement on many issues, even those who speak the same language, and they also suffer from insufficient technical training, so the institution fails to provide significant leadership in standardization outside of its own activities.

The other institutions that are involved in literacy are nongovernmental. A number of development institutions provide at least some materials written in Mayan languages to accompany their development programs; the Proyecto Lingüístico Francisco Marroquín (PLFM) has as its goal the production of materials, many of them technical, in Mayan languages and the training of linguists; the Institute for Linguistics of the Universidad Rafael Landívar produces materials ranging from collections of stories for children to grammars and other technical linguistics studies; the research group Oxlajuuj Keej Maya' Ajtz'iib' does research and publishes in analytical and applied linguistics; the Asociación de Escritores Mayences de Guatemala publishes in Mayan languages; and so on. Of these, some of the members or former associates of the PLFM and the members of Oxlajuuj Keej are the most highly trained and respected linguists in the field. They have no official status, but their work and the contributions they make to the published literature on Maya literacy and the structure of Mayan languages are taken seriously by other institutions. Furthermore, some of the former associates of either the PLFM or Oxlajuuj Keej work for the ALMG, for PRONEBI, at the Institute for Linguistics at Landívar, or in other development or community action groups.

Finally, there are a number of Maya university students who are studying linguistics at the Universidad Mariano Gálvez or the Universidad Rafael Landívar and who are or will be taking an active role in literacy decisions. Many of them are currently working in PRONEBI, in Oxlajuuj Keej, as teachers, or in other positions of importance for the literacy effort.

Criteria for Standardization

Given the diverse dialect situation among Mayan languages, standardization is not a simple process. In general, two major strategies for standardization can be identified: choosing an existing spoken form of a language and promoting it as the standard for the written form, or creating an artificial written standard based on combinations of characteristics from different spoken varieties. Maya seem to be heading toward the latter strategy. The main problem with the first strategy is the lack of an accepted prestige dialect for the majority of the languages. The main problem with the second strategy is that the resulting standard may be unacceptable to everyone.

Oxlajuuj Keej has published a list of "technical criteria" that help in making decisions in the standardization process:

1. Where different terms for the same concept are found in different places, all of them can be taken to be synonyms and they can be taught as such in the places where they are not used.

2. Where variation in the form of the same term (or rule) exists in different places, it is important to select the forms that give more information and that are more readily understood by the majority. This generally means writing the more complete and more basic forms, and at times it also means writing the more original and conservative forms. [For example, the form for "to him/her" varies between *che, chre, chi re* in various languages of the K'ichee' group. The most complete and conservative of these forms is *chi re,* consisting of the full preposition *chi* followed by the word *re,* which preserves the third-person singular marker *r-.*]

3. It is important to avoid localisms; that is, the forms that are restricted to one local variety and that are not found in other varieties.

4. When a decision demonstrates the similarity between one language and another that is closely related to it, it is even better, because there are a number of Mayan languages that are mutually intelligible. [For example, Poqomam has a sound that is pronounced as a glottalized *w* or *m* that corresponds to the glottalized *b* in other Mayan languages. The ALMG and Oxlajuuj Keej have suggested writing this as *b'* rather than using *w'* to represent it, thereby conserving the similarity between Poqomam and other languages.]

5. It is important to include in the standard form all the possibilities for expression that exist in the language and not reduce it to an incomplete or less rich form. (Oxlajuuj Keej 1993: 124, translation mine; examples in brackets are added)

In several respects these criteria demonstrate a concern with historical authority. In particular, the second criterion explicitly states that conservatism (choosing the form that is best preserved from the ancestral language) is an important factor in decision making. Furthermore, the fourth criterion suggests that similarity to other closely related Mayan languages should be emphasized, a clearly historical argument that also promotes convergence, rather than divergence, in the written record. A brief example might be illustrative here.

In K'ichee', there are ten vowels, five short (i, e, a, o, u) and five long vowels of the same quality (spelled ii, ee, aa, oo, uu). Many people who write K'ichee' are inclined not to represent the difference. One of the K'ichee' members of Oxlajuuj Keej was commenting that she encountered some difficulty in reading the difference between phrases such as "you plant the cornfield" and "the cornfield is planted," because while they are often written the same, she heard one of them with a long vowel where the other had none:

    kaatik ri ab'iix   you plant the cornfield

    katik ri ab'iix   the cornfield is planted

The other K'ichee' linguist in the group said that she too heard a difference but that the difference resided in the other vowel of the verb, thus:

    katik ri ab'iix   you plant the cornfield

    katiik ri ab'iix   the cornfield is planted

The team then proceeded to analyze these sentences to see if some agreement could be reached about the standard form. Should the verb be written the same in both cases, or if different, then different in terms of the first or second vowel?

First, the Tz'utujiil member of the team pointed out that the first vowel was the marker of second-person singular in the first sentence and that in Tz'utujiil and in Protomaya this was a long vowel. The first vowel in the second example, however, is part of the time/aspect prefix (*ka*) and is therefore not long in any variety of K'ichee'. The second vowel is part of the verb root and is short. The group recalled, however, that in some dialects of K'ichee' and of Tz'utujiil this vowel is lengthened in the passive form of the verb, which represents a historical *h* infix. The analysis of the two sentences is, therefore:

    k-aa-tik ri ab'iix   you plant the cornfield
    time/aspect—second-person singular—verb

ka—tiik ri ab'iix   the cornfield is planted
time/aspect—third-person singular—passive verb

What has happened in the two contemporary varieties of K'ichee' is that one or the other of the vowels has been shortened, perhaps because the information was redundant, but there is disagreement as to which vowel should be shortened. The conclusion the group drew was that both vowels should be written long in the appropriate context (that is, ka*atik* in the first instance and *katiik* in the second), and that this rule should be followed in all forms that have either a second-person singular marker or a passive verb, whether the possibility for confusion arises or not.

The final decision shows how historical analysis can be applied to a practical problem. Comparison of the equivalent forms in several dialects of K'ichce' and in closely related languages such as Tz'utujiil showed that the historically earlier forms of the second-person singular markers and of passive verb stems had long vowels. The two dialects under consideration differed in terms of which long vowel they preserved. Some writers have chosen to represent neither long vowel, leading to difficulties of interpretation for readers. The suggestion to write the long vowels for both the second-person marker and the passive stem permits distinguishing the two meanings ("you plant the cornfield" and "the cornfield is planted"), and the solution is also in accord with historical accuracy. This last point is very important. In any number of arguments about the proper representation of forms, historical accuracy has proved to be the most convincing argument available. In this case, for instance, each of the K'ichee' linguists began by insisting on her own version to the exclusion of the other version. It was only the historical argument that convinced them to write a version that was not locally accurate but has the advantage of representing the speech of both localities.

It is clear that historical accuracy can be carried too far, for instance, in suggesting written forms that correspond to no spoken variety or in suggesting written forms that are in fact less transparent than the spoken form. Furthermore, it is still unclear how acceptable such forms will be to people who have no knowledge about language history. Actual written usage will eventually test the acceptability of these forms. What is of interest, however, is how forceful historical authority proves to be.[5]

One reason for the force of historical authority is that Mayan languages are almost the only attribute of contemporary Maya culture that can be claimed to be unequivocally *Maya* in genesis and development.[6] Therefore, citing even earlier Maya sources for a decision places it even more firmly within the realm of the "purely" Maya. Many speakers of Mayan languages believe that some of the changes that their languages have undergone are due to influence from Spanish, so reversing a change by calling on Maya history also reverses the negatively perceived Spanish influence on the language.[7] Additionally, this sort of historical argumentation can be seen in the light of the entire revitalization process of reanalyzing history and putting it to specifically Maya use. What better than to discover language history, something that by its very nature must be Maya, and put it to service in the reclaiming of the important linguistic domain of writing.

Putting Standardization into Practice

Standardization has not yet been tested much in practice. There is substantial production of school materials by PRONEBI and some production of school materials by others for private Maya schools. A few other institutions have published occasional pamphlets or other materials in Mayan languages. Some of the writers outside of PRONEBI are going to the recognized linguistic experts for help in the technical aspects of writing, others are making their own decisions on an ad hoc basis, and the PRONEBI writers generally make decisions without consulting very much with anyone outside the institution. Maya writing is appearing more and more in public, in banners and posters for specific events, in names of businesses, and so on. Sometimes it is well written using the unified alphabet, sometimes not. One person, Gaspar Pedro González, has written a novel in Q'anjob'al that has been published in Spanish translation (González 1992); the Q'anjob'al version is being prepared for publication. González had had no experience of writing in his own language and basically made up his alphabet and writing conventions as he went, but he has now given the novel to a Q'anjob'al expert in writing and issues of standardization for complete editing.

Besides the still haphazard nature of writing decisions as they are being put into practice, there is one practical and theoretical issue of some importance that is being worked out. This is the role of speech versus language or, to put it into more concrete terms, the role of the local language versus a wider standard variety. Connected with this is the argument for convergence rather than divergence and for unification of Mayan languages.

Leaders in the revitalization movement are concerned with what they view as the increasing fragmentation of Mayan languages. While they mostly respect the language divisions that have been recognized traditionally, with some arguments over the status of very closely related languages, they are universally opposed in principle to the further division of dialects into new languages. They have also expressed dissatisfaction with language classifications that propose new languages or that stress dialect diversity. The principle of language unification is being used to suggest that wherever differences between languages can be minimized, they should be. While no one has seriously suggested that a single Mayan language can be used to promote Maya unity (this would require large populations to learn a second Mayan language and would be prejudicial to the nineteen Mayan languages that were not chosen to be the single language of unity), most people would like to see somewhat less diversity than currently exists.

At the same time, leaders pay respect to the principle of self-determination, which logically applies to each separate Maya community and language, as well as to the entire Maya population in opposition to the Ladino population. This is one reason why the ALMG, for instance, gives equal representation to each of the language communities, rather than proportional representation by number of speakers or the like. A tension between the principles of unity and of self-determination is thus set up. In addition to the principled recognition of the separate Mayan languages by leaders in the revitalization movement, local language loyalties, as previously alluded to, are very strong. This creates one of the largest obstacles to language standardization, because each community is likely to reject any standard that differs from the way its members actually speak. Even thoroughly trained linguists have some difficulty adjusting to writing something that is not what they say (although many of them have done so). Where there is no already established tradition of literacy, the untrained population is often simply bewildered by being asked to read or write in a way that differs from speech. The only models people have for language are speech.

Standardization, if it succeeds, will in all likelihood be a relatively lengthy process, where local communities are given a chance to accustom themselves to the necessity for new rules and for learning a new dialect. It will inevitably disadvantage some people whose local variety is more different from the emerging norm than others, which may well set up a prestige hierarchy among spoken dialects where almost none has existed. This could potentially be grounds for utter rejection of standardization attempts, which could in turn frustrate the attempts to create meaningful literacy in Mayan languages.

A somewhat extreme example is provided by the arguments that are currently raging about the status of Achi, a dialect of K'ichee' that is spoken in Rabinal, San Miguel Chicaj, San Jerónimo, Salamá, and Cubulco. This variety is clearly a dialect of K'ichee' rather than a separate language, in linguistic terms; it is no more divergent from other dialects of K'ichee' than they are from each other, and its time of separation from other dialects of K'ichee' (using standard lexico-statistic methodology) is relatively short, far short of the time that is usually necessary to establish separate languages. However, Achi at the time of the Spanish invasion was a separate political community from the K'ichee' political community, a difference that was of course eradicated by the subsequent Spanish control of all political power. Many members of the Achi community, especially those from Rabinal, have been accustomed to think of themselves as somehow different from the K'ichee' and call their language by a different name, Achi. The unification argument holds that dialects should never be counted as separate languages because this simply leads to greater and greater fragmentation among Maya. The self-determination argument holds that local wishes must be respected.

There is an excellent linguist in the Achi community who is vigorously supporting the unification argument. She is being equally vigorously opposed by leaders in Rabinal. The arguments that are advanced in favor of unification include the historical argument (even old K'ichee' sources such as the *Poopool Wuuj* say that the people of Rabinal speak K'ichee'), the linguistic argument, and the very practical argument that giving in to local desires for a separate language name will lead, in the long run, to increased isolation for the Achi linguistic community. The arguments advanced in favor of recognizing Achi as a separate language, on the other hand, are largely based on identity. The linguist who is promoting unification has several times been heatedly accused of "destroying our identity" by her Rabinal colleagues.

Another example can be provided by the vowel situation in K'ichee'. The majority of K'ichee' dialects have ten vowels, five short and five long, and this represents the historically earlier situation as well. One dialect, however, has ten vowels that differ on the basis of another characteristic of pronunciation: tense/lax (five tense and five lax). The tense vowels correspond historically to long vowels but sound like short vowels, while the lax vowels correspond historically to short vowels and sound different from either the short or the long vowels. One other dialect has only six vowels, five tense and one lax. The ALMG, for some reason, originally proposed writing the difference between tense and lax rather than between short and long (this is orthographically different, because the tense vowels are written as single vowels [a], like short vowels, while the lax vowels are written with a diaeresis, or two dots, over them [ä] and in spite of repeated petitions on the part of K'ichee' linguists to change the spelling of vowels has not so far done so. The point here is that those who make the difference between tense and lax rather than long and short vowels are not in agreement with the proposed change, even though it makes more sense in terms of the majority position and in terms of history. One K'ichee' linguist who speaks a six-vowel dialect, for example, eventually agreed in principle that long vowels should be written, but when he saw the name of the major K'ichee' book, the *Poopool Wuuj*, written with the long vowels it ought to have, he reacted negatively. The *Poopool Wuuj* is a strong symbol of K'ichee' achievement and identity, and seeing a new spelling of its name elicited a loyalty reaction that had little to do with the intellectual issues.

Achieving agreement, then, on choices for the standard is not easy. Local loyalty often proves to be as powerful as or even more powerful than historical authority. These too are issues that will need to be resolved gradually in the future as the Maya continue to promote literacy and to create the tools that literacy requires. Whether the technical arguments or the local arguments ultimately prevail will depend greatly on whether enough Maya become experts in linguistics soon enough to meet the needs for their services and on whether the Maya continue to respect their expertise. It is clear that the experts must be Maya and not outsiders. Whether widespread and active literacy in Mayan languages achieves success depends on a great many factors, including resolving standardization issues in ways that are acceptable to the public.

Notes

1. Most of what I know about revitalization and the standardization process for Mayan languages in Guatemala has come from discussion with the members of the research group Oxlajuuj Keej Maya' Ajtz'iib', of which I have been the coordinator since 1990. I am grateful to Pakal (José O. Rodríguez Guaján), Waykan (José Gonzalo Benito Pérez), Nik'te' (María Juliana Sis Iboy), Ajpub' (Pablo García Ixmatá), Lolmay (Pedro García Mátzar), Saq Ch'en (Ruperto Montejo Esteban), Saqijix (Candelaria Dominga López Ixcoy), and Pala's (José Francisco Santos Nicolás) for the many discussions and analyses we have shared. I am also grateful to Raxche' (Demetrio Rodríguez Guaján) and Judith Maxwell for other discussions on these themes and to the editors and authors of this book, especially Kay Warren, for comments on this essay.

2. There are, of course, some instrumental domains where Mayan languages are still used, but even here the tendency is to use them locally and not regionally. Thus Mayan languages are used in local agriculture, but Spanish is used more in plantation agriculture, and Mayan languages are used in local markets but not to the same extent in regional markets. Spanish usually is used in organized religion, much more in the schools than are Mayan languages, and for all official state and legal functions.

3. I employ double vowels to represent long vowels in the Maya alphabet. Maya words (including the titles to works such as the *Poopool Wuuj*) and language names are spelled using this convention. Traditional Spanish equivalents for the language names are Kaqchikel = Cakchiquel, K'ichee' = Quiché, Poqomam = Pocomam, Tz'utujiil = Tzutujil, Q'anjob'al = Kanjobal, Achi = Achí, Chikomuselteko = Chicomucelteco, Itzaj = Itzá, and Jakalteko = Jacalteco.

4. It is interesting to speculate on how much standardization was applied to Maya hieroglyphic writing. As far as is known, extant inscriptions were written in either Ch'ol or Yukatek Maya. The writing system has a great number of variants for writing the same thing, but the symbols themselves are very similar over the entire geographic area where they have been found (Linda Schele, personal communication), suggesting that there was, indeed, substantial standardization.

5. There is not always consensus on historical authority. First of all, few Maya have learned enough historical linguistics to be able themselves to construct the arguments. There is some tendency for historical authority to be appealed to even by those who do not know much historical linguistics, and consequently the arguments are sometimes without foundation. As more Maya learn how to do historical analysis, for which there is extensive and well-tested methodology, they are increasingly becoming the recognized authorities for the "facts" about language history.

6. Many other elements of Maya culture (such as clothing or religion) have been characterized as being of Spanish or European origin (in whole or part) and, therefore, or so the argument goes, not truly "Maya." This has been in particular the kind of argument used by the political Left in an attempt to show that the "Indians" of today are the creation of the colonial period. Such arguments have often been faulty in historical accuracy and, even worse, have made the fundamental error of requiring a cultural element to have been existent before European contact for it to "count" as Maya, thus allowing Maya none of the normal cultural change that all groups undergo. The purpose of such arguments, of course, has been to show that Maya are culturally impoverished. The result has been that there is a good deal of confusion about what is truly Maya. Language presents no such confusion, since Mayan languages are of clear pre-Columbian origin.

7. There are indeed some changes that Mayan languages have undergone due to influence from Spanish. My impression, however, is that Maya are far more willing to attribute change to such influence than the facts actually warrant. Many changes that the languages have undergone are due more to internal pressures for change than to external influence.

13.
Prescriptive Grammar and Kaqchikel Revitalization

Judith M. Maxwell (Tulane University)

The Kaqchikels are Maya Indians who live in the central highlands of Guatemala and speak a language of the K'iche'an group. Since the invasion of the Spanish in the sixteenth century, Kaqchikel centers have been either co-opted as seats of non-Indian rule or relocated so that they might serve as suppliers of goods and services to non-Indian political and economic centers. The Kaqchikels, then, to a greater extent than many other Maya groups of highland Guatemala, have been under heavy and constant pressure to adopt non-Indian ways, particularly in language and in dress. Throughout their history, the Kaqchikels have sidestepped direct attempts at assimilation and, whenever possible, have turned colonial policies around to serve their own ends. Petitions from the sixteenth and seventeenth centuries from Kaqchikels to the Spanish crown and its representatives in the New World ask for traditional rights to receive tribute, for exemption from tribute demands, and for the right to exogamous practices. The Kaqchikels, again in part due to their proximity to non-Indian urban centers, are among the most highly educated Maya group in the highlands. Of the small cadre of Indians who have teaching certificates (a high school–level award), approximately 85 percent are Kaqchikels. Of the Kaqchikels finishing high school in 1988, 25 percent had some college-level training by 1990. This compares with less than 1 percent for other Indian ethnicities.[1]

The Kaqchikels are a "modern" people. Many live in or near urban centers such as Guatemala City, Tecpán, Comalapa, and Chimaltenango. They participate in local, national, and world market economies. They are, for a Maya people, relatively prosperous. The income per capita is among the highest for Maya groups, though still well below the non-Indian median. As a result of both this prosperity and the intense promotion of education, the Kaqchikels meet many of the criteria of acculturation described by Adams (1972). Many now live in houses with cement, tile, or ceramic floors, wear sandals or shoes, speak Spanish fluently, and have electricity and potable water in their homes. While most women wear traditional Indian dress as a symbol of their ethnicity, most men dress in Western attire except on ceremonial occasions. Lists of cultural traits, such as those above, have been employed by the Guatemalan census since the 1950s for ethnic classification, but they fail to distinguish the Kaqchikel populace today, and that populace still exists as a strong and separate ethnicity. Irma Otzoy, a Kaqchikel scholar, in her master's thesis at the University of Iowa (1988), explicitly examines and rejects the idea of any trait list being able to identify Kaqchikels versus non-Indians or to set off any Indian minority group. Otzoy and Colop conclude similarly that the official policies of assimilating the Indian populace and the appropriation of past Maya glory as non-Indian national patrimony have failed in that the Maya, the Kaqchikels particularly, are "conscious of their origins, of their identity, of their history, and of their future" (1990: 27). Pop Caal proclaims, "Never have we dreamed of being Ladinos" (n.d.).

Many scholars of the Maya, both foreign (Adams 1991; Annis 1987; Smith 1978, 1990c; Smith and Boyer 1987; McClintock 1985; Stoll 1982) and native (Cojtí Cuxil 1987a, 1990a, 1991; Sam Colop 1984, 1988, 1990; Otzoy 1988), have documented an increasing activism among Indians in the face of the torrent of violence that flowed through the highlands most fiercely in the years 1980 to 1984. This violence, its historical fact, its continued though ameliorated practice, its constant imminence, has been answered by vocal Maya participation in the political process through petitioning, promoting, and seeking to direct or influence governmental education programs and through independently organized cultural societies.

In the mid-1970s a number of culture groups began to organize presentations of short skits and poems in Mayan languages and of Maya cultural practices throughout Guatemala. The violence of the early 1980s dispersed most groups, as leaders sought the anonymity of the masses. But as the violence continued, new leaders emerged, often in the place of their slain predecessors, and these leaders decided that silence was neither golden nor a protection. They made a commitment for themselves and their people to promote Maya culture and Mayan languages. They worked to reestablish the groups doing cultural presentations, while also working through more public and political forums. Despite the relative numerical scarcity of these new leaders, the new Maya elite, they have had great success at the national level.

The Kaqchikels are actively involved in the development and promotion of their language and culture, a process labeled "revitalization." Revitalization includes all the overt political acts mentioned above, but it also includes a daily and personal dimension, one now heavily emphasized by the groups involved in local-level cultural promotion, of a commitment to "practice what you preach": not just to present dramas and read poems in Kaqchikel but to speak it at home, with friends on street corners, in public as well as private places, all of which are acts of quiet daily heroism in the face of constant outside (and lamentably often peer) pressure to relegate Kaqchikel usage to the quaint or ceremonial spheres or to oblivion.

Let us now turn to the Maya as scholar, in particular the Kaqchikel as scholar. Though among the most highly educated Maya, the Kaqchikels do not have a large cadre of professionals. There are some practicing lawyers, several nurses, many accountants, and one sociologist. Since the 1970s, linguistic training has been available to some members of the Kaqchikel community. There is now a relatively large corps of Kaqchikels who understand the structural complexities of their language, not only can define a noun, a verb, and a positional but also know what makes their language an ergative one. They can describe and exemplify the passive and the antipassive. All are committed to disseminating information about their language in scientific terms, terms that make clear that Kaqchikel is a language in its own right, with structures different from those of Spanish but not wrong. The Universidad Mariano Gálvez, funded largely by U.S. sources, caters to the emerging indigenous intelligentsia and offers as one of its few undergraduate degrees one in sociolinguistics. Why all this emphasis on language and linguistics?

The question about language is easily answered. Sociolinguistic studies, such as those of Fishman (1977), Haugen (1959), and Scotton (1963), have documented language as a major marker of ethnicity. Moreover, language is often a symbol of and for an ethnic group. It should come as no surprise that this is true as well of the Maya in general and of the Kaqchikels in particular. The census definition of Indian used in 1954 gave language as the strongest and most secure trait of Indian identity. Unlike other trait-list items that have been explicitly rejected by the Maya, language is considered an important characteristic of their ethnic identity by in-group members. Otzoy (1988), in a survey of Kaqchikel women attending the national Universidad de San Carlos, found that all listed the Kaqchikel language as the single most important feature in maintaining Indian identity and as a symbol thereof. This was true even for those Kaqchikel women who did not speak the language or who were only semispeakers. There is agreement among the more rural Kaqchikels as well that the language is the single most important factor in group identity, cohesion, and self-replication. Surveys by the Programa Nacional de Educación Bilingüe (PRONEBI) find overwhelming support for Kaqchikel language instruction and for the use of Kaqchikel as the medium of education in general, despite the fact that many believe that Kaqchikel is not useful for modern economic conditions and personal life advancement and that Spanish is a sine qua non for their children's education.

Given the importance of language to Kaqchikel culture, the numerical imbalance of professionals involved in the study of the language becomes understandable. These professionals are busy at many levels. Many are employed in the development of teaching materials for PRONEBI, others teach the language in communities, while still others work for private institutions or foundations or donate their time to cultural promotion groups. They prepare reading materials, texts, technical word lists for various fields, primers on Maya numeration (which is vigesimal rather than decimal), information on governmental programs and aid opportunities, translation of official documents, and works of art, all in Kaqchikel.

So now we have a picture of the Kaqchikels as a community primed for and initiating cultural revitalization. Within this picture, the central actors are Kaqchikel linguists who not only prepare materials in the language but can defend the language scientifically against outside denigration. Now let us turn to the role of grammars per se in this process.

Kaqchikel Grammar

For the present discussion, grammar refers to a formal linguistic description of the structure of a language. A brief historical overview will set the scene. The first surviving grammars of Mayan languages were written by Spanish priests with the goal of aiding clerics to efficiently learn the language so that they might use it in predication and the task of conversion. Kaqchikel is no exception to this general rule. The early grammars are often quite good, very thorough, and well equipped with textual material, especially passages useful in the presentation of Christian doctrine. The goal of making Kaqchikel available to outsiders—first the Spanish and later the Ladinos and later yet foreigners—as a tool in proselytizing continues to the present. In the mid-1800s European scholars became interested in Mesoamerica, and a pair of excellent grammars of Kaqchikel and K'iche' appeared in German and French, respectively, for the Western scholarly public (Seler 1873; Brasseur de Bourbourg 1961). In 1885 Daniel Brinton published a grammar of Kaqchikel through the American Philosophic Society (Brinton 1885). Since the 1940s, U.S. academics have become increasingly involved in Guatemala, and several partial grammatical studies have been done in English. A grammar of Kaqchikel was written in Spanish in 1956 by Herbruger. Since 1970 there has been a burgeoning number of books and pamphlets published in Kaqchikel. In 1989 the Proyecto de Desarrollo Integral del Pueblo Maya (PRODIPMA), together with the Proyecto Lingüístico Francisco Marroquín (PLFM), published a grammar of

Kaqchikel written by Kaqchikel speakers, though the technical language and explication were in Spanish. A team of linguists jointly sponsored by Tulane University and the Academia de las Lenguas Mayas de Guatemala is now working on a Kaqchikel grammar which will appear entirely in that language.

All these grammars are descriptive grammars. They seek to explicate the structures of the language, to show the forms that exist, and to explain their derivation, their ordering, and their composition. The grammars deal with various levels of linguistic complexity from phonology through syntax. Now, however, a new kind of grammar is appearing. A group of Maya linguists who call themselves Oxlajuuj Keej Maya' Ajtz'iib', in commemoration of the Maya calendar date of their founding, is producing prescriptive grammars. These grammars do not simply document the forms that exist in the language and describe them, they set a standard for "correct" usage.

At first blush, this may seem retrograde. In the United States linguists are still battling prescriptivists who, in gate-keeping capacities, are prescribing standards of correct usage and using the inability of certain people or peoples to master this usage as reason for and justification of discrimination to limit their access to education, certain employments, and areas of the public sphere. It is considered acceptable to turn down people who apply for jobs as receptionists, secretaries, and hostesses if they do not speak "good English" and "would make a bad impression." The U.S. Office of Equal Opportunity Employment cannot fight prescriptive grammarians. So why is prescriptive grammar appearing in Guatemala and from the pens of activists in cultural revitalization?

The answer to this is that Kaqchikel, like many Mayan languages, is fragmented. The Spanish policy of *reducciones* and *congregaciones* settled people in isolated and nucleated centers and sought to keep them there. Trade and travel beyond the community were reduced from preinvasion levels and regulated. Town festivities and identifications were organized and encouraged by the priests and have persisted to this day. Sol Tax (1937) found that the primary identification of Maya in Guatemala was to their township rather than to a larger polity, be it the language group or the nation-state. This has changed notably. Tum (1991) points to the 1980s as the decade of most radical change, when violence forced an outward look and even remote groups became part of a larger ethnic unit. Now not only are language groups recognized and valued but common Maya roots are claimed as central. Enrique Sam Colop (1990) gives his own identity as first K'iche', then Maya, then as a man from Cantel, and finally, if at all, as Guatemalan. In this decade, when ethnicities are fighting to establish a unity out of a plurality that they see as a deliberate product of both colonialist policies and reductionist foreign scholarship, a uniformity must be created out of the multiplicity of dialectal variation. Haugen (1959) has noted that the process of standardization is first a narrowing as the selection of "standard" forms occurs. This narrowing must be followed by acceptance, dissemination, and subsequent elaboration. Guatemalan Maya are in the first stages of this process. Maya scholars and writers are giving birth to "standard" languages, births knowledgeably midwifed by Maya linguists. A manual of grammar for Kaqchikel, authored by Pakal B'alam (n.d.), serves as forceps for this difficult birth.

Let us look for a moment at the contents of Pakal B'alam's grammar and note how it differs from descriptive equivalents. The themes covered are almost exactly identical to those covered by the PRODIPMA/PLFM grammar (1988) and are presented in identical order. B'alam's *alfabeto* section emulates the PRODIPMA/PLFM phonology section, and the two word-class sections have the same inventory: nouns, numbers, measures, verbs, adjectives, positionals, statives, personal classifiers, affect words, adverbs, particles, and pronouns. Both syntax sections include the same phrases: the noun phrase, the verb phrase, the adjective phrase, the adverbial phrase, the prepositional phrase, the relational noun phrase, and the state verb phrase. They also deal with coordination and order of elements. Both works further elaborate on sentence structure through discussions of subject, predicate, simple and complex sentences, concordance, ergativity, word order, and question formation. B'alam's prescriptive grammar, however, includes several additional, unique sections. Among these are discussions of the Maya hieroglyphic writing system and the Maya numerical system. These do not, perhaps, have a structural place in a grammar, but they are essential in a document of ethnic identity, especially one that seeks to consolidate an identity and deepen it through exploration and elaboration of the tight bonds between the Maya past and Maya present. There is also a section dealing with the decision to use Latin characters and the purpose of the grammar itself, an open invitation to the process of revitalization and community construction. Then follow sections on conventions for writing texts in Kaqchikel, covering use of the hyphen, use of capital letters, word separation, dialectal variation, use of contraction, and use of punctuation marks. The multiplicity of ad hoc solutions found in Kaqchikel literature has been used by opponents of Kaqchikel literacy as proof that the Mayan languages are not adequate vehicles for written expression. The solutions offered in the B'alam grammar not only proffer uniformity but do so in a reasoned way.

Many grammars and many publications in Kaqchikel differ in whether they write pronoun subjects of stative constructions as part of the stative predicate or as separate words. B'alam argues for the separate word solution: "in these cases, it is easy to identify [the absolutive pronouns], because they are always *in, at, ø, oj, ix, e* and they do not alter morphophonemically when they appear before vowel or consonant initial roots. These clitics, because of the position they occupy with respect to the root, are *proclitics*. The proclitics precede the root and are written separately" (n.d.: 41). In those cases, such as before intransitive verb stems, when the absolutives show morphophonemic alternation conditioned by the initial segment of the root, the pronouns are written as part of the verb word.

> preverbal (with alternation)
> > atin "bathe"
> > > y*i*natin y*o*jatin
> > > y*a*tatin y*i*xtatin
> > > natin ye'atin
>
> > muxan "swim"
> > > y*i*muxan y*o*jmuxan
> > > y*a*muxan y*i*smuxan
> > > nimuxan yemuxan
>
> with nonverbal predicates (no alternation)
> > ajanel "carpenter"
> > > in ajanel oj ajanela'
> > > at ajanel ix ajancla'
> > > ajanel e ajanela'
>
> > tikonel "farmer, planter"
> > > in tikonel oj tikonela'
> > > at tikonel ix tikonela'
> > > tikonel e tikonela'

While the sections of the B'alam grammar may mimic predecessor grammars, the content does not always. The PRODIPMA/PLFM grammar rightly states that SVO (subject verb object) is the most common word order and is unmarked. The B'alam grammar gives VOS (verb object subject) and further states that "the basic word order of Kaqchikel is completely opposed to that of Spanish, which is SVO" (n.d.: 137). B'alam bases this observation not on a modern text count but on an analysis of the postinvasion documents *Annals of the Kaqchikels* and the *Títulos de Xpantzay*. This highlights another property of revitalization, a move to define oneself independently of the dominant culture. Borrowings are largely eliminated. The section on coordination in B'alam's grammar does not include the two most common conjunctions heard in spoken Kaqchikel, *y* (and) and *pero* (but). Nor does it include the ubiquitous *entonces* (then) with its variants *tons* and *tonce*. Maya linguists are aware that borrowing is a common phenomenon in languages of the world. They know the statistic that 60 percent of the active American English vocabulary based on the 10,000 most commonly used words in newspaper reporting is borrowed from French. They point out, however, that today the structural relationship of English and French speakers in the United States is not that of the Kaqchikel and Spanish speakers in Guatemala. The Kaqchikels are labeled illegitimate, and proof of that illegitimacy is the "insufficiency" of their language as shown in the "constant" recourse to borrowing. The Kaqchikels counter this in two ways: by seeking to educate the non-Indian populace as they have been educated in linguistics, and by using their linguistic training both to use the morphological and phonological resources of the language to form neologisms and to scan the historical record for older, appropriate forms in disuse. Pakal B'alam has produced a document that can do both, though its primary audience is intended to be the Kaqchikel populace.

Standardization does not occur without repercussions in the structure of the language itself. Natural languages are constantly changing, and within a speech community there is synchronic variation. Those who write the first texts, be they prescriptive grammars, schoolbooks, or readers, codify the emergent standard. Most of the writers of "new" standard Kaqchikel are young writers in their twenties and thirties. The Kaqchikel that these authors speak and represent differs in some systematic ways from that of their parents. Sometimes the grammatical analyses of these young writers suggest that their parents' forms are more "original" or more generalizable, and these forms are often *prescribed*, but they do not always show up in the ordinary writing and production of texts.

One example is the use of the focus antipassive. Linguists describing the common usage of Kaqchikel twenty years ago (Blair 1969; Kaufman 1974; Norman 1974; Krueger 1984) indicate that the most unmarked word order was VOS. All other logically possible word orders were restricted in pragmatic usage and/or marked morphologically and syntactically. Saqijïx and Nik'te' (1993) show this still to be the case for the K'iche'an languages, though the variation is becoming more statistically weighted toward subject-initial collocations in the speech and writing of younger speakers, and some word orders now seem ambiguous or even receive different readings among younger language users. However, a sentence count in books published in Kaqchikel within the past five years reveals that those sentences with two overt, nonoblique noun phrases are subject initial.[2] Moreover, they are subject initial without any complications being added to the verbal morphology. This constitutes a change in the rules of Kaqchikel grammar. The following examples illustrate the state of affairs ten to fifteen years ago.

Word order and verbal morphology
1.   xukamis*aj*   ri äk'   ri achin
         killed   the chicken   the man

2.   ri achin   xkamisan   ri äk'
         the man   killed   the chicken

3.   * ri achin   xukamisaj   ri äk'
         the man   killed   the chicken

At the point in time illustrated above, in order to move the subject noun phrase (NP) to a preverbal position it is necessary to change the verb form. Notice that sentence 1 contains a //u-// pronoun marker that agrees with the subject NP. In sentence 2, with the subject NP appearing before the verb, the verb loses this pronoun-marking agreement, and the verbal suffix changes from the transitive //-aj// to the intransitive //-an//.[3] The loss of verbal agreement with the noun and the marking of the verb with the suffix //-an// are necessary correlates of "extracting" the subject NP and placing it before the verb. Sentence 3, which shows reordering with no change in the verbal morphology, is ungrammatical (marked by the asterisk). Native speakers of Kaqchikel did not use such constructions ten to fifteen years ago.

However, times change. Most young Kaqchikel speakers now attend national or private schools. They become literate in Spanish. One of the permitted and statistically prominent word orders in Spanish is SVO. Many of these young Kaqchikels had been prepared for school by their parents speaking Spanish in the home to avoid schoolroom discrimination and the trauma of facing a new learning situation in an alien language. Kaqchikel instruction was often lacking or nonsystematic in the schools. Later many of these young people became literate in Kaqchikel; some received advanced training in linguistics, participating in technical courses at the PLFM, in short courses offered by PRONEBI, the Coordinadora Cakchiquel de Desarrollo Integral (COCADI), the Comité Nacional de Alfabetización (CONALFA), and in linguistics programs at the Universidad Rafael Landívar and Universidad Mariano Gálvez. This cadre of well-prepared young academicians has begun the enormous task of establishing a body of literature and, in the process, codifying (hence, standardizing) written Kaqchikel.

An examination of the past five years of output from the Universidad

Rafael Landívar's Linguistics Center and of the past ten years of PRONEBI publications shows that the writing now reflects a different set of practices in Kaqchikel. These practices are illustrated briefly below.

Word order and verbal morphology: current practice

4. xukamisaj   ri äk'   ri achin
   killed   the chicken   the man

5. ri achin   xukamisaj   ri äk'
   the man   killed   the chicken

6. ri achin   xkamisan   ri äk'
   the man   killed   the chicken

Today, both sentences 5 and 6 are used. Sentence 5 is no longer considered ill formed, except prescriptively. In fact, the order SVO has become the statistically preponderant one, without any shift in verbal morphology. Sentences such as 6 still occur, but they are very infrequent in writing. In speech they tend to appear only in linguistics lectures in Kaqchikel or in the usage of speakers over age thirty. Sentences such as 4 are also on the decline. Younger speakers often understand them in context, but if asked about the construction in isolation they will reword the sentences as 5 and call 4 confusing or ambiguous.

This represents a change in the language. A previously ungrammatical form has become acceptable and accepted. In fact, it has become predominant. The previously required form for fronted subjects, that with the antipassive marker //-an//, has greatly decreased in usage, and the old "normal" form with "unmarked" word order also occurs less often and is no longer considered clear. The presence of the "new" dominant form (the fronted subject noun with the normal, "unmarked," transitive verbal morphology) is setting the standard in overwhelming numbers in the written texts of Kaqchikel. In the process of standardization, new elements will be and are being codified into Kaqchikel. The example of word order shift and verbal morphology realignment is but one of myriad tokens of language change being encoded into the standard language. Language change with standardization is inevitable and part of the process.

Language changes as particular lexical items are selected as standard. Such choices are commonplace in all standardized and standardizing languages. When there are multiple lexical items with the "same" meaning, a standard often employs one term more than others or exclusively. In English, "pants" is statistically preferred to "trousers" or "britches." "Trousers" and "britches" are assigned connotative loads according to the values associated with the speakers of the English varieties in which the words are normal. In Kaqchikel standardizers, the authors of the new literacy, must choose between disparate lexical items as well. "Cat," for example, may be represented as mis, *mes, lux, syan,* or *si'an.* PRONEBI has established a "lexical" policy, offering the most generally used term in the textbooks, but it instructs teachers, via manuals and training courses, that other terms are available and suggests that the local variant be taught alongside the printed term as a coequal synonym. In practice, the geographically most dispersed term has not always been that printed in PRONEBI materials, since data are skewed by the surveys available at printing and the backgrounds of the technical writers. However, the policy offers a working solution to the problem of multiple lexical variants and tries to avoid stigmatizing those not chosen for the printed page. Other authors have worked without a policy, writing as they themselves speak, so a variety of dialectical usages could potentially appear. Again, in practice, the diversity of Kaqchikel is underrepresented in print, because those writers getting into print seem to be from a few municipalities, those with good avenues to educational opportunities and channels into press. These towns seem to share a variety of features, while maintaining separate identifying characteristics, but the printed word does underrepresent varieties of Kaqchikel spoken away from the central Kaqchikel communities.

Morphology also varies from community to community, and again the writing practice will determine which forms become the norm. For example, there is dialectal variation concerning the suffix //-xtaj//. This suffix added to a verb will alter its meaning. See the examples below.

7.	xutz'ët		s/he saw
	(a)	xutz'etxtaj	s/he saw quickly, s/he glanced
	(b)	xutz'etxtaj	s/he saw suddenly
	(c)	xutz'etxtaj	s/he saw small things, s/he peeked, s/he saw (diminutive)

Not all these meanings for the forms with the //-xtaj// suffix are available in all communities. In some communities, the only meaning is "to do something volitionally quickly" (a). In some towns, the form can only mean "to do something involuntarily quickly or by surprise" (b). In other places, the only form is that the action was somehow "diminutive," in this case, either a small look at something or a look at something small (c). Some communities allow both readings (a) and (b); others allow (a), (b), and (c). Few instances of this suffix as yet appear in the printed Kaqchikel corpus, but usages (a) and (c) have surfaced, while (b) has not. Policy statements typically have not been applied to morphological variation by PRONEBI, though again instructors are asked to use the local variants as alternatives when they differ from those on the printed page. But as morphology is less transparent, it is less available to instructors for systematic analysis and application of relative standards. The morphological standards are being set almost exclusively by what makes it into print.

Variation at the lexical level is accessible. Speakers can easily notice it and express opinions, observations, and judgments about it. Morphology is less accessible; untrained speakers have difficulty pinpointing points of difference and their implications. This is even more true of the syntactic level. People are aware that their speech varieties differ but find it difficult to do more than exemplify the differences. Explanations tend to be prescriptive and often derivative of rules learned for Spanish, rules not applicable to the Mayan linguistic stock.

I will close with a final example of a syntactic change that is being codified de facto by publication. At one point, movement of an adverb to a preverbal position required the insertion of the word *wi* at the extraction site, the place the adverb would occupy in an unmarked word order. As more and more elements began to be accepted preverbally, however, the strictness of this injunction faltered. Over the past twenty years, the movement of adverbs into a preverbal position has become acceptable without *wi*. *Wi* now appears only occasionally, though it seems safely fossilized in questions about location and direction.

8.	pa rutinamit	xb'ey	wi	rija'
	to his-town	he-went	extraction trace	he
9.	pa rutinamit	xb'ey		rija'
	to his-town	he-went		he
10.	akuchi'	xb'ey	wi	rija'?
	where	he-went	extraction trace	he
11.	?akuchi'	xb'ey		rija'?[4]
	where	he-went		he

Sentence 8 represents a construction that was once common but is now seldom heard; it is judged "okay" but stilted; sentence 9, without the *wi* trace, "sounds better." Sentence 10 is the standard question phrase for "where did he go?" This is such a common construction that 10 remains the norm; sentence 11 is heard and accepted without correction, unless attention is drawn to it, as in a text on grammar. When questions are asked about the presence or absence of *wi*, speakers find their judgments waver. The motivation for the *wi* trace, the desensitizing of the preverbal position, is dying out. Many elements, including subject nouns, can now hold that position with impunity. As the markedness of the preverbal position decreases, so does the need to mark movement from a site, the *wi* spot, to that position. In the recently published Kaqchikel texts, the number of *wi* particles in nonquestion constructions is extremely small. Sentences with fronted adverbials occur with no *wi* traces. This statistical distribution is the inverse of the earlier pattern and represents another linguistic change in progress, one given impetus by the weight of the "newly" written word.

Kaqchikel is a vital, expanding language, and as such it is changing. At the same time, social change has brought the cultural and linguistic revitalization movement to a vigorous boil. Language as both the external and internal symbol of a people is a crucial element in emerging ethnic presentation. The standardization, through the weight of publication and under the critical guiding light of autochthonous prescriptive grammars, is capturing a historic moment, gelling linguistic change, and forging a new language, that of a "correct" written standard, a norm. This norm is definitionally new; its dissemination and acceptance will be crucial steps in the new definition of Kaqchikel (and Maya) being.

Let me close with the statement of purpose from B'alam's grammatical treatise, a purpose I share in this presentation, to show the place of prescriptive grammar in Kaqchikel (and Maya) revitalization:

> on this occasion, we have taken as a base [for the work of standardization and normativization] ancient sources, sources from the language itself [as spoken], and also aspects which exist in other Mayan languages, since the degree of similarity is very noticeable and no one can deny the relationship between the said languages, knowing the common terms and grammatical structures; the preceding is palpable evidence of the common trunk that unites the Mayan languages. (N.d.: 9)

Notes

1. These figures are based on estimates by the Proyecto de Desarrollo Integral del Pueblo Maya (PRODIPMA).

2. Eighty percent of the sentences with two nonpronominal, nonoblique noun phrases have SVO order.

3. This particular intransitive marker indicates antipassive, that is, that the NP remaining in direct (nonoblique) relationship to the verb is the patient, the agent having been "removed."

4. The symbol "?" before an example sentence is a linguistic convention that indicates that native speakers find such sentences intelligible but awkward or nonnative.

14.
Maya Education: A Historical and Contemporary Analysis of Mayan Language Education Policy

Julia Becker Richards (Universidad Rafael Landívar)
Michael Richards (Universidad del Valle de Guatemala)

This chapter has a threefold purpose: (1) to provide a historical overview of the state-delivered forms of education to which Maya schoolchildren have been subjected; (2) to examine recent political events that have reshaped the conceptions of society, state, and schooling that Maya hold; and (3) to describe recent trends in Guatemalan language education policy with a focus on the recent phenomenon of Escuelas Mayas (community-based Maya schools that seek to reinforce Mayan languages and culture). Specifically, this chapter describes bilingual education efforts of the past three decades and the current status of the Programa Nacional de Educación Bilingüe (PRONEBI). In the last section of the essay, we analyze the political movement of Maya educational advocacy in the context of the Escuelas Mayas.

Historical Background

Legislation enacted under colonial and republican regimes since the Spanish invasion of Guatemala has cast Maya peoples and their languages as detrimental to national progress. On the one hand, laws have been drafted to subordinate Maya as a labor class within a non-Maya-designed economic order, and, on the other, laws have been crafted to ensure that Maya remain segregated from Ladinos in the social domain. At the core of these legislative acts lie various forms of state language policy.

The Colonial Period

During the early colonial period the conquering Spanish exercised blatant force to subjugate the Maya peoples, extract their labor, and convert them to Christianity (this latter done, in large part, to appease the critical Catholic Church). Using pacification policies that had been effectively applied in medieval Spain, *reducciones* and *congregaciones* did indeed accomplish the intended task of resettling the normally dispersed native Guatemalan population into European-patterned towns (MacLeod 1973).

From the beginning of colonial rule in New Spain, the Spanish crown espoused a policy of Castilianization (see Heath and Laprade 1982), whereby Spanish was to be used as the medium of native conversion to Christianity. Paradoxically, however, the first groups of friars charged with administering newly created Indian towns found it more convenient to provide catechetical instruction in the Mayan languages. For reasons of expediency, they simply overlooked the royal decrees governing language relations between so-called castes and used native languages as the principal medium of communication.

Fearing that native friars were becoming too empathetic toward the ways of the native Maya and diverging too greatly from official church doctrine, the Catholic hierarchy set out to squelch native language use and instruction, and a Castilianization effort of unprecedented proportions was mounted. In 1646 Royal Visitor to Guatemala don Antonio de Lara outlined the crown's Castilianization policy, decreeing (among others things) that Indians had to adopt patronymic surnames; that in Indian towns there had to be a teacher to teach Spanish every day to children age five to eight; that only those Indians who learned Spanish would be entitled to the privilege of wearing Spanish dress, wearing a cape, and riding a saddled horse with bridle and spurs; that the courts not allow speech in any other language but Spanish under threat of public lashing; and that all official and ceremonial recitations be done in Spanish (Aguirre 1972: 373–374).

The Republican Period

After New Spain obtained independence from Spain in 1821, Guatemala's leaders continued to espouse an overt Castilianization policy. After witnessing the disintegration of New Spain and then of the United Provinces of Central America, writers of the Guatemalan Constituent Congress of 1824 worked to ensure that neither Indian groups nor Creole leaders in the Indian hinterlands would further fragment Guatemala through secessionist movements. Toward these ends, they called for the eradication of all indigenous languages:

> The Constituent Congress of the State of Guatemala, considering that it ought to have one national language, and, while those [Mayan languages] still used by Indians are so diverse, incomplete, and imperfect, and are not sufficient to enlighten the [Maya] people, does decree and declare that: The parish priest, in agree-

ment with the municipalities of the people, should, through the most expedient, prudent, and efficient means, extinguish the languages of the Indians. (Skinner-Klee 1954: 20)

Succeeding postcolonial Guatemalan governments continued to propose formal Castilianization policies, but because bureaucratic infrastructure and public education were scant in the indigenous regions of the highlands, there existed little institutional support for implementing these policies. Over the ensuing decades, Indians consequently gained very little communicative knowledge of Spanish. In short, Indian monolingualism in Mayan languages continued to characterize Maya linguistic interactions, as it did until the mid-1970s.

1965 to 1978

Guatemala's rewritten constitution of 1965 declared Spanish as the official language of Guatemala (Article 4) and espoused that the state was to play a key role in facilitating the integration of indigenous groups into the "national culture" (Article 110). The Ley Orgánica de Educación, also enacted in 1965, declared that education should be an instrument of community development and that it should be integrated with other development sectors to promote cultural, economic, and social progress. It stated that "incorporation [of Indians] into the educative process will be considered of national interest" (Article 60). The Ley Orgánica de Educación mandated instruction in the official language at all levels while providing an exemption for teaching prestigious foreign Indo-European languages, which was in the interest of certain immigrant elite groups such as the formidable German-Guatemalan community (see Wagner 1991).

The Ley Orgánica also left open the possibility of using the native languages for instruction (Article 9). Although the law was implemented with the aim of hastening Castilianization of the indigenous population through the transitional use of the mother tongue, it is significant that this was the first time since the early colonial period that the opportunity for Mayan language use in the school was opened.

Under the shelter of this 1965 educational legislation, in combination with the ripple effects of a 1964 UNESCO-sponsored seminar promoting rural education efforts (MINEDUC 1964: 180), a program known as Castellanización Bilingüe was created. This program was explicitly designed to facilitate the integration of Indians into national culture by easing the transition from the mother tongue to Spanish (MINEDUC n.d.: 3). Since the 1940s, there had existed a compensatory *castellanización* program for indigenous children, but this preschool effort was conducted exclusively in Spanish by monolingual Spanish-speaking teachers. Language and cultural barriers between teacher and student naturally brought limited success, with the outcome being that Maya children entering school "were simply spectators, which resulted in an absolute lack of interest in school on the part of those being educated, as well as their parents" (MINEDUC 1964: 180).

Under the new Castellanización Bilingüe program initiated in 1965, the preschool year now was to be taught by "bilingual promoters" who were native speakers of a Mayan language, were bilingual in Spanish, and had completed the sixth grade of primary school. The bilingual promoters received a one-month training course and then were assigned to a school, where, following the three goals of the program, they were to Castilianize the children, alphabetize the adults, and contribute to the social and economic development of the community.

In this new version of *castellanización*, children were to be taught to read and write in the vernacular while they learned to orally communicate in Spanish. After the children had successfully mastered mother-tongue early literacy skills, the transition between the vernacular alphabet and the Spanish alphabet was to be made by teaching Spanish sounds and letters that did not appear in the Mayan languages. Because the *castellanización* program was viewed clearly as a bridge to facilitate literacy in Spanish and to prepare the indigenous child for a course of study disseminated solely in Spanish, every attempt was made to reduce Mayan languages to a writing system that corresponded as closely as possible to the Spanish alphabet and orthography (Richards 1993).

Although the use of the mother tongue in the *castellanización* classroom was viewed only as a transitional step to aid in the acculturative process of Indian children (see Herrera 1987; Richards 1987), the use of even a limited bilingual method by native language speakers helped to increase school achievement and to reduce drop-out rates (Amaro and Letona 1978: 46). By 1982, the bilingual *castellanización* program was extended to 13 linguistic areas and incorporated over 1,200 bilingual promoters and 57,000 students (IIN 1985: 78).

1978 to the Present

In the years 1978 to 1984, Guatemala was racked by violence unparalleled since the Spanish conquest five hundred years ago. Scores of thousands of persons were killed and many more were left homeless as a result of military and insurgency standoffs. Those most affected were Maya civilians caught in their homelands, where the insurgency movement had surfaced after suffering defeat from the Guatemalan army years earlier. Designated by the army-run state as accessories to a

Communist-inspired insurrection, Maya peoples were indiscriminately attacked in a campaign where village massacres became a common counterinsurgency tactic (see Aguilera Peralta 1980; Black 1984; Carmack 1988b). As a result, hundreds of thousands of surviving Maya fled to Mexico or to remote mountain regions in the country or tried to blend into the relative anonymity of the shantytowns in Guatemala City. A survival strategy for them was to adopt non-Maya clothing and to disguise their ethnic identity through speaking Spanish.

Ironically, while the state conducted a terror campaign against Maya communities throughout most of the country, the Ríos Montt and Mejía Víctores military regimes in power during the period 1983 to 1985 opened up a rare political opportunity that actually allowed for the broader exercise of Maya cultural expression, political power, and the use of the indigenous languages. For example, it was the Ríos Montt regime that instituted a Council of State that contained representatives of the major Guatemalan ethnic groups and mandated that some municipal development funds be channeled into reviving traditional Maya ceremonies. Under the subsequent Mejía Víctores regime, the Constituent Assembly drafted the 1985 constitution that reversed the overt assimilationist orientations maintained by successive governments since the colonial period by "recognizing, respecting, and promoting the rights of peoples and communities to their cultural identity in accordance with their values, their language, and their customs" (Article 58).

The Proyecto Nacional de Educación Bilingüe (1981 to 1984)

Although under the Castellanización Bilingüe program school achievement increased and dropout rates fell (USAID 1980), Ministry of Education officials were aware that children leaving the bilingual preschool year still possessed insufficient Spanish literacy skills to succeed in the all-Spanish primary school system. An obvious solution to this problem was to extend bilingual education until schoolchildren did indeed demonstrate sufficient mastery of the Spanish language. With this end paramount, the Proyecto Nacional de Educación Bilingüe was launched in 1980. Two-thirds of the funding for the project came from the U.S. Agency for International Development (USAID).

Under this bilingual education project, academic content areas, from the preschool year (now called *preprimaria* instead of *castellanización*) to second grade, were translated from Spanish into the four major Mayan languages: K'iche', Mam, Kaqchikel, and Q'eqchi'. Operating still under a clearly transitional model of bilingual education, the bilingual curriculum was introduced in stepwise fashion in consecutive years in ten pilot schools in each of the four language regions. The project experienced fundamental setbacks during its four-year existence, the most notable being the nefarious murders of three of its senior Maya technicians at the hands of the army (see Taubman 1983). In addition to these three project technicians, scores of teachers and *promotores bilingües*, both from the bilingual schools as well as from the general public education system, were murdered.

The Programa Nacional de Educación Bilingüe (PRONEBI)

In 1984, as the project termination date was drawing close, bilingual education in Guatemala became institutionalized within the context of the mercurial political currents operating at the time. General Mejía Víctores had come to power in 1983 through a coup d'état against General Ríos Montt. The brutal counterinsurgency policy carried out by his predecessor continued at the same magnitude and then subsided as state terror achieved the desired result of driving the insurgents farther into the hinterlands. The record of human rights violations by this time had gained Guatemala notoriety in the world community (Richards 1985). International pressure was mounting against a pariah government, and, due largely to international sanctions, the ruling army elite set the country on a more democratic course. The army had largely succeeded in squelching the guerrillas, and international negative sanctions were damaging the country's economy. An additional reason for the army wanting to relinquish its rule was the expectation that Guatemala, like neighboring El Salvador, could benefit from massive infusions of military and economic aid if indications of lessening human rights violations were forthcoming.

Mejía Víctores's minister of education, Eunice Lima, was influential in drafting a new education law; she in turn was heavily influenced by members of the national and international academic community on the merits of bilingual education. With USAID poised to help fund projects that would empower sectors that stood to benefit from rural primary education, the mandate was set for unprecedented Maya participation in the education of the indigenous population.

With the new legislation, PRONEBI was created (MINEDUC 1985). As an institution, PRONEBI assumed a vanguard posture in a growing Mayanist movement that cast the Mayan languages as central to the cultural heritage of the nation and a national treasure to be fortified and preserved through bilingual education. Because PRONEBI was chartered with the mission to mass-produce textbooks and other ancillary materials for mother-tongue literacy (and was provided with the financial and technical means to do so), it was congruous that it would assume a leading role in education as well as in broader currents surrounding language revitalization and the affirmation of ethnic identity.

To be certain, PRONEBI has had to cross formidable obstacles trying to implement its goal of "providing preprimary and primary education in bilingual and bicultural form to the school age indigenous population of the country" (MINEDUC 1985). From 1986 to 1990, PRONEBI expanded its coverage from the original forty pilot schools of the Proyecto Nacional de Educación Bilingüe to operating in over four hundred schools providing instruction at preprimary level through fourth grade. The program today serves an additional eight hundred schools in the four most populous language regions as well as in the Q'anjob'al, Ixil, Poqomchi', and Tz'utujil regions, where only preprimary programs are offered.

PRONEBI operates under a bilingual education model it terms "parallelism," which calls for the parallel development of the Mayan language and Spanish from preprimary through fourth grade. Its leading officials, however, express hope that the program will eventually expand its coverage to provide bilingual education in all six grades of primary.

There are inherent contradictions within the power hierarchies of PRONEBI in that most of its Maya leaders embrace a more emphatic maintenance model than the program's state and international donor agencies permit. Within the Ministry of Education itself, as well as within other government agencies, PRONEBI has met resistance precisely because it is run largely by Indians for Indians. The autonomy it enjoys, combined with the fact that the leaders of the institution increasingly espouse an adamant Mayanist orientation, magnifies the institution to a level of perceived threat to the customary integrationist approaches of the state apparatus.

Compounding the obstructivist bureaucracy are hundreds of teachers in the PRONEBI system who oppose the more Mayanist stance taken by most of the technicians and administrators in the central PRONEBI office. Many teachers in rural schools have not yet come to embody the Mayanist self-affirming ethos. In the classroom they continue to teach in the manner in which they were taught, with Spanish being the object and the vehicle for instruction. To these teachers, who more often than not lack Mayan language reading and writing skills and even oral proficiency skills, the instruction of the mother tongue is seen as a burden for themselves as well as an educational obstacle for their students (Richards 1989).

These teachers also note that they are obliged to respond to the constituency of parents who are even more adamant in demanding that their children learn the official language of the state. Five hundred years of an educational system defined in and by Spanish is not easily transformed, especially when Spanish is undeniably the language of power and the vehicle for economic opportunity in Guatemala. For most Maya parents the instrumentality of Mayan language literacy simply is not apparent (Richards 1990). Teachers frequently charge PRONEBI's central office technicians (all of whom are former rural teachers) with having lost touch with the realities of rural life; in the words of one teacher, "They have forgotten how it is out here."

While some Ministry of Education and donor organization officials, teachers, and parents reject PRONEBI because it is "too Maya," members of the emerging Maya intelligentsia, on the other hand, reject the official program because it is "not Maya enough." They see PRONEBI as little more than an extension of its assimilationist forebears, and that beneath the thin veneer of Mayan language and cultural content inclusion, it is an insidious apparatus leading to Mayan language extinction and ultimately to ethnocide (Cojtí Cuxil 1987b; Sam Colop 1988; CECMA 1992). The sentiment from this camp is that PRONEBI, as a state institution, has an apologist function that attempts to exculpate the recent and present regimes. It is argued that although these governments appear to be democratic, they still operate in an insidious fashion against Maya and the movement of ethnic assertiveness.

Many of the educators in PRONEBI empathize or openly embrace the Mayanist orientation yet are frustrated with having to negotiate conflicting agendas surrounding bilingual education. For a minority of teachers in the general system, and for many professionals and leaders outside of PRONEBI, bilingual education has come to represent the crucible for the attainment of Indian equity. Individuals at the forefront of an emerging cultural revitalization movement have promoted Indian consciousness through generating interest in the preservation, purification, and standardization of the Mayan languages. Having succeeded in casting the Mayan languages as the hallmark of Maya heritage and modern-day Indian ethnicity, valorization of the languages has assumed major stature as a political strategy in the contemporary struggle for cultural and ethnic equality in Guatemala.

For the many criticisms that can be leveled against PRONEBI's implementation of a national bilingual education program, numerous changes affecting Guatemalan education and language policy directed toward Maya peoples have been instituted. To summarize Herrera's (1987) appraisal of officialized bilingual education in Guatemala, in just a decade PRONEBI has been instrumental in:

1. launching research, which, although cursory and sometimes incomplete, has provided a basic linguistic profile of Guatemala;
2. advancing the level of language standardization and modernization;

3. opening up areas wherein certain collective interests have pressured the state to implement language-planning policies designed to reduce barriers that hinder access of Maya to state resources, that enhance communication, and that reduce discrimination;
4. creating an atmosphere that has directed the attention of authorities and the society in general to examine critical linguistic issues that affect the country;
5. advancing the option of bilingual-intercultural education for the country;
6. generating a corpus of written materials in the Mayan languages;
7. expanding the knowledge base of Maya culture;
8. training Maya personnel at the level of teacher certification and university degree in the areas of bilingual education and applied linguistics;
9. involving Maya in projects dealing not only with primary education but with the current situation and future destiny of the Mayan languages; and
10. being a catalyst institution, or a generating force, behind important milestone events for Maya groups, organizations, and national legislation.

At present, PRONEBI is firmly ensconced within an ethos of ethnic unification and linguistic fortification. As mentioned, however, substantial opposition has largely neutralized these initiatives. Because of PRONEBI's apparent inability to forge ahead with its philosophical goals, Maya leaders question its capacity and willingness to respond to the needs of the Maya communities.

The historical forces outlined above and the raising of consciousness over ethnic identity have brought about independent, community-controlled attempts at Mayanist primary education. For many of these emergent schools, the fundamental question has become one of direct Maya community control over the education of its youth. The conservation of Maya cultural values in the school setting has become a prominent focus of the language revitalization and ethnic affirmation movement. In the next section, the principal initiatives in Maya education are examined.

The Emergence of Escuelas Mayas

Prior to becoming minister of education in September 1993, Alfredo Tay Coyoy (the first Maya appointed to a cabinet position in Guatemalan history) remarked that under PRONEBI "Western culture is simply being translated into the Mayan languages" (CECMA 1992: 28). This statement epitomizes the frustration many Maya leaders feel about PRONEBI—that although a bilingual approach is used to educate indigenous children in the early primary grades, they still continue to be schooled through the memorization of culturally inappropriate facts in an alienating and disarticulated ambience.

As another Maya spokesperson further delineated,

We do not wish to totally dismiss the mid-1980s efforts of the PRONEBI . . . but this institution truly lacks in-depth objectives for maintaining, developing, and fortifying its own languages and cultures . . . we point out that it is not sufficient to concern ourselves only about language, the construction of some school buildings, the filling of them with desks, and the handing out of some teaching and learning materials if [these actions] are not accompanied by conceptualizations, philosophies, and actions coming from within the indigenous cultures. (CECMA 1992: 11)

Out of a combination of factors ranging from generalized disaffection with the official bilingual education program to a growing language revitalization and ethnic affirmation sentiment, and with more and more Maya themselves possessing increased technical capability in all aspects of formal education, there have emerged in the past few years private, community-based Maya schools. These Escuelas Mayas have developed their own unique pedagogical approaches to bilingual and intercultural education. The Escuelas Mayas are in an embryonic stage and are undergoing considerable change at the time of the writing of this chapter.

In 1994 approximately two dozen Escuelas Mayas elected to become loosely federated into the Asociación de Escuelas Mayas de Guatemala. This association operates under the stewardship of the Centro de Documentación e Investigación Maya (CEDIM), with start-up funding provided by UNICEF. After obtaining legal recognition, the principal task of the association has been the development of a curricular model for the Escuelas Mayas.

Eight of the Escuelas Mayas are secondary schools (*básico*) with a teacher-training and certification component (*magisterio*). Alongside these teacher-training schools are primary schools that serve as "application schools" for the student teachers. Some of these schools work in collaboration with adult literacy programs, such as Comisión Nacional de Alfabetización (CONALFA) and the Instituto Guatemalteco de Radiofónica (IGER), to teach the alphabet to adults in the evenings. In

Map 3. Escuelas Mayas in Guatemala

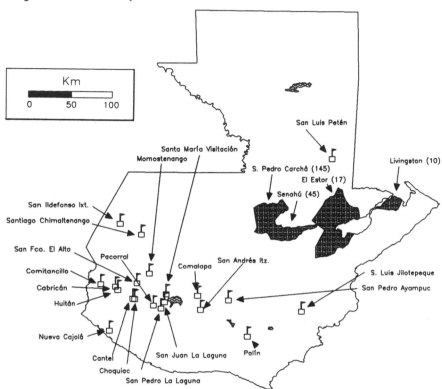

Note: Q'eqchi' multiple site regions are encompassed throughout shaded *municipio* areas.

addition to these schools there are sixteen others that serve primary school–age children.

Four of the Escuelas Mayas located within the Q'eqchi' language area are made up of clusters of satellite schools, increasing the number of actual schools within the association to a significant degree. For example, the Centro Don Bosco in San Pedro Carchá, Alta Verapaz, groups 145 rural primary satellite schools in addition to the central school in Carchá; Senahú has 45 additional schools; El Estor has 17; and Livingston has 10. The satellite schools of Centro Don Bosco also function as adult literacy centers (bilingual Q'eqchi'-Spanish) in the evenings. Map 3 depicts the location of the Escuelas Mayas; the multiple cluster schools in the Q'eqchi' region are shown through a cross-hatching of their operational radii.

While all the schools were established to serve indigenous youth and all the schools incorporate some degree of Mayan language and culture within the curriculum, the sociolinguistic profile and the raison d'être of each of the schools are very different. For example, the one-room Escuelas Mayas in the Q'eqchi' area were established by the Catholic parishes to satisfy a demand for schooling in very remote areas. These children come to school monolingual in Q'eqchi', and the school curriculum was devised to accommodate and cultivate their language abilities. Currently the first two grades are taught exclusively in Q'eqchi'; third grade is a transition year to Spanish; and in grades four to six Spanish is the language of instruction, with Q'eqchi' and Maya culture taught as subjects.

In many of the urban Escuelas Mayas of the highlands, the schools were established for the purposes of "rescuing" and "revitalizing" Mayan language and culture. The Maya children attending the schools in these areas are predominantly Spanish speakers, and their parents have turned to the school to teach the Mayan language "correctly" (that is, free from Spanish borrowings) and to inculcate the children with "traditional Maya cultural values." In other schools, where the children enter school as bilingual Maya-Spanish speakers, parents have looked to the school as a way to stem the tide of accelerated language shift that is occurring in many highland communities.

The amount of Mayan language use in the classroom and direct instruction of the Mayan language and cultural content currently varies within each of the schools. Under the association, the goal is to increase the use of Mayan language within the curriculum so that within the next few years 70 to 90 percent of all instruction in all grades will be delivered in the Mayan languages (CEDIM 1994a, 1994b). The region-specific Mayan language is to be taught as a subject, and Maya culture is to form the core of all integrated subject matter instruction. Because all schools lack instructional materials in the respective languages (as well as in Spanish) and all teachers lack training in Mayan language literacy skills as well as the use of the mother tongue as a pedagogical tool, many school directors and teachers do not foresee attaining that goal for quite some time.

The Escuelas Mayas are all *escuelas de auto-gestión,* or community-controlled schools, designed to serve the interests and needs of the community. Although the schools are largely self-sustaining, most receive some economic assistance from outside sources. Many of the schools were established as an outgrowth of parish community development efforts and receive funding from abroad; others have obtained resources from universities, private donor organizations, and individual

Maya and non-Maya donors. Tuition for the schools ranges from the equivalent of U.S.$.50 to $4.00 per month, and most offer some form of financial aid or scholarships for families who cannot afford school costs. In the Livingston communities, families do not pay tuition but rotate in providing the teachers their meals.

Most of the Escuelas Mayas have relied on the PRONEBI bilingual textbooks, supplemented by Mayan language and Spanish-as-a-second-language materials published by the Universidad Rafael Landívar, as their primary didactic resources. In the Kaqchikel regions, some of the schools have used the methodology and the educational materials produced by the Universidad Rafael Landívar's project Franja de la Lengua y Cultura Maya, a Kaqchikel language and cultural enrichment program designed for Maya and Ladino schoolchildren living in urban centers (see Dávila 1993). Other schools have developed their own teachers' guides and instructional materials or have adapted existing ones to meet specific program objectives.

Each of the Escuelas Mayas has a set of delineated objectives that tend to include the following:

1. enhancing the child's personal and group Maya identity;
2. conserving, revitalizing, and promoting the Mayan languages;
3. offering an integrated, intercultural education oriented toward work and the application of school learning to the daily life of students;
4. developing an "authentic" bilingual teaching and learning environment;
5. forming students and professionals with an ethnic consciousness so that they will be capable of effectively serving in the region through communication in the native language and Spanish; and
6. providing a well-rounded education founded on Maya principles (in some cases, on Christian principles), typically based on the conceptualization of humans as part of nature; the importance of maintaining equilibrium; a view of science, art, and religion as one interdependent relation; and the sacredness and centrality of maize.

From the perspective of language education policy, three fundamental principles have emerged from the Escuelas Mayas experience: (1) the possibility of articulating Maya cultural knowledge through the school setting (as one spokesperson said, "The goal of Escuelas Mayas is to incorporate schooling into Maya culture, not incorporate Maya culture into schooling"); (2) the possibility of enhancing intercultural commu-nication through the use of the Mayan language and the cultivation and protection of Maya cultural values and knowledge within the school setting; and (3) the possibility of the school serving as an effective agent of language maintenance and revitalization.

Although it is not clear how "Maya" and "official" school philosophies are defined and less clear how they are to be operationalized, these issues are of lesser concern to those running, planning, and teaching in the Escuelas Mayas. What is of paramount importance, however, is that the efforts of the Escuelas Mayas are fundamentally a matter of Maya themselves controlling the education of Maya children.

Bibliography

Adams, Richard N. 1970. *Crucifixion by Power: Essays on Guatemalan National Social Structure, 1944–1966.* Austin: University of Texas Press.

———. 1972. *Community Culture and National Change.* New Orleans: Middle American Research Institute.

———. 1990. Ethnic images and strategies in 1944. In *Guatemalan Indians and the State, 1542–1988,* ed. Carol Smith, pp. 141–162. Austin: University of Texas Press.

———. 1991. Strategies of ethnic survival in Central America. In *Nation-States and Indians in Latin America,* ed. Greg Urban and Joel Sherzer, pp. 181–206. Austin: University of Texas Press.

Aguilera Peralta, Gabriel. 1980. Terror and violence as weapons of counterinsurgency in Guatemala. *Latin American Perspectives* 25: 91–113.

Aguirre, Gerardo. 1972. *La cruz de Nimajuyu: Historia de la parroquia de San Pedro La Laguna.* Guatemala City: Iglesia Católica de Guatemala.

Ajpub' (Pablo Garcfa Ixmatá). 1993. *Gramática pedogógica Tz'utujil.* Guatemala City: Programa para el Desarrollo Integral de la Población Maya de la Universidad Rafael Landívar.

Allen, Arthur. 1992. Unriddling the glyphs: A new generation of Mayanists lets the Maya in on their secrets. *Lingua Franca* 3(1): 52–58.

Altbach, Philip G., and Gail P. Kelly. 1984. Introduction. In *Education and the Colonial Experience,* ed. Philip G. Altbach and Gail P. Kelly, pp. 1–5. New Brunswick, N.J.: Transaction Publications.

Amaro, Nelson, and Marta Angelica Letona. 1978. *Estrategias y modalidades de la educación bilingüe en Guatemala durante la última década.* Guatemala City: USIPE-UNESCO-CEPAL-PNUD.

Anawalt, Patricia Rieff. 1990. *Indian Clothing before Cortés: Mesoamerican Costumes from the Codices.* 2nd ed. Civilization of the American Indian Series No. 156. Norman: University of Oklahoma Press.

Anderson, Benedict. 1983. *Imagined Communities.* London: Verso.

Annis, Sheldon. 1987. *God and Production in a Guatemalan Town.* Austin: University of Texas Press.

Arias, Arturo. 1990. Changing Indian identity: Guatemala's violent transition to modernity. In *Guatemalan Indians and the State, 1542–1988,* ed. Carol Smith, pp. 230–257. Austin: University of Texas Press.

Asturias, Miguel Angel. 1923. *Sociología guatemalteca: El problema social del indio*. Guatemala City: Tipografía Sánchez y de Guise.
Asturias, Miguel Angel, and J. M. Gonzales de Mendoza. 1937. *Anales de los Xahil de los indios cakchiqueles*. 2nd ed. [Translation of the original French edition by Georges Raynaud.] Guatemala City: Tipografía Nacional.
Asturias de Barrios, Linda. 1985. *Comalapa: El traje y su significado*. Guatemala City: Museo Ixchel del Traje Indígena.
AVANSCO (Asociación Para el Advance de las Ciencias Sociales en Guatemala). 1988. *La política de desarrollo del estado guatemalteco 1986–1987*. Cuadernos de Investigación No. 2. Guatemala City: AVANSCO.
———. 1992. *¿Donde está el futuro? Procesos de reintegración en comunidades de retornados*. Cuadernos de Investigación No. 8. Guatemala City: AVANSCO.
B'alam, Pakal (José Obispo Rodríguez Guaján). N.d. Manual de redacción del idioma Kaqchikel. Guatemala City: Programa para el Desarrollo Integral de la Población Maya de la Universidad Rafael Landívar, in press.
Barre, Marie Chantal. 1982. Políticas indigenistas y reivindicaciones indias en América Latina, 1940–1980. In *América Latina: Etnodesarrollo y etnocidio*, ed. Guillermo Bonfil et al., pp. 39–82. San José, Costa Rica: Ediciones de la Facultad Latinoamericano de Ciencias Sociales.
Barth, Fredrik. 1969. Introduction. In *Ethnic Groups and Boundaries: The Social Organization of Cultural Difference*, ed. Fredrik Barth, pp. 9–38. Boston: Little, Brown and Company.
Bastos, Santiago, and Manuela Camus. 1993. *Quebrando el silencio: Organizaciones del pueblo maya y sus demandas (1986–1992)*. Guatemala City: Facultad Latinoamericano de Ciencias Sociales–Guatemala.
Benjamin, Walter. 1968. *Illuminations: Essays and Reflections*. Ed. and with an introduction by Hannah Arendt. New York: Schocken Books.
Berlin, Heinrich. 1958. El glifo "emblema" en las inscripciones mayas. *Journal de la Société des Americanistes*, n.s. 47: 111–119.
———. 1959. Glifos nominales en el sacrcófago de Palenque. *Humanidades* 2(10): 1–8.
———. 1977. *Signos y significados en las inscripciones mayas*. Guatemala City: Instituto de Antropología e Historia.
Berlo, Janet Catherine, and Raymond E. Senuk. 1982. *Maya Textiles of Highland Guatemala*. St. Louis: University of Missouri–St. Louis.
Berryman, Phillip. 1984. *The Religious Roots of Rebellion: Christians in Central American Revolutions*. Maryknoll, N.Y.: Orbis Books.
Black, George. 1984. *Garrison Guatemala*. New York: Monthly Review Press.
Blair, Robert Wallace. 1969. *Cakchiquel Basic Course*. Provo, Utah: Brigham Young University Press.
Bonfil Batalla, Guillermo. 1981. Utopía y revolución: El pensamiento político contemporáneo de los indios en América Latina. In *Utopía y revolución: El pensamiento político contemporáneo de los indios en América Latina*, ed. Guillermo Bonfil Batalla, pp. 11–53. Mexico City: Editorial Nueva Imagen.
Branfman, Judy. 1987. Politics affect fiber arts development. *Cultural Survival Quarterly* 11(1): 53–56.
Brasseur de Bourbourg, Charles Etienne. 1861. *Popol Vuh: Le Livre sacré et les*

mythes de l'antiquité Americaine, avec les livres héroiques e historiques de Quiches. Paris.

———. 1961. *Gramática de la lengua Quiché*. Guatemala City: José de Pineda Ibarra.

Brinton, Daniel G. 1885. *The Annals of the Cakchiqueles*. New York: Brinton's Library of Aboriginal American Literature.

———. 1969. *The Annals of the Cakchiquels: The Original with a Translation, Notes and Introduction*. New York: AMS Press.

Britnell, George E. 1951. Problems of economic and social change in Guatemala. *Canadian Journal of Economic and Social Change* (17)4: 398–401.

———. 1958a. Problemas del cambio económico y social en Guatemala. In *Economía de Guatemala*, ed. Seminario de Integración Social Guatemalteca, pp. 47–77. Guatemala City: Editorial del Ministerio de Educación Pública.

———. 1958b. Reseña de la economía guatemalteca. In *Economía de Guatemala*, ed. Seminario de Integración Social Guatemalteca, pp. 29–43. Guatemala City: Editorial del Ministerio de Educación Pública.

Brown, Cecil H. 1991. Hieroglyphic literacy in ancient Mayaland: Inferences from linguistic data. *Current Anthropology* 32(4): 489–495.

Brown, R. McKenna. 1991. Language maintenance and shift in four Kaqchikel towns. Ph.D. dissertation, Department of Latin American Studies, Tulane University.

Bruce, R. D. 1983. El Popol Vuh y el libro de Chan K'in. In *Nuevas perspectivas sobre el Popol Vuh*, ed. Robert Carmack and Francisco Morales Santos, pp. 273–292. Guatemala City: Editorial Piedra Santa.

Burgos Figueroa, Rafael. 1991a. ¿Te deum o misa de réquiem por el V centenario del descubrimiento de América? I. *La Hora* 4(24,750): 9, 21.

———. 1991b. ¿Te deum o misa de réquiem por el V centenario del descubrimiento de América? II. *La Hora* 4(24,751): 11, 21.

———. 1991c. ¿Te deum o misa de réquiem por el V centenario del descubrimiento de América? III. *La Hora* 4(24,752): 11, 25.

Calder, Bruce J. 1970. *Crecimiento y cambio de la iglesia católica guatemalteca, 1944–1966*. Seminario de Integración Social Guatemalteca Estudio No. 6. Guatemala City: Editorial José de Pineda Ibarra.

Camacho, Daniel, et al. 1982. Declaración de San José sobre el etnocidio y el etnodesarrollo. In *América Latina: Etnodesarrollo y etnocidio*, ed. Guillermo Bonfil et al., pp. 23–27. San José, Costa Rica: Ediciones de la Facultad Latinoamericano de Ciencias Sociales.

Campbell, Lyle. 1977. *Quichean Linguistic Prehistory*. University of California Publications in Linguistics, 81. Berkeley: University of California Press.

Cardoza y Aragón, Luis. 1989. La conquista de América. In *Nuestra America frente al V Centenario: Emancipación e identidad de América Latina (1492–1992)*, ed. Mario Benedetti, pp. 30–34. Mexico City: Joaquín Mortiz/Planeta.

———. 1990. Los indios de Guatemala. In *1492–1992, la interminable conquista: Emancipación e identidad de América Latina (1492–1992)*, ed. Mario Benedetti, pp. 13–22. Mexico: Joaquín Mortiz/Planeta.

Carlsen, Robert. 1985. Analysis of the Early Classic period textile remains: Tomb 23, Río Azul, Guatemala. In *Río Azul Reports Number 3: The 1985*

Season, ed. R. E. W. Adams, pp. 152–160. San Antonio: Center for Archaeological Research of the University of Texas at San Antonio.

————. 1986. Analysis of the Early Classic period textile remains: Tomb 19, Río Azul, Guatemala. In *Río Azul Reports Number 2: The 1984 Season*, ed. R. E. W. Adams, pp. 122–155. San Antonio: Center for Archaeological Research of the University of Texas at San Antonio.

————. N.d. Discontinuous warps: Textile production and ethnicity in contemporary highland Guatemala. In *Crafts in Global Markets: Changes in Artisan Production in Middle America*, ed. June Nash. Albany: State University of New York, in press.

Carlsen, Robert, and David A. Wenger. 1991. The dyes used in Guatemalan textiles: A diachronic approach. In *Textile Traditions of Mesoamerica and the Andes: An Anthology*, ed. Margot Blum Schevill, Janet Catherine Berlo, and Edward B. Dwyer, pp. 359–380. New York: Garland Press.

Carmack, Robert M. 1973. *Quichean Civilization: The Ethnohistoric, Ethnographic, and Archaeological Sources*. Berkeley: University of California Press.

————. 1981. *The Quiché Mayas of Utatlán: The Evolution of a Highland Guatemala Kingdom*. Norman: University of Oklahoma Press.

————. 1988a. The story of Santa Cruz Quiché. In *Harvest of Violence: The Maya Indians and the Guatemalan Crisis*, ed. Robert M. Carmack, pp. 39–69. Norman: University of Oklahoma Press.

————, ed. 1988b. *Harvest of Violence: The Maya Indians and the Guatemalan Crisis*. Norman: University of Oklahoma Press.

Carrillo, Hugo. 1992. "Nuestros" inditos. *Siglo Veintiuno* 3(778): 31.

Carrillo Ramírez, Alfredo. 1971. *La evolución histórica de la educación secundaria en Guatemala, desde el año 1831 hasta 1969*. Vol. 1. Guatemala City: Editorial José de Pineda Ibarra.

Casalis, Georges. 1978. Los derechos de los Pueblos. In *Carter y la logica del imperialismo*, vol. 2, ed. Hugo Assmann. Costa Rica: Ediciones de la Editorial Universitaria Centroamericana.

Casaus Arzú, Marta. 1992. *Guatemala: Linaje y racismo*. Costa Rica: Ediciones de la Facultad Latinoamericano de Ciencias Sociales.

Castañeda, Ester S. de. 1962. *Estudios sociales (primer curso)*. Guatemala City: Talleres Imprel.

CECMA (Centro de Estudios de la Cultura Maya), eds. 1992. *Hacia una educación maya: Primero encuentro taller de escuelas con programas de cultura maya*. Guatemala City: Editorial Cholsamaj.

CEDIM (Centro de Documentación e Investigación Maya). 1992. *Foro del pueblo maya y los candidatos a la presidencia de Guatemala*. Guatemala City: CEDIM.

————. 1993. Ixim 1(1). Guatemala City: CEDIM.

————. 1994a. Marco conceptual y modelo educativo de las Escuelas Mayas. Unpublished MS.

————. 1994b. Modelo de la Educación Maya. Unpublished MS.

Celaya Ibarra, Adrian, and Adrian Celaya Ulibarri. 1992. *Derecho autonómico Vasco*. Balboa, Spain: Universidad de Deusto.

Cernea, Michael M. 1991. Knowledge from social science for development policies and projects. In *Putting People First: Sociological Variables in Rural Development*, ed. Michael M. Cernea. New York: World Bank.

Chacach, Martin. 1987. Los dialectos del Kaqchikel. Paper presented at the IX Taller de Lingüística Maya, Antigua, Guatemala.

Chávez, Adrián Inés. 1974. *Kí-chè Tzib: Escritura Kí-chè y otras temas.* Quetzaltenango.

———. 1984. Academia de la Lengua Maya Ki-che. In *Ponencia No. 4 del Segundo Congreso Lingüístico Nacional: Simbologías de los alfabetos mayas,* pp. 26–32. Special edition of *Guatemala Indígena.* Guatemala City: Instituto Indigenista Nacional.

Cholba'l Samaj. 1991. *Agenda con el calendario maya.* 2nd ed. Guatemala City: Editorial Maya Wuj.

Clendinnen, Inga. 1988. *Ambivalent Conquests: Maya and Spaniards in Yucatan, 1517–1570.* Cambridge: Cambridge University Press.

Clifford, James. 1988. *The Predicament of Culture: Twentieth-Century Ethnography, Literature, and Art.* Cambridge, Mass.: Harvard University Press.

COCADI (Coordinadora Cakchiquel de Desarrollo Integral). 1985. *El idioma, centro de nuestra cultura.* Chimaltenango, Guatemala: COCADI.

———. 1987. *Maya Kaqchikel ajlab'al: Sistema de numeración maya Kaqchikel.* Guatemala City: COCADI.

———. 1992. *Agenda 1992.* Guatemala City: COCADI and el Consejo Kaqchikel Moloj Ri'il Pa Runik'ajal Tinamit "Kaji' Imox."

Coe, Michael D. 1992. *Breaking the Maya Code.* New York: Thames and Hudson.

Coj Ajbalam, Pedro. 1981. Algo sobre la naturaleza del Ixim. In *Utopía y revolución: El pensamiento político contemporáneo de los indios en América Latina,* ed. Guillermo Bonfil Batalla, pp. 366–370. Mexico City: Editorial Nueva Imagen.

Cojtí Cuxil, Demetrio. 1984. Problemas de la identidad nacional guatemalteca. *Revista Cultura de Guatemala* 5(1): 17–21.

———. 1987a. *Ensayo sobre variedades de enseñanza bilingüe.* Guatemala City: Ministerio de Educación.

———. 1987b. *La educación bilingüe: ¿Mecanismo para la uniformidad o para el pluralismo lingüístico?* Guatemala City: Universidad Rafael Landívar.

———. 1988. *Lingüística e idiomas mayas en Guatemala.* Colección Cuadernos de Investigación No. 4-88. Guatemala City: Ediciones de la Dirección General de Investigación, Universidad de San Carlos.

———. 1989. Sistemas colonialistas de definición del indio y atribución de su nacionalidad. *Tradiciones de Guatemala, Revista del Centro de Estudios Folklóricos* (1989): 67–100.

———. 1990a. Lingüística e idiomas mayas en Guatemala. In *Lecturas sobre la lingüística maya,* ed. Nora England and Stephen R. Elliot, pp. 1–25. Antigua, Guatemala: CIRMA.

———. 1990b. Los censos nacionales de población: ¿Medios de opresión de pueblo indio? *A Saber* 1: 36–44.

———. 1991. *La configuración del pensamiento político del pueblo maya.* Quetzaltenango, Guatemala: Asociación de Escritores Mayances de Guatemala.

————. 1992. The contours of Mayan political thinking. Paper presented at the XVII International Congress of the Latin American Studies Association, Los Angeles.

————. 1994. *Políticas para la reivindicación de los mayas de hoy (fundamento de los derechos específicos del pueblo maya)*. Guatemala City: Cholsamaj.

Cojtí Macario, Narciso. 1984. Principios ortográficos del Dr. Kaufman y PLFM. In *Ponencia No. 4 del Segundo Congreso Lingüístico Nacional: Simbologías de los alfabetos mayas*, pp. 21–25. Special edition of *Guatemala Indígena*. Guatemala City: Instituto Indigenista Nacional.

Colby, Benjamin, and Lore M. Colby. 1976. *El contador de los días: Vida y discurso de un adivino Ixil*, trans. Juan José Utrilla. Mexico City: Fondo de Cultura Económica.

Comaroff, Jean, and John Comaroff. 1991. *Of Revelation and Revolution: Christianity, Colonialism, and Consciousness in South Africa*. Chicago: University of Chicago Press.

COMG (Consejo de Organizaciones Mayas de Guatemala). 1991. *Rujunamil ri mayab' amaq': Derechos específicos del pueblo maya*. Guatemala City: COMG.

Cordry, Donald, and Dorothy Cordry. 1968. *Mexican Indian Costumes*. Austin: University of Texas Press.

Culbert, T. Patrick, ed. 1973. *The Classic Maya Collapse*. Albuquerque: University of New Mexico Press.

Dávila, Amilcar. 1993. *Dos culturas y una escuela: Experiencia de la franja de lengua y cultura maya*. Guatemala City: Universidad Rafael Landívar.

Davis, Shelton H. 1988. Introduction: Sowing the seeds of violence. In *Harvest of Violence: The Maya Indians and the Guatemalan Crisis*, ed. Robert M. Carmack, pp. 3–38. Norman: University of Oklahoma Press.

Early, John D. 1982. *The Structure and Evolution of a Peasant System: The Guatemalan Case*. Gainesville: University of Florida Press.

Ebel, Roland H. 1988. When Indians take power: Conflict and consensus in San Juan Ostuncalco. In *Harvest of Violence: The Maya Indians and the Guatemalan Crisis*, ed. Robert M. Carmack, pp. 174–191. Norman: University of Oklahoma Press.

Economist Intelligence Unit. 1992. *Country Report: Guatemala, El Salvador, Honduras*. No. 3. London: Economist Intelligence Unit.

Edmonson, Munro S. 1971. *The Book of Counsel: The Popol Vuh of the Quiche Maya of Guatemala*. Middle American Research Institute Publication 35. New Orleans: Middle American Research Institute.

Ehlers, Tracy Bachrach. 1990. *Silent Looms: Women and Production in a Guatemalan Town*. Boulder, Colo.: Westview Press.

Ejército de Guatemala. 1963. *La muerte de Tecún Umán*. Guatemala City: Editorial del Ejército.

Enciso, Jorge. 1953. *Design Motifs of Ancient Mexico*. New York: Dover Publications.

England, Nora. 1992a. Doing Mayan linguistics in Guatemala. *Language* 68(1): 24–31.

————. 1992b. *Autonomía de los idiomas mayas: Historia e identidad;*

Rukutamil, Ramaq'il, Rutzijob'al: Ri Mayab' Amaq'. Guatemala City: Editorial Cholsamaj.

Escobar, Arturo, and Sonia E. Alvarez. 1992. *The Making of Social Movements in Latin America: Identity, Strategy, and Democracy.* Boulder, Colo.: Westview Press.

Experiencias de otros países plurilingües: Belgica, España, Suiza. 1990. *A Saber* 1: 65–69.

Fabian, Johannes. 1991. *Time and the Work of Anthropology: Critical Essays 1971–1991.* Chur, Switzerland: Harwood Academic Publishers.

Falla, Ricardo. 1978a. *Quiché rebelde: Estudio de un movimiento de conversión religiosa, rebelde a las creencias tradicionales, en San Antonio Ilotenango, Quiché (1948–70).* Guatemala City: Editorial Universitaria de Guatemala.

―――. 1978b. El movimiento indígena. *Estudios Centroamericanos* 33(356–357): 437–461.

―――. 1988. Struggle for survival in the mountains: Hunger and other privations inflicted on internal refugees from the Central Highlands. In *Harvest of Violence: The Maya Indians and the Guatemalan Crisis,* ed. Robert M. Carmack, pp. 235–255. Norman: University of Oklahoma Press.

―――. 1992. *Masacres de la selva: Ixcán, Guatemala (1975–1982).* Guatemala City: Editorial Universitaria de Guatemala.

Ferguson, Brian, ed. N.d. State at siege. Unpublished MS.

Fernández Fernández, José Manuel. 1988. *El Comité de Unidad Campesina: Origen y desarrollo.* CERCA Cuaderno No. 2. Guatemala City: Centro de Estudios Rurales Centroamericanos (CERCA).

Fischer, Edward F. 1992. Creating political space for cultural pluralism: The Guatemalan case. Paper presented at the 91st Annual Meeting of the American Anthropological Association, San Francisco.

―――. 1993. The West in the future: Cultural hegemony and the politics of identity. *American Anthropologist* 95(4): 1000–1002.

―――. 1996. The Pan-Maya Movement in Global and Local Context. Ph.D. dissertation, Department of Anthropology, Tulane University.

Fishman, Joshua A. 1977. *Sociolinguistics.* New York: Penguin.

―――. 1988. *Language and Ethnicity in Minority Sociolinguistic Perspective.* Philadelphia: Multilingual Matters.

Fletcher, Lehman B., Eric Graber, William C. Merrill, and Erik Thorbecke. 1970. *Guatemala's Economic Development: The Role of Agriculture.* Ames: Iowa State University Press.

Foucault, Michel. 1979. *Discipline and Punish.* New York: Vintage Books.

Fox, John W. 1978. *Quiche Conquest: Centralism and Regionalism in Highland Guatemalan State Development.* Albuquerque: University of New Mexico Press.

Friedman, Jonathan. 1992. The past in the future: History and the politics of identity. *American Anthropologist* 94(4): 837–859.

Galeano, Eduardo. 1986. *El descubrimiento de América que todavía no fue y otros escritos.* Barcelona: Editorial Laia.

―――. 1991. *El libro de los abrazos.* Mexico City: Siglo XXI.

García Hernández, Abraham. 1986. Breve historia de la Asociación de Escritores

Mayences de Guatemala. *Winak Boletín Intercultural* 2(3): 138–160.
Garzón, Susan Tharp. 1985. Language death in a Mayan community in southern Chiapas. Master's thesis, University of Iowa.
——. 1991. Grammatical acceptability and something else. Ph.D. dissertation, University of Iowa.
Geertz, Clifford. 1963. *Peddlers and Princes: Social Development and Economic Change in Two Indonesian Towns*. Chicago: University of Chicago Press.
——. 1985. *Local Knowledge: Further Essays in Interpretive Anthropology*. New York: Basic Books.
Ghai, Dharam. 1988. *Participatory Development: Some Perspectives from Grass-Roots Experiences*. UNRISD Discussion Paper 5. Geneva: United Nations Research Institute for Social Development.
Ghelert Mata, Carlos. 1984. *Vida, enfermedad y muerte en Guatemala*. Guatemala City: Ediciones de la Dirección General de Extensión, Universidad de San Carlos.
González, Gaspar Pedro. 1992. *La otra cara*. Guatemala City: Ministerio de Cultura y Deportes.
Gordillo Barrios, Gerardo. 1987. *Guatemala historia gráfica*. Guatemala City: Editorial Piedra Sanata.
Grindle, Marilou. 1986. *State and Countryside: Development Policy and Agrarian Politics in Latin America*. Baltimore: Johns Hopkins University Press.
The Guatemalan economy. 1992. *Guatemala News Watch* 7(1): 3.
Guzmán Bockler, Carlos, and Jean-Loup Herbert. 1971. *Guatemala: Una interpretación histórico-social*. Mexico City: Siglo Veintiuno.
Hale, Charles, and Carol Smith. 1991. Reframing the national question in Central America: The challenge from Indian militancy in the 1980's. Unpublished MS, Department of Anthropology, University of California, Davis.
Hanchard, Michael. 1993. Culturalism versus cultural politics: Movimento Negro in Rio de Janeiro and São Paulo, Brazil. In *The Violence Within: Cultural and Political Opposition in Divided Nations*, ed. Kay B. Warren, pp. 57–85. Boulder, Colo.: Westview Press.
——. 1994. *Orpheus and Power: The Movimento Negro of Rio de Janeiro and São Paulo, X, 1945–1988*. Princeton, N.J.: Princeton University Press.
Handy, Jim. 1984. *Gift of the Devil: A History of Guatemala*. Toronto: Between the Lines Press.
Haugen, Einar. 1959. Dialect, language and the nation. In *Readings in Sociolinguistics*, ed. Joshua Fishman. New York: Academic Press.
Hawkins, John. 1984. *Inverse Images: The Meaning of Culture, Ethnicity and Family in Postcolonial Guatemala*. Albuquerque: University of New Mexico Press.
Heath, Shirley, and Richard La Prade. 1982. Castilian colonization and indigenous languages: The cases of Quechua and Aymara. In *Language Spread: Studies in Diffusion and Social Change*, ed. Robert Cooper. Bloomington: University of Indiana Press.
Hendrickson, Carol. 1986. Handmade and thought-woven: The construction of dress and social identity in Tecpan Guatemala. Ph.D. dissertation, Department of Anthropology, University of Chicago.

———. 1991. Images of the Indian in Guatemala: The role of indigenous dress in Indian and Ladino constructions. In *Nation-States and Indians in Latin America*, ed. Greg Urban and Joel Sherzer, pp. 287–306. Austin: University of Texas Press.

———. 1995. *Weaving Identities: Construction of Dress and Self in a Highland Guatemala Town.* Austin: University of Texas Press.

Héraud, Guy. 1963. *L'Europe des ethnies.* Paris: Presses de L'Europe.

Herbruger, Alfredo. 1956. *Metodo para aprender a hablar, leer, y escribir la lengua Cakchiquel.* Guatemala City.

Herrera, Guillermina. 1987. *Estado del arte sobre educación bilingüe en Guatemala.* Guatemala City: Universidad Rafael Landívar.

———. 1990a. Las lenguas indígenas de Guatemala:Situación actual y futuro. In *Lecturas sobre la lingüística maya*, ed. Nora C. England and Stephen R. Elliot, pp. 27–50. Guatemala City: CIRMA.

———. 1990b. Untitled talk given at the Seminario Internacional de Pueblos Indios, December 1990.

Hill, Robert M., and John Monaghan. 1987. *Continuities in Highland Maya Social Organization: Ethnohistory in Sacapulas, Guatemala.* Philadelphia: University of Pennsylvania Press.

Hirschman, Albert O. 1983. The principle of conservation and mutation of social energy. *Grassroots Development* 7(2): 6–8.

Hobsbawm, Eric. 1983. Introduction: Inventing traditions. In *The Invention of Tradition*, ed. Eric Hobsbawm and Terence Ranger, pp. 1–14. Cambridge: Cambridge University Press.

Horowitz, Ronald. 1985. *Ethnic Groups in Conflict.* Berkeley: University of California Press.

IBRD (International Bank for Reconstruction and Development). 1951. *The Economic Development of Guatemala.* Washington, D.C.: IBRD.

IIN (Instituto Indigenista Nacional). 1985. *Informe del Segundo Congreso Lingüístico Nacional.* Special publication. Guatemala City: Ministerio de Educación.

Indian Law Resource Center, ed. 1984. *Derechos indios, derechos humanos: Manual para indígenas sobre procedimientos de reclamaciones en el campo de los derechos humanos internacionales.* Washington, D.C.: Indian Law Resource Center.

INE (Instituto Nacional de Estadística). 1988. *Encuesta nacional socio-demográfica 1986–1987.* Vol. 3, Fascicle 1. Guatemala City: INE.

Johnson, Irmgard Weitlaner. 1954. Chiptic cave textiles from Chiapas, Mexico. *Journal de la Société des Americanistes*, n.s. 43: 137–147.

Juárez-Paz, Rigoberto. 1992. La hazaña de los tiemos modernos. *Crónica* 5(221): 69.

Kaufman, Terrence S. 1974. *Idiomas de Mesoamérica.* Guatemala City: José de Pineda Ibarra.

———. 1976a. *Proyecto de alfabetos y ortografías para escribir las lenguas mayances.* Guatemala City: Editorial José de Pineda Ibarra.

———. 1976b. Archaeological and linguistic correlations in Mayaland and associated areas of Mesoamerica. *World Archaeology* 9(1): 101–118.

Kellman, Julia Ann. 1991. Weaving huipiles: Narratives of three Maya women weavers. Ph.D. dissertation, Department of Anthropology, University of Iowa.

Kleymeyer, Charles D. 1992. Cultural energy and grassroots development. *Grassroots Development* 16(1): 22–31.

Krueger, Chris, and Kjell Enge. 1985. *Security and Development Conditions in the Guatemalan Highlands*. Washington, D.C.: Washington Office on Latin America.

Krueger, Roberta Hendricks. 1984. Cakchiquel verbs. Ph.D. dissertation, Department of Linguistics, University of Chicago.

Le Page, R., and L. Tabouret. 1980. *Language and Social Identity*. New York: Academic Press.

Liano, Dante. 1984. *La palabra y el sueño: Literatura y sociedad en Guatemala*. Rome: Bulzoni Editore.

———. 1992. Los santos inocentes. *Crónica* 5(225): 15–21.

Lima, Ricardo M. 1992. *Héroes de la vida cotidiana: Personajes mayas*. Vol. 2. Guatemala City: Universidad Rafael Landívar.

Lolmay (Pedro Oscar García Mátzar). 1993. *Gramática pedogógica Kaqchikel*. Guatemala City: Programa para el Desarrollo Integral de la Población Maya de la Universidad Rafael Landívar.

López Raquec, Margarita. 1989. *Acerca de los alfabetos para escribir los idiomas mayas de Guatemala*. Guatemala City: Ministerio de Cultura y Deportes.

Lovell, W. George. 1988. Surviving conquest: The Maya of Guatemala in historical perspective. *Latin American Research Review* 23(2): 25–37.

———. 1991. *Conquista y cambio cultural: La sierra de los Cuchumatanes de Guatemala, 1500–1821*. Guatemala City: CIRMA.

Lovell, W. George, and Christopher H. Lutz. 1992. Conquest and population: Maya demography in historical perspective. Paper presented at the 1992 International Congress of the Latin American Studies Association, Los Angeles.

Lutz, Christopher. 1976. Santiago de Guatemala, 1554–1773: The socio-demographic history. Ph.D. dissertation, University of Wisconsin.

MacLeod, Murdo. 1973. *Spanish Central America*. Berkeley: University of California Press.

Martínez Peláez, Severo. 1970. *La patria del criollo: Ensayo de interpretación de la realidad colonial guatemalteca*. Guatemala City: Editorial Universitario.

Maxwell, Judith M. 1992. Linguistic markers of solidarity among the highland Maya. Paper presented at the XVII International Congress of the Latin American Studies Association, Los Angeles.

McClintock, Barbara. 1985. The Maya and the *violencia*. Paper given at the Annual Meeting of the Association of American Anthropologists, Washington, D.C.

McQuown, Norman A. 1990. Introducción. In *Lecturas sobre la lingüística Maya*, ed. Nora C. England and Stephen R. Elliott, pp. ix–xiv. Guatemala City: CIRMA.

Mejia, Marco Vinicio. 1992. Quinto centenario: El autodescubrimiento. *Siglo Veintiuno* 3(717): 12.

Menchú, Rigoberta, with Elizabeth Burgos. 1985. *Me llamo Rigoberta Menchú y así me nació la conciencia*. Mexico City: Siglo Veintiuno Editores.

Méndez de la Vega, Luz. 1989. Folclore, intromisión y discriminación. *Crónica* 89(2): 51.

Miller, Hubert J. 1990. Catholic leaders and spiritual socialism during the Arévalo administration in Guatemala, 1945–1951. In *Central America: Historical Perspectives on the Contemporary Crisis*, ed. Ralph Lee Woodward, pp. 85–105. New York: Greenwood Press.

MINEDUC (Ministerio de Educación de Guatemala). N.d. Programa de Castellanización. Unpublished MS.

————. 1964. *Primer seminario sobre problemas de la educación rural guatemalteca.* Guatemala City: Ministerio de Educación.

————. 1985. *Reglamento del PRONEBI.* Guatemala City: Ministerio de Educación.

Mitchell, W. J. 1980. Introduction. In *The Language of Images*, ed. W. J. Mitchell, pp. 1–8. Chicago: University of Chicago Press.

Montejo, Víctor. 1987. *Testimony: Death of a Guatemalan Village*, ed. Víctor Perera. Willimantic, Conn.: Curbstone Press.

————. 1991. In the name of the pot, the sun, the broken spear, the rock, the stick, the idol, ad infinitum and ad nauseam: An exposé of Anglo anthropologists' obsessions with and invention of Mayan gods. Paper presented at the Annual Meeting of the American Anthropological Association, San Francisco.

Morley, Sylvanus G. 1989. *La civilización maya.* Mexico City: Fondo de Cultura Económica.

Morley, Sylvanus G., George W. Brainerd, and Robert J. Sharer. 1983. *The Ancient Maya.* 4th ed. Stanford, Calif.: Stanford University Press.

Morris, Walter F., and Jeffrey J. Foxx. 1987. *Living Maya.* New York: Harry N. Abrams.

Nelson, Diane M. 1991. The reconstruction of Mayan identity. *Report on Guatemala* 12(2): 6–7, 14.

Nemerov, Howard. 1980. On poetry and painting, with a thought of music. In *The Language of Images*, ed. W. J. Mitchell, pp. 9–13. Chicago: University of Chicago Press.

Neuberger, Benjamin. 1986. *National Self-Determination in Postcolonial Africa.* Boulder, Colo.: Lynne Rienner Publishers.

Norman, William M. 1974. *A Comparison of Cakchiquel and Quiché Verbal Morphology.* Guatemala City: Proyecto Lingüístico Francisco Marroquín.

Obeyesekere, Gananath. 1992. *The Apotheosis of Captain Cook: European Mythmaking in the Pacific.* Princeton, N.J.: Princeton University Press.

O'Neale, Lila M. 1942. Early textiles from Chiapas, Mexico. In *Middle American Research Records 1*, ed. Robert Wauchope, pp. 1–6. New Orleans: Middle American Research Institute.

Osborne, Lilly'de Jongh. 1965. *Indian Crafts of Guatemala and El Salvador.* Norman: University of Oklahoma Press.

Osborne, William T. 1993. The ethical symbiosis between anthropologists and the peoples they study. *Anthropology Newsletter* 34(9): 1, 6.

Otzoy, Irma. 1988. Identity and higher education among Mayan women. Master's thesis, Department of Anthropology, University of Iowa.

————. 1992. Identidad y trajes mayas. *Mesoamérica* 23: 95–112.

Otzoy, Irma, and Enrique Sam Colop. 1990. Identidad étnica y modernización

entre los mayas de Guatemala. *Mesoamérica* 19: 97–100.
Oxlajuuj Keej Maya' Ajtz'iib' (Ixkem, Ajpub', Lolmay, Nik'te', Pakal, Saqijix, Waykan), trans. 1992. Anales de los Kaqchikeles. Unpublished MS.
———. 1993. *Maya' Chii': Los idiomas mayas de Guatemala*. Guatemala City: Cholsamaj.
Pacheco, Luis. N.d. *La religiosidad contemporánea Maya-Kekchí*. Quito, Ecuador: Ediciones Abya-Yala.
Payeras, Mario, and Héctor Díaz-Polanco. 1990. *Diálogo sobre la cuestión étnico-nacional*. Mexico City: Ediciones de Octubre Revolucionario.
Paz, Marco Antonio de. 1993. *Maya' amaaq' xuq junamilaal, pueblo Maya y democracia*. Seminario Permanente de Estudios Mayas, Cuaderno No. 3. Guatemala City: Editorial Cholsamaj.
Paz, Octavio. 1987. Review of "The blood of kings: A new interpretation of Maya art." *New York Times Review of Books*, 26 February 1987.
Pellecer, Carlos Manuel. 1991a. ¡Cuidado con la guerra indianista! I parte. *Prensa Libre* 41(12,798): 12, 38.
———. 1991b. ¡Cuidado con la guerra indianista! II parte. *Prensa Libre* 41(12,802): 12, 83.
———. 1991c. ¡Cuidado con la guerra indianista! III parte. *Prensa Libre* 41(12,805): 12, 126.
———. 1991d. ¡Cuidado con la guerra indianista! IV parte. *Prensa Libre* 41(12,806): 12, 63.
———. 1991e. ¡Cuidado con la guerra indianista! V parte y final. *Prensa Libre* 41(12,807): 12, 70.
Pettersen, Carmen L. 1976. *Maya of Guatemala: Life and Dress/Maya de Guatemala: Vida y traje*. Guatemala City: Museo Ixchel del Traje Indígena.
PLFM (Proyecto Lingüístico Francisco Marroquín). 1993. *Agenda maya*. Antigua, Guatemala: PLFM.
Poitevin, René. 1993. *Guatemala: La crisis de la democracia—dudas y esperanzas en los golpes de estado de 1993*. Facultad Latinoamericano de Ciencias Sociales-Guatemala Debate No. 21. Guatemala City: Facultad Latinoamericano de Ciencias Sociales–Guatemala.
Pop Caal. N.d. La resistencia maya y la violencia. Unpublished MS.
Porras Castejón, Gustavo. 1978. Guatemala: La profundización de las relaciones capitalists. *Estudios Centroamericanos* 33(356–357): 368–377.
Prakash, Gyan. 1992. Writing post-Orientalist histories of the Third World: Indian historiography is good to think. In *Colonialism and Culture*, ed. Nicholas B. Dirks, pp. 353–388. Ann Arbor: University of Michigan Press.
Prechtel, Martín, and Robert S. Carlsen. 1988. Weaving and cosmos amongst the Tzutujil Maya of Guatemala. *RES* 88: 122–132.
PRODIPMA (Programa para el Desarrollo Integral de la Población Maya) and PLFM (Proyecto Lingüístico Francisco Marroquín). 1988. *Gramática de idioma Kaqchikel*. Guatemala City: PRODIPMA/PLFM.
Quemé, Rigoberto, Guillermo Rodríguez Guaján, Ricardo Mejía, and Otilia Lux de Cotí. 1990. Estrategias para la consolidación de la Academia de las Lenguas Mayas de Guatemala. In *Reporte del II Seminario: Situación actual y futuro de la Academia de las Lenguas Mayas de Guatemala*, pp. 68–74. Guatemala City: ALMG.

Main Picking Quan   1 Wgt   1.19#

TOTAL SHIPPING WEIGHT

PACKED BY

SHIPPING CHARGES

DATE SHIPPED

OF CTNS.

Raxche' (Demetrio Rodríguez Guaján). 1992. *Cultura maya y políticas de desarrollo.* Chimaltenango, Guatemala: COCADI.

Recinos, Adrián. 1950. *Memorial de Sololá: Anales de los Cakchiqueles.* Mexico City: Fondo de Cultura Económica.

———. 1984. *Crónicas indígenas de Guatemala.* Academia de Geografía e Historia de Guatemala Publicación Especial No. 29. Guatemala City: Serviprensa Centroamericano.

Recinos, Adrián, and Delia Goetz. 1953. *The Annals of the Cakchiquels: Title of the Lords of Totonicapan.* Norman: University of Oklahoma Press.

Richards, Julia Becker. 1987. Learning Spanish and classroom dynamics: School failure in a Guatemalan Mayan community. In *Success or Failure?: Linguistic Minority Children at Home and in School,* ed. H. Trueba. New York: Newbury House/Harper and Row.

———. 1989. Mayan language planning for bilingual education in Guatemala. *International Journal of the Sociology of Language* 77: 93–115.

———. 1993. First Congress of Mayan languages of Guatemala. In *The Earliest Stage of Language Planning: The "First Congress" Phenomenon,* ed. Joshua A. Fishman. The Hague, Netherlands: Mouton de Gruyter.

———. 1994. Mayan language literacy in Guatemala: A socio-historical overview. Paper presented at the Annual Meeting of the American Anthropological Association, Atlanta.

Richards, Michael. 1985. Cosmopolitan world-view and counterinsurgency in Guatemala. *Anthropological Quarterly* 3: 90–107.

———. 1990. *Un perfil de los idiomas y las comunidades del Programa Nacional de Educación Bilingüe.* Guatemala City: Ministerio de Educación.

Rojas, Rosa, and Hans-Joachim Löwer. 1993. Blick zurück nach vorn. *Geo* 5: 46–55.

Rowe, Ann Pollard. 1981. *A Century of Change in Guatemalan Textiles.* New York: Center for Inter-American Relations.

Ruiz Recinos, M. Julia. 1972. *Nociones de historia de Guatemala.* Guatemala City: Cultural Centroamerica.

Sahlins, Marshall. 1981. *Historical Metaphors and Mythical Realities: Structure in the Early History of the Sandwich Islands Kingdom.* Ann Arbor: University of Michigan Press.

———. 1985. *Islands of History.* Chicago: University of Chicago Press.

Sam Colop, Enrique. 1984. Hacia una teoría de educación bilingüe. Master's thesis, Universidad San Carlos.

———. 1988. La educación bilingüe y los idiomas mayas en Guatemala. *Boletín de Lingüística* 2(11–12): 1–5.

———. 1990. Introducción al discurso K'iche'. Paper given at the XXII Taller Maya, Coban, Guatemala.

———. 1991. *Jub'aqtun omay kuchum kaslemal: Cinco siglos de encubrimiento.* Seminario Permanente de Estudios Mayas, Cuaderno No. 1. Guatemala City: Editorial Cholsamaj.

———. 1992. Derecho del hombre bicultural en Guatemala. In *Cultura maya y políticas de desarrollo,* ed. Raxche', pp. 101–115. Chimaltenango, Guatemala: Ediciones COCADI.

Saqijïx (Candelaria Dominga López Ixcoy) and Nik'te'(María Juliana Sis Iboy).

1993. *Gramática pedagógica K'ichee'*. Guatemala City: Programa para el Desarrollo Integral de la Población Maya de la Universidad Rafael Landívar.

Schele, Linda. 1991. *Notebook for the XVth Hieroglyphic Writing Workshop at Texas*. Austin: Art Department, University of Texas.

Schevill, Margot Blum. 1985. *Evolution in Textile Designs from the Highlands of Guatemala*. Berkeley: Lowie Museum of Anthropology.

Schutz, Alfred. 1970. *On Phenomenology and Social Relations*. Chicago: University of Chicago Press.

Scott, James C. 1976. *The Moral Economy of the Peasant: Rebellion and Subsistence in Southeast Asia*. New Haven, Conn.: Yale University Press.

——. 1990. *Domination and the Arts of Resistance: Hidden Transcripts*. New Haven, Conn.: Yale University Press.

Seler, Eduard. 1873. *Gramatische Quiche*. Bonn: Universität Bonn.

Scotton, Carol. 1963. *Language and Identity Negotiation*. Bloomington: University of Indiana Press.

Simon, Jean-Marie. 1987. *Guatemala: Eternal Spring, Eternal Tyranny*. New York: W. W. Norton.

Skinner-Klee, Jorge, ed. 1954. *Legislación indigenista de Guatemala*. Mexico City: Instituto Indigenista Interamericano.

Smith, Carol A. 1978. Beyond dependency theory. *American Ethnologist* 5(3): 615–617.

——. 1990a. Conclusion: History and revolution in Guatemala. In *Guatemalan Indians and the State, 1542–1988*, ed. Carol A. Smith, pp. 258–285. Austin: University of Texas Press.

——. 1990b. Introduction: Social relations in Guatemala over time and space. In *Guatemalan Indians and the State, 1542–1988*, ed. Carol A. Smith, pp. 1–30. Austin: University of Texas Press.

——, ed. 1990c. *Guatemalan Indians and the State, 1542–1988*. Austin: University of Texas Press.

——. 1991. Maya nationalism. *NACLA Report on the Americas* 23(3): 29–33.

Smith, Carol A., and Jeff Boyer. 1987. Central America since 1979. Part 1. *Annual Review of Anthropology* 16: 197–221.

Smith, Waldemar R. 1977. *The Fiesta System and Economic Change*. New York: Columbia University Press.

Spinden, Herbert J. 1975. *A Study of Maya Art: Its Subject Matter and Historical Development*. New York: Dover Publications.

Stavenhagen, Rodolfo. 1988. *Derecho indígena y derechos humanos en América Latina*. Mexico City: Ediciones del Colegio de México and the Instituto Interamericano de Derechos Humanos.

Stoll, David. 1982. *Fishers of Men or Founders of Empire? The Wycliffe Bible Translators in Latin America*. London: Zed Press.

——. 1988. Evangelicals, guerrillas, and the army: The Ixil Triangle under Ríos Montt. In *Harvest of Violence: The Maya Indians and the Guatemalan Crisis*, ed. Robert M. Carmack, pp. 90–116. Norman: University of Oklahoma Press.

——. 1993. *Between Two Armies in the Ixil Towns of Guatemala*. New York: Columbia University Press.

Stuart, L. 1956. El ambiente del hombre en Guatemala. In *Integración social en*

Guatemala, ed. Jorge Luis Arriola. Guatemala City: Seminario de Integración Social Guatemalateca.

Sturm, Circe. 1992. The resurrection of Mayan hieroglyphics: An examination of their use by highland Maya in modern Guatemala. Unpublished MS, Department of Anthropology, University of California at Davis.

Suarez, Jorge. 1982. *Mesoamerican Indian Languages*. Cambridge: Cambridge University Press.

Taubman, Philip. 1983. Slaying case in Guatemala angers U.S. aides. *New York Times*, 11 September.

Taussig, Michael. 1993. *Mimesis and Alterity: A Particular History of the Senses*. New York: Routledge.

Tax, Sol. 1937. The *municipios* of the midwestern highlands of Guatemala. *American Anthropologist* 39(3): 423–444.

Tay Coyoy, Alfredo. 1993. Analisis de la situación de la educación en Guatemala. Photocopied MS, UNICEF-Guatemala.

Tedlock, Barbara. 1992. *Time and the Highland Maya*, rev. ed. (orig. 1982). Albuquerque: University of New Mexico Press.

Tedlock, Barbara, and Dennis Tedlock. 1985. Text and textile: Language and technology in the arts of the Quiché Maya. *Journal of Anthropological Research* 41(2): 121–146.

Tedlock, Dennis. 1983. *The Spoken Word and the Work of Interpretation*. Philadelphia: University of Pennsylvania Press.

———. 1985. *Popol Vuh: The Definitive Edition of the Mayan Book of the Dawn of Life and the Glories of Gods and Kings*. New York: Simon and Schuster.

———. 1992. The Popol Vuh as a hieroglyphic book. In *New Theories on the Ancient Maya*, ed. Elin C. Danien and Robert J. Sharer, pp. 229–240. Pennsylvania: University Museum of the University of Pennsylvania.

———. 1993. Torture in the archives: Mayans meet Europeans. *American Anthropologist* 95(1): 139–152.

Thompson, J. Eric S. 1984. *Grandeza y decadencia de los mayas*. Mexico City: Fondo de Cultura Económica.

Todorov, Tzvetan. 1984. *The Conquest of America*, trans. Richard Howard. New York: Harper.

Tozzer, Alfred M. 1957. *Chichen Itza and Its Cenote of Sacrifice: A Comparative Study of Contemporaneous Maya and Toltec*. Cambridge, Mass.: Peabody Museum of Archaeology and Ethnology.

Trinh, Minh-ha T. 1982. *Reassemblage*. Ethnographic film, Senegal/United States.

Tum, Pedro Coyote. 1991. Actitudes hacia los idiomas mayas. Master's thesis, Universidad Mariano Gálvez, Guatemala.

Turner, Terence. 1991. Representing, resisting, rethinking: Historical transformations of Kayapo culture and anthropological consciousness. In *Colonial Situations: Essays on the Contextualization of Ethnographic Knowledge*, ed. George W. Stocking. Madison: University of Wisconsin Press.

Tzaquitzal Zapeta, Alfonso Efraín. 1993. *Titulo de los señores Coyoy*. Guatemala City: Comisión Interuniversitaria Guatemalteca de Conmemoración de Quinto Centenario del Descubrimiento de America.

Tzian, Leopoldo. 1994. *Kajlab'aliil maya'iib xuq mu'siib': Ri ub'antajiik iximuleew; Mayas y Ladinos en cifras: El caso de Guatemala.* Guatemala City: Cholsamaj.

UNESCO (United Nations Educational, Scientific, and Cultural Organization). 1976. *Circula la televisión en un solo sentido.* Colección Estudios y Documentos de Comunicación Social No. 70. Paris: Editorial UNESCO.

United Nations. 1978. *Human Rights: A Compilation of International Instruments.* New York: United Nations.

————. 1987. *Estudio del problema de la discriminación contra las poblaciones indígenas.* New York: UN Subcommission for the Prevention of Discrimination and Protection of Minorities.

USAID (U.S. Agency for International Development). 1980. *Bilingual Education in Guatemala.* Washington, D.C.: U.S. Agency for International Development.

Varela, Fr. Francisco de. N.d. Calepino en lengua cakchiquel. Seventeenth-century MS in the American Philosophical Society, Philadelphia, Pa.

Vargas Llosa, Mario. 1990. Questions of conquest: What Columbus wrought, and what he did not. *Harper's,* December.

Vela, David. 1990. Preocupaciones lingüísticas en Guatemala. *La Hora* 4(24,394): 3, 29.

Villacorta, J. Antonio. 1934. *Memorial de Tecpán-Atitlán por Francisco Hernández Arana Xajilá y Francisco Díaz Gebutá Quej.* Guatemala City: Tipografía Nacional.

Villagutierre Soto-Mayor, Juan de. 1933. *Historia de la conquista de la provincia del Itzá.* Guatemala City: Sociedad de Geografía e Historia.

Wagner, Regina. 1991. *Los alemanes en Guatemala 1828–1944.* Guatemala City: Editorial IDEA/Universidad Francisco Marroquín.

Wallace, Anthony F. C. 1956. Revitalization movements. *American Anthropologist* 58: 264–281.

————. 1972. *The Death and Rebirth of the Seneca.* New York: Vintage.

Warren, Kay B. 1978. *The Symbolism of Subordination: Indian Identity in a Guatemalan Town.* Austin: University of Texas Press.

————. 1992. Transforming memories and histories: The meaning of ethnic resurgence for Mayan Indians. In *Americas: New Interpretive Essays,* ed. Alfred Stepan, pp. 189–219. New York: Oxford University Press.

————. 1993. Interpreting *la violencia* in Guatemala: Shapes of Kaqchikel silence and resistance in the 1970s and 1980s. In *The Violence Within: Cultural and Political Opposition in Divided Nations,* ed. Kay B. Warren, pp. 25–56. Boulder, Colo.: Westview Press.

————. 1995. Each mind is a world: Dilemmas of feeling and intention in a Kaqchikel Maya community. In *Other Intentions: Culture and the Attribution of States of Mind,* ed. Lawrence Rosen, pp. 47–67. Seattle: University of Washington Press and School of American Research.

————. N.d. *Mayan Public Intellectuals and Indian Cultural Resurgence in Guatemala.* Austin: University of Texas Press, forthcoming.

Watanabe, John M. 1990. Enduring yet ineffable community in the western periphery of Guatemala. In *Guatemalan Indians and the State, 1542–1988,* ed. Carol A. Smith, pp. 183–204. Austin: University of Texas Press.

———. 1992. *Maya Saints and Souls in a Changing World.* Austin: University of Texas Press.

———. 1995. Unimagining the Maya: Anthropologists, others, and the inescapable hubris of authorship. *Bulletin of Latin American Research* 14(1): 25–45.

Wauchope, Robert. 1942. Notes on the age of the Cieneguilla Cave textiles from Chiapas. In *Middle American Research Records No. 1*, ed. Robert Wauchope, pp. 7–8. New Orleans: Middle American Research Institute.

Weiner, Annette B. 1992. *Inalienable Possessions: The Paradox of Keeping-While-Giving.* Berkeley: University of California Press.

Weiner, Tim, and Sam Dillon. 1995. In Guatemala's dark heart, CIA tied to death and aid. *New York Times*, April 2, A1, A6.

Wilson, Richard. 1991. Machine guns and mountain spirits: The cultural effects of state repression among the Q'eqchi' of Guatemala. *Critique of Anthropology* 11(1): 33–61.

———. 1993. Anchored communities: Identity and history of the Maya-Q'eqchi'. *Man* 28(1): 121–138.

———. 1995. *Maya Resurgence in Guatemala: Q'eqchi' Experiences.* Norman: University of Oklahoma Press.

Wolf, Eric R. 1957. Closed corporate peasant communities in Mesoamerica and Central Java. *Southwestern Journal of Anthropology* 13(1): 1–18.

———. 1969. *Peasant Wars of the Twentieth Century.* New York: Harper and Row.

Wood, Josephine, and Lilly Osborne. 1966. *Indian Costumes of Guatemala.* Graz: Akademische Druck– und Verlaganstalt.

Woodbury, Anthony C. 1993. *A Defense of the Proposition, "When a Language Dies, a Culture Dies."* Texas Linguistics Forum 33.

Worsley, Peter. 1984. *The Three Worlds: Culture and World Development.* London: Weidenfeld and Nicolson.

Wright, Robin M. 1988. Anthropological presuppositions of indigenous advocacy. *Annual Review of Anthropology* 17: 365–390.

Wyss, Juan. 1992a. La polvareda de 500 años no es para asfixiarse. *El Gráfico* 29(9,811): 9.

———. 1992b. La polvareda de 500 años no es para asfixiarse. *La Hora* 4(24,881): 11, 29.

Ximénez, Francisco. 1967. *Escolios a las historias del orígen de los indios.* Publicación Especial 13. Guatemala City: Sociedad de Geografía e Historia de Guatemala.

Young, Crawford. 1976. *The Politics of Cultural Pluralism.* Madison: University of Wisconsin Press.

———. 1993. *The Rising Tide of Cultural Pluralism: The Nation-State at Bay?* Madison: University of Wisconsin Press.

Index